THE
ORTHODOX CHURCH

**Recent Titles in
Denominations in America**

THE
ORTHODOX CHURCH

THOMAS E. FITZGERALD

Denominations in America, Number 7
Henry Warner Bowden, *Series Editor*

Greenwood Press
Westport, Connecticut • London

Library of Congress Cataloging-in-Publication Data

FitzGerald, Thomas E.
   The Orthodox Church / Thomas E. FitzGerald.
     p. cm. — (Denominations in America, ISSN 0193–6883 ; no. 7)
    Includes bibliographical references and index.
    ISBN 0–313–26281–0 (alk. paper)
    1. Orthodox Eastern Church—United States. 2. Orthodox (Orthodox
Eastern Church)—United States. I. Title. II. Series.
  BX735.F57   1995
  281.9'73—dc20   94–21685

British Library Cataloguing in Publication Data is available.

Library of Congress Catalog Card Number: 94–21685
ISBN: 0–313–26281–0
ISSN: 0193–6883

First published in 1995

Greenwood Press, 88 Post Road West, Westport, CT 06881
An imprint of Greenwood Publishing Group, Inc.

Printed in the United States of America

The paper used in this book complies with the
Permanent Paper Standard issued by the National
Information Standards Organization (Z39.48–1984).

10 9 8 7 6 5 4 3 2 1

To Kyriaki with love

Orthodoxy cannot be maintained simply by inertia. No tradition can survive unless it is continued through creative effort. The message of Christ is eternal and always the same, but it must be reinterpreted again and again so as to become a challenge to every new generation, to be a message which may appeal to man in his concrete situation. We have not simply to keep the legacy of the past, but must first realize what we have inherited and do everything we can to present it to others as a living thing.

Father Georges Florovsky
The Responsibility of Orthodox Believers in America

CONTENTS

SERIES FOREWORD

The Greenwood Press Denominations in America Series follows a distinguished precedent. These current volumes improve on earlier works by including more churches than before and by looking at all of them in a wider cultural context. The prototype for this series appeared almost a century ago. Between 1893 and 1897, twenty-four scholars collaborated in publishing thirteen volumes known popularly as the American Church History Series. These scholars found twenty religious groups to be worthy of separate treatment, either as major sections of a volume or as whole books in themselves. Scholars in this current series have found that outline to be unrealistic, with regional subgroups no longer warranting separate status and others having declined to marginality. Twenty organizations in the earlier series survive as nine in this collection, and two churches and an interdenominational bureau have been omitted. The old series also excluded some important churches of that time; others have gained great strength since then. So today, a new list of denominations, rectifying imbalance and recognizing modern significance, features many groups not included a century ago. The solid core of the old series remains in this new one, and in the present case a wider range of topics makes the study of denominational life in America more inclusive.

Some recent denominational histories have improved with greater attention to primary sources and more rigorous scholarly standards. But they have too frequently pursued themes for internal consumption alone. Volumes in the Greenwood Press series strive to surmount such parochialism while remaining grounded in the specific materials of concrete ecclesiastical traditions. They avoid placing a single denomination above others in its distinctive truth claims, ethical norms, and liturgical patterns. Instead, they set the history of each church in the larger religious and social context that shaped the emergence of notable denominational features. In this way the authors in this series help us understand the interaction that has occurred between different churches and the broader aspects of American culture.

Each of the historical studies in this current series has a strong biographical focus, using the real-life experiences of men and women in church life to highlight significant elements of an unfolding sequence. The first part of every volume singles out important watershed issues that affected a denomination's outlook and discusses the roles of those who influenced the flow of events. The second part consists of biographical sketches, featuring those persons and many others who contributed to the vitality of their religious heritage. This format enables authors to emphasize the distinctive features of their chosen subject and at the same time recognize the sharp particularities of individual attributes in the cumulative richness that their denomination possesses.

The author of this volume has produced a remarkable study, despite almost overwhelming difficulties. Various forms of Eastern Orthodoxy stem from the beginnings of Christianity itself, and they acquired different emphases while spreading into disparate cultures. Their many versions were ancient when the Western Hemisphere was new to Europeans. This sense of longevity gave Eastern Orthodox churches a special reverence for tradition, which they brought with them to America. As representatives of Greek, Russian, Syrian, Ukrainian, and other Orthodox groups immigrated here, they resisted any alteration of their imported confessions and liturgies vis-à-vis the rest of American spirituality. Indeed, they usually refused to pool their resources or to cooperate more closely with each other, even when such marginality reduced their influence. This spirit of isolated integrity has perpetuated separate institutions, ethnic identities, hierarchies, and theological priorities in an American context where neither geography nor politics any longer justifies them. FitzGerald is at his best in accounting for the complex reasons behind the continuance of numerous Orthodox entities. He is also cogent and persuasive in analyzing the cultural and ecumenical factors that slowly move these groups toward closer interaction. As professor of religious studies and history at Hellenic College, Holy Cross Greek Orthodox School of Theology, he is fortuitously placed to comprehend this ecclesiastical spectrum. His balanced perspective and sympathetic treatment of these communions mark a notable advance in our effort to understand what these churches mean to each other and what future role all American denominations might play in national life.

HENRY WARNER BOWDEN

PREFACE

Orthodox monks from Russia established a mission on Kodiak Island in Alaska in 1794. It marked the formal entrance of organized Orthodox Church life into North America. Two hundred years later, the Orthodox Church in the United States is firmly established. The presence of over 3 million Orthodox Christians gathered into over 1,500 parishes is the fruit of those missionaries and of the pious immigrants who struggled to establish the Orthodox Church in this land. All the problems associated with the organizational unity of the Orthodox in America have not been fully resolved as yet. However, the Orthodox have reached a significant point in their maturation. This is evident in the vitality of parish life, in the renewal of worship, in theological education, in ecumenical witness, as well as in social and missionary concerns. The presence of the Orthodox Church not only has begun to contribute to this society and to religious life in America but also has begun to contribute to the witness of the Christian faith throughout the world.

This book is the first attempt to describe in a comprehensive way the story of the origins and developments of the Orthodox Church in the United States during the past 200 years. It is the story of missions and immigrants, of the quest for survival and the desire for recognition, of the intention to preserve the faith and of the willingness to share that faith with others. For the Orthodox, it is ultimately a story that has its roots in Palestine and its origin in the message of Jesus Christ. Yet, it is a story colored by the life of distant places such as Constantinople, Alexandria, Antioch, Jerusalem, and Moscow.

This study has some important limitations. It examines only the Orthodox Church in the United States. Presently, the Orthodox Church here is actually composed of a number of ecclesiastical jurisdictions, usually a diocese or a number of dioceses that constitute an archdiocese or a church. These ecclesiastical jurisdictions are related to the family of autocephalous Orthodox churches throughout the world. This family is frequently referred to as the "Eastern Orthodox Church." While the term "Eastern" is used less and less, it often serves to distinguish this family of churches from the family known as the "Oriental Orthodox Churches." The ecclesiastical jurisdictions in this country that are associated with the Oriental Orthodox churches are not covered in this study. It should also be noted that only limited reference is made to those ecclesiastical jurisdictions that call themselves Orthodox but that are not related to the autocephalous Orthodox churches. These limitations have been imposed primarily because of space.

As with other books in this series, a biographical dictionary follows the chapters. This dictionary follows the format of Henry Warner Bowden's *Dictionary of American Religious Biography,* Second Edition, Revised and Enlarged (Westport, CT: Greenwood Press, 1993). In selecting the biographies, I have sought to identify persons who have made or are presently making contributions in ministry, teaching, or scholarship that go beyond their own particular ecclesiastical jurisdiction. The biographies clearly indicate the rich diversity of Orthodox leaders in America.

ACKNOWLEDGMENTS

As a teacher, I am deeply conscious of the influence that others have had upon my own reflections, research, and writing. Space does not permit me to acknowledge everyone who has assisted me in bringing this project to fruition. But, I am obliged to acknowledge those who have been especially helpful.

My wife, Kyriaki, deserves special mention. I have greatly benefited from her continuous support and her own insight into the themes discussed in this book. I am especially happy that she not only has read the story with interest but also has been an important part of the story.

My formal research into the development of the Orthodox Church in this country began during my doctoral studies under the direction of Professor Anthony-Emil Tachiaos of the School of Theology of the University of Thessaloniki. I have greatly benefited from his example as both a scholar and a theologian and from his constant support, which has carried over into the writing of this book.

During the course of my research, I had the opportunity to speak at length on a number of occasions with Father John Meyendorff, dean and professor of church history at St. Vladimir's Orthodox Theological School. His own broad understanding of history and theology enabled him to offer me many very insightful perspectives on the development of Orthodox Christianity in this country.

I am deeply honored that Professor Henry Warner Bowden of Rutgers University selected me to prepare this volume as part of the series of which he is the general editor. Throughout the process, often marked by delays and frustrations on my part, he has been a source of helpful direction, generous encouragement, and scholarly perspective.

During the research for and writing of this book, I have had the opportunity to be part of a number of important communities. I appreciate the assistance of many of my colleagues and my students at Hellenic College–Holy Cross Greek Orthodox School of Theology and St. Vladimir's Orthodox Theological Seminary. I have also benefited from the assistance offered by the members of the communities of New Skete and from my colleagues at the World Council of Churches in Geneva, Switzerland. Likewise, I also express my special gratitude to the good people of St. Nicholas Orthodox Church in Manchester, New Hampshire.

Finally, I want to express a special word of appreciation to Archbishop Iakovos, Primate of the Greek Orthodox Archdiocese and Chairman of the Standing Conference of Canonical Orthodox Bishops. Throughout his episcopal ministry in this country, which has spanned thirty-six years, he has contributed immeasurably to the witness of the Orthodox Church. I am deeply grateful for his encouragement of my scholarly work and especially for his interest in seeing this study brought to completion.

Part One
THE ORTHODOX
CHURCH: A HISTORY

1
THE ORTHODOX CHURCH: AN INTRODUCTION

Orthodox Christians in America today believe that their church had its origins not in this country but in the land of Palestine nearly 2,000 years ago. This unique community of faith was established by Jesus Christ in a public manner with the call of the first apostles in Galilee. This community of believers was enlivened by the Holy Spirit on the first Pentecost when the apostles and disciples were empowered to begin their missionary activity. This is described in the Book of Acts of the Apostles.

Orthodox Christians in America today remember that the first Christians were faithful to the commandment of Christ to preach the gospel to all peoples. Guided by the Holy Spirit, they set out to establish Christian communities in the cities of the Mediterranean world and beyond. These first communities became the bases from which other missionaries went forth to spread the gospel of Christ to the wide varieties of peoples in Europe, Africa, and Asia. Christian communities speaking languages such as Aramaic, Syriac, Greek, Coptic, and Latin came into being despite persecution from the pagan Roman government during the first three centuries of the Christian era. The early Christians knew that their faith was a universal one, not to be confined to a particular place, people, or time. In the early fourth century, the governmental persecution ceased, and in 381 Christianity became the official religion of the Roman Empire, whose capital had been moved to Constantinople in 324. The cessation of persecution led to greater missionary activity, a flowering of liturgical rites, and greater reflection upon the apostolic faith.

Orthodox Christians in America today claim to profess the same apostolic faith that was preached by the apostles and other early Christian missionaries. Orthodox Christians claim to confess and teach this faith without addition or diminution.

Rooted in God's own revelation as manifested most especially in the person and activity of Christ, this apostolic faith expresses the fundamental affirmations about the Trinitarian God and his relationship to human persons and the rest of the creation.[1]

EASTERN AND WESTERN CHRISTIANITY

The church was not a monolithic community from the beginning. The church was diligent in preserving unity in the authentic apostolic faith. It was meant to be a guide toward salvation, and so any distortion in teaching was viewed with alarm. Yet, from the earliest days, there was a healthy diversity in the manner in which the church expressed the one faith and celebrated the faith in worship. The apostolic faith was expressed in the languages and through the various cultures of the Mediterranean world. In the eastern portion of the Christian Roman Empire, Greek was the preferred language of education and culture. In the western portion, Latin predominated. On the borders of the Roman Empire and beyond them, the church was composed of other peoples of different cultures who used languages such as Syriac and Armenian.

Because of these developments in the early church, it has been common to speak broadly about Eastern and Western Christianity. These designations certainly have their limitations. But, they do help us to understand the development of the church as it grew and matured during the first millennium, especially in Europe, the Middle East, and North Africa.

The development of the Eastern and the Western expressions of Christianity was affected by the particular challenges that the church faced and to which it responded, especially in the fourth and fifth centuries. The heresies of Arianism, Nestorianism, and Eutychianism, for example, affected primarily the Eastern parts of the church. The heresies of Donatism and Pelagianism affected primarily the Western parts of the church. The writings of St. Basil the Great, St. Gregory the Theologian, and St. Gregory of Nyssa must be understood primarily in light of pastoral concerns and the distortions of the faith in the eastern portion of the church, which they opposed. Likewise, the writings of St. Ambrose of Milan, St. Hilary of Poitiers, and St. Augustine of Hippo must be understood against the background of their times and the pastoral concerns that they faced in Western Europe and North Africa.[2]

Within this same time frame many books claiming to have an apostolic authority were in circulation. While some of these texts originated from within the confines of the church and claimed apostolic authority, others were the work of sectarians. The church, therefore, had to determine which books were worthy of being regarded as genuine Scripture and which were not. This process of selection took place over a period of about 300 years. The New Testament as we know it today contains the twenty-seven books that came out of the life of the early communities and that the church determined to be authentic and salutary. Only in the middle of the fourth century was a firm consensus on the entire collection reached.[3]

From the earliest days of Christianity, the authentic teachings of the church were challenged by pagan philosophies or seriously threatened by false teachings from within the Christian communities. In order to meet major challenges, it was common for the bishops of the church to gather in council, especially from the second century onward. In imitation of the Apostolic Council of Jerusalem (Acts 15), the bishops of a particular region would gather under the leadership of the regional primatial bishop, who by the fifth century was designated as a metropolitan or a patriarch.

Among these councils, the ecumenical councils were important events in the life of the church from the fourth to the eighth centuries. These councils gathered together bishops and other teachers from throughout the Mediterranean world to respond to major challenges affecting the entire church. Usually these challenges involved distortions of the apostolic faith and, thereby, the misunderstanding of the Scriptures. The decisions of these councils bore witness to the faith of the church and were valuable expressions of the unity of the church. During this period the terms "Catholic" and "Orthodox" came to be used by the church to affirm that it taught the apostolic faith fully and authentically. These terms were also used by the church to distinguish itself from sectarian movements.[4]

The Statement of Faith fashioned at the Councils of Nicaea in 325 and elaborated upon at the Council of Constantinople in 381 became an important creed. This creed not only bore witness to the apostolic faith expressed in the Scriptures but also served as a bond of unity among the various regional churches. From the fourth century, this creedal statement has had a significance that has transcended the subsequent Christian divisions of the fifth, the eleventh, and the sixteenth centuries. Today, it is an affirmation of faith used not only by Orthodox but also by Roman Catholics and many Protestants.[5]

DIVISIONS AMONG CHRISTIANS

The legitimate differences that characterized the Eastern and Western traditions of early Christianity were complicated by political and cultural tensions that provided a basis for divisions among Christians. Moreover, serious distortions in the expression of the faith and in ecclesiastical practices were left unchecked in places and were often presented by some as being normative for the entire church.

In the wake of the Council of Chalcedon in 451, a major division erupted, primarily in the eastern portion of the Roman–Byzantine Empire. This division came about chiefly over the terms used to express the relationship of Christ's full humanity and full divinity. It reflected differences in theological approach to Christology that characterized the Alexandrian and the Antiochian traditions throughout the early fifth century. The regional churches within the Roman–Byzantine Empire accepted the terminology used by the council. The regional churches on the periphery of the empire did not accept the terminology used by the council.[6]

Major attempts to heal the division took place at the Councils of Constantinople in 553 and 681. However, the differences in theological emphasis, which were compounded by political, ethnic, and cultural differences, could not be overcome at the time. This division was further exacerbated both by the political changes accompanying the rise of Islam and by subsequent divisions among Christians.

Today, the Orthodox Church accepts the decision of the Council of Chalcedon in 451 as well three subsequent ecumenical councils. The Oriental Orthodox Churches do not formally accept the Council of Chalcedon or the subsequent councils of 553, 681, or 787. While these two families of churches have not been in full communion since the fifth century, recent formal consultations have affirmed that they share the same Orthodox faith. Leaders in both families are presently studying the possible manner in which full communion can be affirmed and celebrated.[7]

The Great Schism is a division that is generally much better known. This division is between the Church of Rome and the Church of Constantinople, together with those regional churches in communion with it. Following the Germanic invasions in Western Europe and the growth of the Frankish Empire, this division occurred gradually between the ninth and thirteenth centuries. The date of 1054 is simply a convenient one that marked the exchange of limited excommunications but certainly not the formal division of the regional churches. This schism can be dated only after the tragic sack of Constantinople and the unfortunate temporary establishment of a Western Christian hierarchy there in 1204.[8]

Numerous attempts were made throughout the Middle Ages to restore full communion. The most significant were councils held in Lyons in 1274 and Florence in 1439. Strongly reflective of medieval Roman Catholic theology, the decisions of both these councils were eventually repudiated by the Orthodox. The tragic fall of Constantinople in 1453 and the accompanying political changes only led to further isolation of Orthodox Christianity and Roman Catholicism and solidified the division.

Two major theological differences at the time led to this division. The first was the *filioque*. This Latin word means "and from the son." It was inserted into the Nicene-Constantinopolitan Creed of 381 after the affirmation that the "Holy Spirit, the Lord and Giver of life proceeds from the Father." This addition was first made to the creed in Spain in the sixth century and was eventually accepted in Rome in the eleventh century. After that it became part of the creed used by Christians throughout Western Europe.

Beginning in the ninth century, St. Photios of Constantinople identified the *filioque* as an unwarranted alteration of the creed. In addition to this, he viewed the addition as an expression of an understanding of the Trinity that diminished both the unique dignity of the Father and the Spirit. The opposition of St. Photios and others also reflected Constantinople's repudiation of the claims of the pope in Rome to have jurisdiction over the Eastern parts of the church.[9]

The second theological difference centered upon the understanding of the authority of the bishop of Rome, the pope. In the wake of the Germanic invasions and the growth of feudalism in Western Europe during the early Middle Ages, the church there developed a highly centralized and monarchical structure that was centered upon the bishop of Rome and his authority. The East recognized that the bishop of Rome had a "primacy of honor," which was rooted in the experience of the early church. However, the absolute authority of the bishop of Rome over and above all other bishops was consistently repudiated by the Eastern bishops as being contrary to the church's teaching as expressed in its Scripture and tradition. The Orthodox never recognized papal claims of "universal jurisdiction" or, later, of "infallibility," which was proclaimed by the Roman Catholic Church in the nineteenth century.[10]

During the period of estrangement from the ninth to the thirteenth centuries, these major differences were complemented by others related to the Sacraments, clerical marriages, and liturgical customs. The many attempts to investigate these differences and to resolve them were frequently stymied by misunderstandings, a lack of historical perspective, cultural prejudices, political intrigues and additional Christian divisions.[11]

The Protestant Reformation began in 1517, less than seventy years after the fall of Constantinople. Much had taken place in those intervening years. The Renaissance exposed Western Europe not only to elements of the Greek classical tradition but also to elements of the Eastern Christian heritage, which had also been generally neglected in the medieval West. Moreover, the knowledge of the physical world had been considerably enlarged due to the voyages of the great explorers.

In their opposition to medieval Roman Catholic teachings and practices, the Protestant Reformers raised important questions about Scripture and tradition, about faith and works, about worship and Sacraments, and about church authority. While they sought to return to the faith and practice of the Apostolic Church, the Reformers were very much children of their times. Both the Reformers and the Counter-Reformers were Westerners who debated topics with precious little reference to the perspectives and experience of the Christians of the East.[12]

Some of the Protestant Reformers did show concern for the Christian East. Lutheran theologians at Tübingen, for example, entered into correspondence with the Patriarchate of Constantinople during the sixteenth century. However, these and other contacts led to little genuine dialogue up until this century. The debates between the Reformers and Rome and the debates among the Protestants themselves were carried on with theological terms with which the Orthodox had little appreciation.[13]

Moreover, the Orthodox, living in lands dominated by Ottomans, Muslims, and, more recently, atheistic Communists, had little opportunity for a genuine dialogue with the Christian West from the fifteenth century down to our own century. In those places where the Orthodox did have contact either with Roman Catholicism or Protestantism, the relationships were seldom cordial. During this difficult period of time, the Christian West, both in its Roman Catholic and Protestant expressions, was frequently more concerned with proselytism than with genuine dialogue and cooperation with the Orthodox.[14]

A TIME OF RENEWAL AND DIALOGUE

The Orthodox Church in many parts of the world is only beginning to recover from tremendous limitations on its life and mission resulting from hostile political regimes in the old Ottoman Empire, in the former Soviet Union, and in the Balkans. Signs of significant growth and revival are evidenced in places where only a few years ago the vitality of the Orthodox Church was questioned by many.

A profound renewal of the principle of conciliarity is to be found in the relationships among the regional autocephalous churches. Under the leadership of the Patriarchate of Constantinople, four historic pan-Orthodox conferences were held in 1961, 1963, 1964, and 1968. These conferences identified a number of critical challenges facing the church and began to plan for a "Great and Holy Council of the Orthodox Church." Since 1976, regular meetings of a Pre-Conciliar Commission have been studying ten topics in anticipation of the council.[15]

Since the early decades of this century, the Orthodox Church has been a participant in the ecumenical movement. From the perspective of the Orthodox, the quest for Christian unity has as its goal the visible unity of Christians who profess the same apostolic faith. The ecumenical movement in general and the World Council of Churches in particular are providing new and exciting opportunities for Christians of different traditions to meet together, to examine differences, to affirm what is held in common, and to work toward the restoration of visible unity.[16]

Today, the Orthodox Church is a family of autocephalous and autonomous churches that are united in the same faith and sacramental life. The number of autocephalous and autonomous churches has varied throughout history. Presently there are the thirteen autocephalous churches, of Constantinople, Alexandria, Antioch, Jerusalem, Russia, Serbia, Romania, Bulgaria, Georgia, Cyprus, Greece, Poland, and Albania. There are two autonomous churches: the Church of the Czech Lands and Slovakia, and the Church of Finland.[17]

Among these churches, the ecumenical patriarch of Constantinople is recognized as the first among the bishops. The ecumenical patriarch has a special responsibility for coordinating the common witness of these churches and of overseeing the development of new regional churches.[18]

There are today about 300 million Orthodox Christians belonging to these regional churches. These Orthodox Christians are sometimes referred to as "Eastern Orthodox." The official designation of the church found in canonical and liturgical texts is the "Orthodox Catholic Church." Often adjectives such as Greek, Russian, or Antiochian are used to refer primarily to historical expressions of the Orthodox Church. Most Orthodox today believe that it is misleading to designate the Orthodox Church as Eastern, given the present geographical and cultural realities.[19]

During the past 200 years, some of the Orthodox autocephalous churches have established jurisdictions in places such as America, Western Europe, Australia, and the Far East. While these new lands are beyond the canonical boundaries of the autocephalous churches, actions were taken to form parishes and dioceses both to engage in missionary activity and to serve Orthodox immigrants. While the Patriarchate of Constantinople has traditionally claimed ecclesiastical jurisdiction over these new lands, historical factors frequently prevented it from exercising appropriate oversight in the past. As we shall see, the Church of Russia was the first to establish a mission in North America in 1794 in the newly discovered territory of Russian Alaska.

Today, the status and organization of the Orthodox Church in North and South America, Western Europe, Australia, and the Far East are receiving a great deal of attention. The Pre-Conciliar Commission addressed the topic of the so-called Orthodox Diaspora at its meetings in 1990 and 1993. The commission affirmed the desire of all the autocephalous churches to work toward a structuring of the church in these lands in a manner that would conform with the canonical principles of ecclesiastical organization and that would better contribute to Orthodox mission and witness.[20]

ORTHODOX SPIRITUALITY

The historical development of the Orthodox Church is distinctive and quite different from that of both Roman Catholicism, especially after the Middle Ages, and the various expressions of Protestantism. Partially because of this, the Orthodox Church has also a distinctive spirituality that differentiates it from most expressions of Western Christianity. While the Orthodox Church has been required to face difficult challenges, it has not passed through the same historical and political processes as has Western Christianity. As has been noted, the Orthodox were not directly involved in the Reformation and Counter-Reformation debates. Indeed, from the time of the Cappadocian fathers in the East and St. Augustine in the West, Orthodox Christianity has understood and celebrated the Christian faith in a manner that is distinctive, sometimes complementary to the Christian West and sometimes dramatically opposed to it. As a result of this, the Orthodox believe that their church has not only preserved the apostolic faith but also emphasized aspects of the faith that are quite distinctive.

The Triune God

"The Lord is God and has revealed himself to us" (Ps. 118:26). This joyous proclamation is sung as part of the Morning Prayers in the Orthodox Church. For the Orthodox, these words declare that their faith, prayers, and perspectives on life are founded upon the reality of the divine self-disclosure. While not diminishing the value of human reason, the Orthodox affirm that God is a mystery who is ultimately beyond human definition. The limited knowledge that we have of God results chiefly from the divine disclosure and not from human speculation, important though it may be. The One who is beyond all has chosen to be revealed because of his love for his creation. Through this divine self-disclosure, the Orthodox hold that they have come to experience and to know the one God as Father, as Son, and as Holy Spirit.[21]

The event of Christ's coming is the core of this revelation according to Orthodox teaching. The revelation of God to the ancient Israelites is fulfilled in the coming of Christ, who is the promised Messiah. In the person of Jesus Christ, divinity is united with humanity in such a way that the distinctive character of each is maintained. This means that the event of the Incarnation reveals in a profound way the intimate bond between living God and the human person together with the entire cosmos. Through his words and deeds, Jesus Christ has revealed the Triune God and the theocentric nature of the human person. Christ shows that the human person belongs to God the Father and is meant to live in fellowship with him through the Spirit. The Resurrection of the Lord is a bold proclamation that not even death can keep human persons from the Father, who loves us. In all that he has done, Jesus offers human persons life in abundance (John 10:10).[22]

The Orthodox teach that the principal task of the Holy Spirit is to reveal the presence of the Risen Christ to persons of every age and every place and to enable human persons to share in his saving work. The Holy Spirit leads persons from a life of self-centeredness to a life centered upon Christ and his gospel. The person of the Spirit is not subordinate to Christ, nor is the ministry of the Spirit inferior to that of Christ. The Spirit unites human persons to Christ, who leads them to the Father. Both Son and Spirit work in harmony to accomplish the will of the Father, who desires that "everyone be saved and come to the knowledge of truth" (1 Tim. 2:4).

Salvation

According to Orthodox teaching, the entire purpose of God's self-disclosure is to restore the human person to fellowship with himself. From the very beginning, the human person was fashioned in the "image and likeness" of God and given the vocation to live in communion with God (Gen. 1:26). Although sin distorts the relationship between God and the human person, it never destroys the fundamental bond between the Father and his sons and daughters. The Orthodox believe that in the coming of Christ, God the Father demonstrates his love for the alienated and calls human persons back to his friendship. Thus, the Orthodox affirm with St. Irenaeus that "the glory of God is the human person fully alive."[23]

The Orthodox place a special emphasis upon an understanding of salvation, which is viewed primarily as sharing. Through the coming of Christ, the Orthodox believe that God has shared fully in human life, thereby enabling human persons to share in his life of unselfish love. Salvation is, therefore, both a free gift of fellowship with the Father and the process by which human persons respond freely to that gift given in Christ through the Spirit. Salvation certainly involves the forgiveness of sin but is not limited to this alone. It is essentially a new relationship freely offered by the Father through Christ and in the Spirit. For this reason, the fathers of the church often declare, "God became human so that human persons may become divine."[24]

The term "deification" (*theosis*) is frequently used by the Orthodox to describe the process of sanctification whereby the human person responds to the divine initiative and moves ever closer to the living God through a life that reflects and imitates the divine love. The human person experiences the presence of the divine in a specific and deeply personal way. So, the Orthodox believe that persons are most fully human when they live their lives in communion with the Source of life. Those who live in Christ know that the process of deification begins at the very moment of creation and continues through the life to come. Love knows no limit and no boundary. The Virgin Mary, honored as the Mother of God, and the other saints bear witness to this reality.[25]

Salvation is not simply personal but also communal. The Orthodox teach that believers grow in their relationship with the Triune God within the fellowship of the church, the community of faith. Established by Christ with the call of the first apostles and enlivened by the Spirit from the day of Pentecost, the church is an integral part of the divine plan of salvation. Persons become members of the church through baptism. Within this unique community of faith, the members of the church have the opportunity to cultivate the bond of love not only with each other but also with the Triune God. The Orthodox affirm the old adage that says, "A solitary Christian is no Christian."[26]

Salvation also has a cosmic dimension. The Orthodox teach that human persons are not saved from the world but in and through the world. The soul is not saved separately from the body but rather together with the body. The whole person, body and soul, is meant to share in the process of sanctification, beginning with the relationships and responsibilities of this life. Far from rejecting the body and the rest of the material creation, the Orthodox look upon the physical as the work of God and a medium through which the divine is manifest. The entire creation, fundamentally good from the beginning, is related to the reality of the Incarnation. Thus, the ultimate transfiguration of the entire cosmos is already prefigured in the lives of the faithful, in the Eucharist, in the icons, and in the relics of the saints.[27]

The Orthodox see the human person as a liturgical being who is meant to glorify God in all things. There cannot be any discontinuity between believers' formal act of worship and their life in society. Through every relationship and responsibility in life, believers have the opportunity to remember God and his mighty acts of salvation. With this remembrance, believers have the opportunity to offer back to the Father, in thanksgiving, their life and all they have received in union with Christ and through the Spirit. The believer's life is ultimately a prayer. Every responsibility and obligation in life has the potential of being undertaken to the glory of the Triune God and in love for other persons.

The Eucharist

The Orthodox certainly do not diminish the importance of formal acts of common prayer and worship. In fact, the Orthodox strongly emphasize the value of communal prayer, especially the Eucharist. Communal prayer is a special time when believers not only respond to the presence of the Living God but also are nurtured by the Scriptures, hymns, and prayers of the church. When believers gather together, they are reminded of their baptismal unity with Christ and of their baptismal unity with all of his followers. The needs and concerns of others are brought to their attention through petitions. Their personal prayer is strengthened through their common prayers. Through their creedal affirmations, the Orthodox faithful profess their faith and are challenged to be faithful in all their words and deeds.[28]

The Eucharist is the most important act of communal prayer for Orthodox Christians. In obedience to the command of the Lord given at the Last Supper (Luke 22:19), the community of believers gathers to hear the Word of God, to offer prayers, to present the gifts of bread and wine, to recall the mighty acts of God, to seek the blessing of the Spirit, and to receive Holy Communion as an expression of union with Christ and with one another. It is an action, the Orthodox believe, that manifests the reign of God in their midst and is an expression of the Kingdom to come.

The Orthodox believe that the Eucharist typifies human life as it is lived in fellowship with God. The bread and the wine are the fruit of creation given by God and fashioned by human hands. The offering placed on the altar signifies not only what has been received but also who the believers are. This reminds them that ultimately their life is a eucharist, an offering of thanksgiving. Through this offering, the Orthodox seek not simply their own salvation but the salvation of the world. At the offering, the believers stand before God with uplifted hands of gratitude, praying the words of the liturgy: "We offer to you your own from what is already yours, always and everywhere."[29]

These faith affirmations characterize Orthodox Christianity. These affirmations are central to the lives of Orthodox believers. They have also been at the very center of the church's missionary endeavors throughout the ages.

Orthodox explorers from Russia sighted the coast of North America on the evening of 19 July 1794. The majestic snow-covered mountain they saw was named in honor of the Prophet Elias, whose feast day had begun. The following morning, the Eucharist was celebrated on board the ship *Saint Peter*. It was a solemn act of thanksgiving. It was also a celebration that heralded the entrance of the Orthodox Church into North America.

2
THE ALASKAN MISSION

The discovery and explorations of the islands that stretch between Asia and North America led directly to the establishment of an Orthodox mission on Kodiak Island in 1794. From this center, missionaries from Russia began to introduce the Orthodox Christian faith to the natives of Alaska. By the time that Alaska was sold by Russia to the United States in 1867, the missionaries had established churches and schools on most of the Aleutian Islands as well as along the Alaskan coast of North America. The Russian Orthodox mission in Alaska marked the formal entrance of Orthodox Christianity into North America. Moreover, the mission in Alaska was one of the last and greatest missionary endeavors to be sanctioned by the Orthodox Church of Russia and the imperial Russian Empire prior to the Bolshevik revolution. On the eve of the October 1917 revolution in Russia, it is estimated that there were over 10,000 Orthodox Christians in Alaska and nearly one hundred churches or chapels.[1]

EXPLORERS AND MERCHANTS

Throughout the sixteenth and seventeenth centuries, Russian explorers traveled eastward across the vast plains of Siberia to the Pacific Ocean. Known in Russian history as the time of the Eastern Conquest, this period was the one in which the various river basins of Siberia were colonized. These rivers acted as natural highways by which Russians could explore the eastern regions of their own vast empire. With the discovery of Kamchatka in 1697, the authority of imperial Russia became more firmly established along the Pacific coast.[2]

In the years prior to his death in 1725, Peter the Great inaugurated plans for a formal and systematic exploration of the land off the coast of Siberia.[3] Vitus

Bering, a Dane by birth, was selected to lead the first exploration supported by the imperial government. Bering had joined the Russian navy in 1704 and had served in both the Sea of Azor and in the Baltic Sea. In the same year that Peter the Great died, Bering left St. Petersburg with orders given to him by Empress Catherine I.[4]

After a treacherous, yearlong journey across Siberia, Bering and his companions reached the coast of Kamchatka and began their exploratory venture on 21 July 1728, when they set sail in a small boat known as the *Saint Gabriel*. In this first expedition, Bering sighted an island that he named Saint Laurence. This island, which is the most westerly landmass of North America, was the first discovery of American territory by Bering. Sailing north along the Asian coastline, Bering reached the most northeastern point of Asia, but he failed to sight the mainland of North America.

A second expedition left the Kamchatka peninsula on 4 June 1741. Two sturdy ships were part of this endeavor. The *Saint Peter* was commanded by Bering, and the *Saint Paul* was commanded by Alexis Chirikov. After the ships became separated during a violent storm, Chirikov first sighted the coast of Alaska on 15 July 1741. The North American mainland was sighted by Vitus Bering four days later. The majestic mountain that was sighted by Bering and his crew was named in honor of the prophet Elias. As the ship was anchored off the coast, the Eucharistic Liturgy was celebrated on board the following morning, 20 July 1741, which was the feast day of the prophet Elias. At the conclusion of the liturgy, members of the crew went ashore and undertook a preliminary exploration.[5]

Alexis Chirikov returned to Kamchatka on 8 October 1741 with greatly diminished crew. The company of seventy men had been reduced to forty-nine. Vitus Bering never returned. During the voyage back to Kamchatka, scurvy broke out among the crew, and Bering also contracted the disease. Shortly after this, the ship was wrecked along the coast of the island that now bears his name. On this island Bering died on 8 December 1741. A handful of survivors constructed a small boat from the wreckage and returned to Kamchatka.

Despite the tragedies that accompanied the expeditions, the explorations of Bering and Chirikov were very successful. The expeditions accurately established two points on the North American mainland and also established the location of a number of the Aleutian Islands. Moreover, the report of the existence of the sea otter, fox, seal, and sea cow provided the stimulus for the fur hunters and merchants to support and to continue the work of exploration. By 1743, there were nearly forty Russian trading companies engaged in gathering furs from the islands and the mainland of North America.[6]

Empress Catherine the Great formally placed the newly discovered land in North America under her rule in 1766.[7] The first permanent settlement based upon the rule of law was established on Kodiak Island in 1784. This colony was established primarily through the efforts of Prince Gregory Shelikov. By 1781, Shelikov had become one of the most wealthy merchants in Siberia and one of the first to recognize that the activities of Russian merchants in North America had to be consolidated. Together with Ivan Golikov, he established a colony on Kodiak Island in the name of the Shelikov-Golikov Company and sought to expand Russian control and influence as far as possible into northwestern America.[8]

The colony on Kodiak was dedicated to the Three Hierarchs. Since the twelfth century, this is the title given to St. Basil the Great, St. John Chrysostom, and St. Gregory the Theologian, who were outstanding bishops and theologians of the late fourth century. The colony rapidly became the center of economic and political life for the Russian merchants and explorers. The Shelikov-Golikov Company became the basis for the Russian-American Company, which was established by Emperor Paul I in 1799. This company became the extension of the Russian imperial government in North America.

THE FIRST MISSIONARIES

Gregory Shelikov and Ivan Golikov sent a letter to Metropolitan Gabriel of St. Petersburg on 10 April 1793. The letter requested the metropolitan to send a scholarly and talented priest to the Kodiak colony. Shelikov and Golikov also stated in their letter that all the expenses of the priest and his missionary activity would be paid by their company.[9]

The request of Shelikov and Golikov was eventually brought to the attention of Empress Catherine the Great, who instructed Metropolitan Gabriel to select a number of clerics for a mission to America. Well aware of some of the difficulties that the missionaries would have to face, Metropolitan Gabriel selected eight monks for the journey to America. Most of the missionaries came from the monastery of Valaam, which had a reputation as a center of spirituality and missionary activity. The leader of the group was Father Joseph Bolotov, who had studied at both the Tver and Rostov seminaries. He was raised to the rank of abbot (Archimandrite) just before the mission began.[10]

Prior to the departure of the missionaries, Metropolitan Gabriel provided them with vestments, liturgical articles, and books that would be necessary for the celebration of the liturgical services. In addition to traveling expenses that the missionaries received from the Holy Synod, the empress also gave 500 rubles to Abbot Joseph and 250 rubles to each of the other missionaries. This money came from the Palestine Fund, which was normally used only for the financial support of the churches and monasteries in the Holy Land.[11]

Metropolitan Gabriel also gave to Abbot Joseph a document that contained instructions for the missionaries. Based upon similar instructions given to Siberian missionaries in 1769, the document is of great historical significance. First, it clearly shows that the missionaries were going to America not simply to serve the spiritual needs of the Russian colonists and merchants but to undertake missionary work among the natives. Second, the document emphasizes that Orthodox Christianity must spread among the natives chiefly through the personal example and the love that the missionaries were expected to demonstrate. A portion of the instructions of Metropolitan Gabriel says:

When Jesus Christ leads you to meet those who do not know the Law of God, your first concern will be to serve as an example of good works to them, so as to convert them by your personal life into obedient servants of the Lord.[12]

The missionaries left the city of St. Petersburg on 25 December 1793 and arrived in Irkutsk on 16 March 1794. After accepting four additional companions, they traveled up the Lena River to the city of Yakutsk. Following a journey by horseback, they arrived at Okhotsk, from which they sailed for Kodiak Island and arrived on 24 September 1794. Throughout the course of the journey, the missionaries frequently stopped to baptize many people, especially in the Yakutsk region and later in Unalaska, where they stopped prior to their arrival at Kodiak. The journey of the first missionaries to America took 293 days. They traveled about 7,400 miles (11,840 km). Even before they reached their mission field, the monks had traveled about one-third of the circumference of the world and never left the confines of the vast Russian Empire.[13]

The Alaskan mainland and the islands of the coast were inhabited by a number of native tribes. Among the most important were the Tlingits, who lived on the southern coastal area; the Aleuts, who lived on the islands off the coast; and the Eskimos, who lived along the Arctic Ocean coast. These and other, smaller tribes were descendants of nomadic peoples from Asia who crossed into North America at least 5,000 years before the discovery of Alaska by the Russians.[14]

A valuable foundation for the work of the missionaries had been laid by some of the more pious explorers and merchants who had come into contact with the natives. While some of the merchants seriously mistreated the natives, other merchants considered it their duty to introduce them to the Orthodox Christian faith. Both Ivan Golikov and Gregory Shelikov, for example, had baptized a number of natives on both Fox Island and Kodiak Island. When the missionaries finally arrived on Kodiak Island in 1794, many natives had already been converted to the Orthodox Christian faith.

When the missionaries arrived on Kodiak Island, there were about 225 Russians and 8,000 natives living there. Under the direction of Shelikov, the missionaries lived in a small monastery located in the village of Saint Paul. As the first Orthodox monastery in North America, it was constructed in such a way that the monks were able to observe the activities of the village. Yet, at the same time, the monks were separated from village life so that they could better follow their monastic discipline.[15]

The missionaries undertook their labors with exceptional zeal and piety between 1794 and 1798. A church building dedicated to the Holy Resurrection of Christ was constructed in the village of Saint Paul, and this became the center of missionary activity on Kodiak Island. The monks subsequently traveled to the other islands and to the mainland of North America. Wherever they journeyed, the monks built small chapels, taught the natives, and baptized them. It is estimated that over 12,000 natives became Orthodox Christians within the first few years of missionary activity.[16]

FATHER HERMAN

Of the original missionaries to Russian America, one has attracted special attention and devotion. His name is Father Herman (German), the monk who was the last of the original missionaries in Alaska when he died in the year 1837 on Spruce Island. Very little is known about Father Herman. Most of the information that is known about his life both before and after his coming to America is contained in a brief biography published in 1894 by the Valaam Monastery to commemorate the centenary of the Alaskan mission.[17]

We know from this source that Father Herman was born in Serpukhov near Moscow probably in 1756. His family name as well as his baptismal names are not known. At the age of sixteen, he left his hometown and entered the Holy Trinity–Saint Sergius Monastery. This monastery was founded in 1354 by Saint Sergius of Radonezh. Father Herman was tonsured a monk in 1783 and then went to dwell in the Valaam Monastery of Lake Ladoga. While at Valaam, the young monk came under the spiritual direction of the famous abbot Nazary. Following the direction of his elder, the monk Herman eventually began to live a semi-eremitical life in a small hut located not very far from the monastery. Father Herman would return to the monastery only to participate in the daily prayers and Eucharistic liturgy. Only a year after becoming a monk, Herman left for Alaska.

Following the return of Abbot Joseph to Irkutsk in 1798 and his death at sea in 1799, Father Herman appears to have become recognized as the head of the monastic community, although he was not ordained and had little formal education. At about the same time, difficulties began to arise in the relationship between the monks and the Russian merchants. At the center of these difficulties was the quality of life of the natives. The treatment of the Alaskan natives by the merchants associated with the Russian-American Company became more abusive. Led by Father Herman, the missionaries became more outspoken in defending the rights of the natives and in criticizing the immorality of many of the Russian merchants. As a result of the activity of the monks, they were briefly placed under arrest in 1800. Several attempts were made to kill Father Herman. The antagonism that developed between the monks and many of the Russian merchants led to a serious decline in the activities of the missionaries. As a result of the monks' activity, an investigation by the Russian government led to positive changes in the activities of the merchants by 1818.[18]

At about the same time, Father Herman left Kodiak Island and went to Spruce Island, which he affectionately called New Valaam. On Spruce Island Father Herman was better able to immerse himself in the ascetical ways of a monk. Yet, even there he did not neglect the material and spiritual needs of the natives. Until the time of his death in 1837, Father Herman worked among the natives on Spruce Island. He cared for orphans, constructed a chapel, and organized a school. In addition to preaching the gospel and leading the services of prayer, Father Herman fed the natives from an experimental garden that he cultivated. His piety and sanctity were recognized by the natives, who referred to him as Apa, which means grandfather.[19]

Prior to his death, Father Herman revealed to the natives of Spruce Island the details of what was ahead. He told them that there would be no priest available to bury him and that they would be required to do it. Herman also told the natives that he would be forgotten for thirty years, then remembered by those beyond Spruce Island. In the manner that he had predicted, Herman died on 13 December 1837. Although the natives of Spruce Island revered his memory and honored him as a saint, not until 1867 did the Church of Russia begin to investigate the life of Father Herman. He was formally declared a saint on 9 August 1970.[20]

BISHOP INNOCENT

The work of evangelization, begun in 1794, did not come to an end when Father Herman died. In the years prior to his death, a small number of priests began to arrive in Alaska from the diocese of Irkutsk in order to reactivate the mission. These priests received financial support from the Russian-American Company. In a revision of the charter in 1821, it was clearly stated that the company was responsible for the financial welfare of the mission of Alaska. In spite of this, the activity of some of these missionaries left much to be desired. "The priests from Irkutsk," writes Serge Bolshakoff, "looked upon the Alaskan parishes as a place of exile and neglected to translate the liturgical and devotional books into the native dialects. They thought only how to return to Siberia as soon as possible."[21] Not until 1824 did this unhappy state of affairs begin to change.

Father John Veniaminov, with his wife, child, and mother, arrived on the Island of Unalaska on 29 July 1824. This new missionary in Alaska and future bishop was born on 27 August 1797 near Irkutsk. At the age of nine, he entered the Irkutsk Seminary School and became one of its most outstanding students. At the age of seventeen, his name was changed from Popov to Veniaminov in honor of the deceased bishop of Irkutsk. Although the young student was recommended to attend the Moscow Theological Academy, John Veniaminov chose to marry and to be ordained. After serving as deacon and priest for a number of years, Father John accepted the request of Bishop Michael of Irkutsk to serve in Alaska. Against the wishes of many of his friends, Father John and his family left Irkutsk on 7 May 1823.[22]

Within the first year of his arrival on Unalaska, Father John constructed both a church and a school, which served as the center of his mission parish. Eager to be fully involved in the life of the natives, the young priest began to learn the language and their customs. The Aleuts of the island had no written language, and the language was especially difficult for Europeans to pronounce because of the number of guttural sounds.

This, however, did not deter Father John. Following the example of the great ninth-century missionaries, Saints Cyril and Methodius, Father John not only learned the language of the Aleuts but also wrote a grammar. He then translated the Eucharistic Liturgy, other prayers, and the Gospel of Saint Matthew. He even wrote a small catechism in the Aleut language, which was called *Indication of the Pathway into the Kingdom of Heaven.*[23] Undoubtedly, the fact that Orthodox Christianity became so well established among the natives of Unalaska was the direct result of both the personal missionary work of Father John as well as his translations.

When Father John was transferred to Sitka in 1834, there were about 2,000 Orthodox Christian natives on the island of Unalaska. Known then as New Archangel, Sitka had become one of the most important centers of Alaskan life. Located not far from the mainland, Sitka had a very good harbor and was the center of the commercial activity, with foreign traders frequently visiting the port. At this time, Sitka was the only port along the northern Pacific coast where ships could be repaired. These factors made Sitka the most important city in Russian Alaska in the early nineteenth century.

Upon his arrival in Sitka, Father John began his missionary work among the natives there who were known as the Tlingits. Unlike most of the other native tribes, the Tlingits had been extremely hostile to the Russian merchants. They had refused to be baptized because they feared that they would become slaves of the Russian merchants. Reacting against the Russian presence, they strongly embraced their pagan customs and rituals.[24]

As was the case in Unalaska, Father John immediately began to learn the language of the natives of Sitka. Conversions among the Tlingits were very slow, however, until 1836. In that year a severe smallpox epidemic spread among the natives. When their own pagan priests were unable to arrest the disease, the natives sought the help of Father John. By demonstrating a genuine love for the natives, Father John not only helped in the cure of the disease but also began to receive many of the natives into the Orthodox Church.[25]

During his service in Sitka, Father John was not required to travel as much as he had while on the island of Unalaska. However, included within the jurisdiction of his parish was the settlement of Fort Ross, which was located about 1,500 miles (2,400 km) south in Spanish California. On 18 July 1836, Father John left Sitka by ship for Fort Ross, which had been established in 1821 by the Russian-American Company to house Russian merchants. After a sixteen-day voyage by ship, Father John finally arrived in California and traveled by horse to Fort Ross.

While attending to the needs of the Orthodox Christians in the Fort Ross colony, Father John also took advantage of his trip to California to visit a number of Roman Catholic missions that were operated by Spanish priests of the Franciscan Order. During a two-week period, Father John visited the missions in San Rafael, San Jose, Santa Clara, and San Francisco. At every stop, Father John spoke to the Roman Catholic priests in the Latin language and attended Mass. On one occasion, he also had the opportunity to witness both a baptism and a burial. In addition to gaining a personal knowledge of the Roman Catholic missions and liturgical services, Father John learned that the rumors that the natives were treated harshly by the Roman Catholics were false. His contacts with the Roman Catholic missionaries were quite significant due to the fact that relationships between Roman Catholicism and Orthodoxy were both limited and strained during the nineteenth century.[26]

After his return to Sitka, Father John began to make plans for a trip back to Russia. The purpose of his trip was threefold. First, he wanted to present the Holy Synod with a detailed report on the Alaskan mission. Second, he wanted to offer to the leaders of the Russian-American Company a plan for the improvement of the educational facilities for the Alaskan natives. Finally, he wanted to receive official approval for his liturgical translations. With these goals in mind, Father John and his family departed for Russia in the fall of 1838.[27]

While in St. Petersburg, Father John received news that brought him great joy and great sorrow. His report on the Alaskan mission was very well received by both Metropolitan Philaret of Moscow and Count N. A. Protasov, who was the ober-procurator of the Holy Synod. However, in the spring of 1840, Father John also received the news that his wife had died in the city of Irkutsk. During this period, Father John received much comfort from Philaret, who subsequently encouraged him to become a monk. Assured that his children would be cared for by the church, Father John became a monk one year after the death of his wife and received the name Innocent. In the same year, he was elected the bishop of the newly established diocese of Kamchatka, the Kurile and Aleutian Islands. He was consecrated on 15 December 1840 in the Cathedral of St. Petersburg.[28]

Bishop Innocent returned to Sitka on 26 September 1841. About one hundred years after its discovery, Alaska received a man as its bishop who had already spent more than ten years preaching the gospel both to Russians and to native Orthodox. With the return of the beloved missionary as bishop of the new diocese, Russian America entered into what has been called the "golden age of Alaska." Under the direction of the new bishop, a cathedral was established in Sitka, new mission parishes were opened, education of the natives was strengthened, and a seminary to train native clergy and teachers was opened in Sitka. In addition to this, Bishop Innocent undertook journeys to many distant mission posts in Alaska and Siberia, especially in the period between 1842 and 1849.[29]

Bishop Innocent was elevated to the rank of archbishop in 1850, and his diocese was enlarged to include areas in Siberia near the Amur River. The headquarters of the diocese was also moved from Sitka to Blagoveschensk in Siberia. Vicar bishops for Sitka and for Yakutsk were subsequently consecrated to assist Archbishop Innocent minister to the vast territory.[30]

During the time when he began to establish new missions in eastern Siberia, Archbishop Innocent continued to have a deep interest in the development of the church in North America. He made some very farsighted recommendations in a letter sent to the ober-procurator of the Holy Synod on 5 December 1867. Although the archbishop assumed that the Russian Orthodox Church had jurisdiction over the North American continent, he did make some bold proposals for the growth of Orthodox Christianity in the New World:

It reached my attention from Moscow that I allegedly wrote to someone saying that I was not pleased that our American colonies had been sold to the Americans. This is completely untrue. On the contrary, I see in this event one of the ways of Providence by which our Orthodoxy can insert itself into the United States, where at the present time serious attention is being given. If I had been asked concerning this subject, this is what I would have advised: a) The American vicariate should not be closed. b) Rather than New Archangel, the residence of the vicar bishop should be located in San Francisco, where climatic conditions are incomparably better and from where it is at least as convenient to have connections with the churches in the colonies as it is from Sitka. c) The present vicar and the whole New Archangel clergy except for one sacristan, should be recalled to Russia, and a new vicar should be appointed who has knowledge of the English Language. Likewise his entourage should be composed of persons who know English. d) The bishop should choose his own staff and be permitted to change members of his staff as well as to ordain to the priesthood American citizens who will accept Orthodoxy with all its traditions and customs. e) The ruling Bishop and the clergy of the Orthodox Church in America should be permitted to serve the Divine Liturgy and other church services in English. And, as is self-evident, translations of the service books into English must be made. f) In pastoral schools, which will be created in San Francisco and elsewhere for the preparation of candidates for missionary and priestly duties, the curriculum must be in English and not in Russian, which will sooner or later be replaced by the former language.[31]

At the age of seventy-two, Archbishop Innocent was appointed metropolitan of Moscow on 26 May 1868. As the successor to Metropolitan Philaret, the new metropolitan of Moscow continued to emphasize the missionary activity of the church, although he was nearly blind and in constant pain. In 1870, Metropolitan Innocent reformed the Society for Promoting Christianity among the Pagans and renamed it the Orthodox Missionary Society. Through the work of this society, many Orthodox rediscovered the importance of missions. After serving as metropolitan of Moscow for almost eleven years, the great missionary died on 31 March 1879 at the age of eighty-two. His body was buried next to the body of Metropolitan Philaret in the Church of the Holy Spirit at the Holy Trinity–Saint Sergius Monastery near Moscow. He was formally declared a saint by the Church of Russia in 1978 and honored with the title Enlightener of the Aleuts and Apostle to America.[32]

THE DECLINE OF THE ALASKAN MISSION

The Alaskan territory was sold by the imperial Russian government to the government of the United States in 1867 for the sum of $7,200,000. This sale took place at a time when the government of the United States was enlarging the territory of the country, chiefly through negotiations with European nations that had claims in North America. Although the rights of the Orthodox Church in Alaska were clearly guaranteed at the time of the sale, a number of factors contributed to the decline of the Alaskan mission.

The Russian-American Company ceased to exist four years before the sale. This organization had been the immediate source of financial support for the mission.

With the closing of the company in 1863, most Russians either returned to Russia or went to settle in San Francisco, California. It has been estimated that in 1870 there were only ninety poor Russian families remaining in Sitka, which had been the center of intense commercial activity throughout the first half of the nineteenth century.[33]

Another very important factor that contributed to the decline of the Alaskan mission was the decision of the Church of Russia to transfer the see of the bishop from Sitka to San Francisco in 1872. Three years after the sale of Alaska to the United States, the Holy Synod of the Church of Russia established the new diocese of the Aleutian Islands on 10 June 1870. Shortly after his arrival in Alaska, Bishop John (Mitropolsky) requested that the see be moved from Sitka to San Francisco. This request was undoubtedly based upon the fact that most Russians had left Alaska. In 1872, the Holy Synod granted the request. Bishop John subsequently established his cathedral and the pastoral school in San Francisco, which had a small Russian colony.

When the see of the bishop was transferred from Sitka to San Francisco in 1872, it was located outside the stated boundaries of the diocese. San Francisco is located about 600 miles (960 km) south of Sitka. This peculiar situation existed until 1900. At that time, the name of the diocese was changed by the Church of Russia to include all North America. In 1905, the ecclesiastical administration of the diocese was transferred to New York City. These peculiarities represented the beginnings of the canonical irregularities that would characterize Orthodox Christianity in America throughout the twentieth century.

The absence of a resident bishop in Alaska and an inadequate number of priests weakened the presence and authority of the Orthodox Church in the territory. While there were over 10,000 native Orthodox in Alaska in 1870, there were only four priests to serve them. When Protestant and some Roman Catholic missionaries entered Alaska in the last quarter of the nineteenth century, the Orthodox Church was not in a very vital position from which it could serve all its faithful and discourage proselytism.[34] Despite this tragic fact, the Orthodox Church in Alaska continued to exist and to provide subsequent Orthodox leaders in North America with a powerful reminder of the missionary dimension of church life.

By the end of the nineteenth century, Orthodox missionaries, both clergy and laity, had traveled throughout all the islands of the Aleutian chain and throughout the coastline of the Alaskan mainland. The mission in Alaska was perhaps the most important missionary endeavor of the Orthodox Church in the late eighteenth and nineteenth centuries. At a time when much of the Orthodox Church throughout the world was confronted with political systems and rival religions that prevented much missionary work, the mission in Alaska heralded the entrance of Orthodox Christianity into a new land.[35]

3
EARLY PARISH DEVELOPMENTS

The foundation of Orthodox Christianity in the continental United States was established during the last quarter of the nineteenth century and the first two decades of the twentieth century. During this time, the focus of Orthodoxy dramatically shifted from Alaska to the major cities of the continental United States. The principal cause of this was the massive influx of immigrants from Greece, Asia Minor, Carpatho-Russia, and other parts of Eastern Europe and the Middle East. Exclusive of the Alaskan territory, there were only 3 Orthodox parishes in the United States in the year 1870. However, fifty years later there were over 250 Orthodox parishes located in major cities throughout the country. These parishes were established chiefly by immigrants who were determined to preserve their Orthodox Christian faith in the New World.

THE EARLY PARISHES

Even before the great flux of immigrants from Eastern and Southeastern Europe, a small number of Orthodox Christians lived in the continental United States. The first Orthodox parish to be established in the United States was founded in the year 1864 in New Orleans, Louisiana. This parish was organized by Greek merchants under the direction of Nicholas Benakis, the consul of the kingdom of Greece in New Orleans. Because of this, the parish is viewed not only as the first organized parish in the United States but also as the first Greek Orthodox parish. Nonetheless, members of this parish included not only Greeks but also Russians and Serbians who were living or working temporarily in the city.

While much of the history of the early years of this parish is lost, a few facts are known. The liturgical services were conducted in English, Church Slavonic, and

Greek. The official records of the parish were in English until 1904. The first priest, Father Agapius Honcharenko, was of Slavic background and had been ordained at the great monastic center of Mount Athos in 1865. Although the parish had accepted gifts of vestments from Czar Alexander II, there is no indication that the parish was ever under the jurisdiction of the Russian Orthodox Archdiocese. It subsequently became part of the Greek Orthodox Archdiocese in 1921.[1]

At about the same time that the parish in New Orleans was established, a number of Orthodox Christians in San Francisco gathered to organize the Greek Russian-Slavonic Church and Philanthropic Society. In 1867, the state of California granted a charter to the society, which intended to establish an Orthodox church. Among the members of the society were Martin Klinkovsterem, who was the Russian consul, and George Fisher, who was the Greek consul in San Francisco. On 13 June 1868, the society requested the Holy Synod of the Church of Russia to assign a priest. In September of the same year, Father Nicholas Kovrygin was transferred from Sitka to San Francisco, and regular liturgical services began to be held.

From 1868 to 1872, the building in which the liturgical services were held was known as the Prayer House of the Orthodox Oriental Church. The liturgical services were conducted in both Slavonic and Greek because the congregation was composed of persons from various backgrounds. In 1872, a new building was purchased, and it became the cathedral and diocesan center of the Russian Orthodox bishop.[2]

More than 2,000 miles (3,200 km) from San Francisco, another parish was established in New York City in 1870. Unlike the other two parishes, this one was not organized by merchants or diplomats. Rather, the parish in New York was founded by Father Nicholas Bjerring with the authorization of the Holy Synod of the Church of Russia. A former Roman Catholic professor of theology, Father Bjerring was an American of Danish background. Following the promulgation of the dogma of papal infallibility at the First Vatican Council, he left the Roman Church. Father Bjerring then traveled to St. Petersburg, where he joined the Orthodox Church and was subsequently ordained a priest on 9 May 1870.[3]

Upon the direction of Metropolitan Philaret of Moscow, Father Bjerring returned to the United States and established a parish in New York City in the same year. Although a permanent church building was never constructed, Father Bjerring celebrated the liturgical services in his home. The sign over the door read, "Greek-Russian Church." The congregation was composed chiefly of members of the Greek and Russian consulates, as well as about one hundred other Orthodox Christians who lived in New York. Records indicate that Father Bjerring also received into the Orthodox Church a number of persons who were raised in other religious traditions. After slightly more than twelve years of existence, however, the Russian government withdrew all financial support, and Father Bjerring had to close the chapel in 1883. While the actual reasons for this decision are not known, it may be assumed that the Russian government at that time did not appreciate the missionary value of the chapel and the activity of Father Bjerring.[4]

Although his chapel was closed, Father Bjerring made an outstanding contribution to the development of Orthodoxy in America. He was responsible for translating and publishing a number of liturgical services. He also wrote a brief history of the Orthodox Church and a commentary on its customs and liturgical practices. One of the most outstanding contributions of Bjerring was the publication of the *Oriental Church Magazine* from November 1879 to October 1881. This journal was the first English-language Orthodox periodical to be published in the United States. Its purpose was to acquaint Americans with the beliefs and practices of the Orthodox Church. The articles that appeared in the journal clearly indicate that Father Bjerring was very deeply committed to the task of Orthodox Christian evangelization in America.[5]

THE GREEK IMMIGRANTS AND THEIR PARISHES

The United States has been called a nation of immigrants. From the time when the first settlements were established along the Atlantic coast in the early seventeenth century, America has been a haven for persons of all races and backgrounds who have sought freedom and opportunity. Until about the year 1880, the majority of the immigrants who came to the United States were from Western and Northern Europe. After 1880, however, the majority of the immigrants who came to the United States prior to 1921 were from Eastern and Southeastern Europe. It has been estimated that between 1800 and the period of World War I, about 15 million immigrants entered the United States. Because many of these immigrants were Orthodox Christians, they provided a powerful impetus to the growth of Orthodoxy in the United States.

A substantial migration of Greeks to the United States began during the last quarter of the nineteenth century and continued until 1921. Prior to this period, Greeks had come to America, but their numbers were not significant. About 200 Peloponnesians came to Florida in 1762, when it was still part of the Spanish Empire.[6] Later, during the early nineteenth century, some American philanthropists helped a small number of Greeks to come to the United States to study. As we have already noted, throughout the middle of the nineteenth century, Greek merchants and government officials could be found in most of the port cities of the United States.[7]

Migration of Greeks from the kingdom of Greece and from the Ottoman Empire began to increase noticeably after 1891. Between then and 1920, statistics show that more than 400,000 immigrants from Greece arrived in the United States. Moreover, this figure does not include Greeks who emigrated from the Ottoman Empire or other countries. Although no exact official figures exist, it has been estimated that the number of Greeks entering the United States from Asia Minor between 1891 and 1920 was about 200,000. However, of the total number of Greek immigrants, only about 75 percent remained. Many subsequently returned to Greece.[8]

The Greek immigrants who arrived before 1921 were not entirely homogeneous. There was a clear distinction between those from the kingdom of Greece and those from Asia Minor. Some of the latter could not even speak the Greek language. Furthermore, it was quite common for Greek immigrants from particular regions, islands, or villages to remain in close contact and even to settle together in certain cities in America. The early social organization and parishes of the immigrants frequently reflected these geographical differences. Most of the immigrants during this period were males who came to America with the hope for economic and social advancement. They preferred the larger cities to the countryside. They began to work in textile mills, steel mills, coal mines, and railroad construction. In the course of time, some established their own small businesses.[9]

Once a sizable number of immigrants settled in a city, they would join together to form a mutual aid society. Sometimes named after a saint, a revolutionary hero, or a place in a fatherland, the society assisted the new immigrants in becoming settled. Perhaps the most important and enduring task of these societies was to organize a parish. During the period between 1891 and 1921, the parish of the Holy Trinity in New York City was the first to be organized, in 1892. Within a matter of a few years, a second parish was established in New York City, as well as one in Chicago and in Lowell, Massachusetts.[10]

Between 1900 and 1921, 138 parishes were organized by the Greek immigrants throughout the United States. Many metropolitan areas had more than one parish. Although the liturgical services were held in rented halls in some cities, the majority of these parishes by 1921 had either constructed their own church buildings or purchased abandoned church buildings. This fact is a powerful testimony to the role that religion played in the life of the immigrants. These church buildings, often constructed in traditional fashion, became the visible expression of the Orthodox faith of the immigrants.

However, the parishes of the immigrants were prone to many problems that they had not found in the homeland. Among these were the need to raise money, the shortage of qualified priests or the presence of uncanonical priests, and the proselytism undertaken by some Protestant sects. Yet, the most serious problem was the absence of a resident bishop who could bring unity and direction to the developing church in America and the establishment of an ecclesiastical organizational structure that would unite the parishes.

In the absence of both a bishop and a formal diocesan structure, each of the early parishes was not only established by the immigrants but also entirely controlled by the immigrants through an elected board of trustees. In accordance with the civil charter of incorporation granted by the state government, the board of trustees was responsible for every aspect of the life of the parish. Although some parishes appealed for a parish priest either to the synod of the Patriarchate of Constantinople or to the synod of the Church of Greece, the board of trustees viewed itself as having ultimate authority within the parish. Contrary to Orthodox tradition, the parish priest was viewed as an employee by the board and dismissed by the board when he did not meet its expectations.[11]

In the absence of a resident bishop and inspired by the democratic ideals of America, most of the immigrants viewed their parish as free and independent of all external ecclesiastical authority. With little knowledge of canon law, the immigrants followed the example of Protestantism and adopted a polity of congregationalism that emphasized the autonomy of the local parish and de-emphasized the need for hierarchical authority.[12]

The Patriarchate of Constantinople, the ranking episcopal see in the Orthodox Church, claimed to have ultimate jurisdiction over the developing Orthodox Church in North America in virtue of canons and precedents reaching back to the fourth century. However, the Patriarchate temporarily transferred its jurisdiction over the so-called diaspora in America to the autocephalous Church of Greece in 1908. While the difficulties in the parishes in America may have contributed to the decision, it appears that the Turkish government had become concerned with anti-Turkish activities of the Greek immigrants in the United States.[13]

However, from 1908 to 1918 the Church of Greece undertook no major action to unify and direct the parishes in the United States. While many believed that the synod of the Church of Greece would provide America with a resident bishop, none was sent. Some believed that the synod took no action because of the influence of Lambros Coromilas, who was the Greek ambassador to the United States. He was accused of viewing religion as a "medieval hindrance" and of wanting the church to remain "headless" so that he could become the unquestioned leader of his compatriots in the United States.[14]

Regardless of whether this accusation was entirely accurate, the fact remains that the status of the parishes in the United States did not improve during the ten years in which they were temporarily under the jurisdiction of the Church of Greece. As we shall see in the next chapter, not until 1918 did the Holy Synod of the Church of Greece, under the presidency of Metropolitan Meletios (Metaxakis), pass a resolution to organize the parishes in America.

THE CARPATHO-RUSSIAN IMMIGRANTS
AND THEIR PARISHES

Prior to the October revolution of 1917 and the Russian civil war, migration of Orthodox Christians from imperial Russia to the United States was not significant. By 1910, there were only about 90,000 Russian immigrants living in the United States. Approximately 80 percent of these immigrants were Russian Jews. Of the small minority of Russian immigrants who were Orthodox Christians, most lived either in San Francisco or in New York City. By the time of World War I, these two cities had communities of Russian Orthodox immigrants that numbered no more than 1,000.[15]

As we have already noted, the Russian Orthodox Cathedral and Pastoral School was transferred from Sitka to San Francisco in 1872. About the year 1896, a Russian Orthodox mission parish was reestablished in New York City to serve the needs of the immigrants. While this mission might be seen as the continuation of the efforts of Father Bjerring, the fact is that the new parish served chiefly the immigrant Russian population.[16]

The most significant migration of Slavs to the United States prior to World War I did not come from imperial Russia but rather from the Austro-Hungarian Empire. These immigrants came from the areas about the Carpathian Mountains that were known as Cherbonnaya Rus or Russian Rubra. Until 1918, this area was part of the northeastern kingdom of Hungary, which was part of the Hapsburg-ruled, Austro-Hungarian Empire. Those persons who migrated to the United States from this area were usually known as Carpatho-Russians (Rusyns). This name indicates both the geographic location of their homeland as well as their ethnoreligious affiliation.[17]

The exact number of Carpatho-Russians who entered the United States prior to 1914 is not known. The United States government listed immigrants only by country of origin until 1899. Only after that date were immigrants classified according to race and peoples. However, it has been estimated that about 150,000 Carpatho-Russians entered the United States between 1880 and 1914. The vast majority of these immigrants were peasants who left their homeland because of poor agricultural conditions. At the time of their arrival, industry in the United States was expanding, and there was a great need for cheap labor. As a consequence of this, most of the Carpatho-Russian immigrants settled in the northeastern part of the United States, especially in Pennsylvania and Ohio. There the immigrants found employment in mines and steel mills.[18]

Upon their arrival in the United States, the Carpatho-Russians were Eastern-Rite Roman Catholics. Although they generally referred to themselves as *pravoslavni* (Orthodox), the Carpatho-Russian immigrants were Eastern Catholics who were known as either Greek Catholics or Ruthenian Catholics. Prior to the sixteenth century, the people of Carpatho-Russia had been Orthodox Christians. However, they were integrated into the Roman Catholic Church during the sixteenth century chiefly as a result of political changes. The Carpatho-Russians were permitted to retain their Orthodox liturgical traditions and many of their Orthodox religious customs. Among these was the practice of a married priesthood. However, the bishops of these Eastern Catholic dioceses were under the ultimate authority of the Roman Catholic pope. Over the course of time, these Eastern Catholics were frequently referred to as "Uniates" to emphasize their union with the Roman Catholic Church.[19]

The Carpatho-Russians were deeply religious people, and the immigrants sought to preserve their religious customs in the United States. Almost as soon as a significant number of immigrants settled in a particular city, they would band together to establish a parish, seek out a priest, and construct a church building. However, their religious identity created a great problem for them. While they followed most Orthodox liturgical practices, they were not members of the Orthodox Church. Although they were known as Greek Catholics, they were generally not accepted by the Latin-Rite Catholics in the United States. At that time, the Roman Catholics in this country had little appreciation of the diversity in Roman Catholicism that had existed in Central and Eastern Europe for centuries.

When the Carpatho-Russians began to organize their parishes, they usually encountered opposition from Roman Catholic priests and bishops, who regarded the

Slavic immigrants with suspicion. Moreover, while there were many Carpatho-Russian priests among the immigrants, there was no bishop. As a consequence of this, the Carpatho-Russian priests had been instructed by the bishops in their homeland to report to the local Roman Catholic bishops in America to receive permission to serve the immigrants. Generally, the Roman Catholic bishops either knew very little about the Eastern-Rite Catholics or had very little desire to encourage Greek Catholic parishes in their diocese.[20]

The difficulties between the Carpatho-Russians and the Roman Catholic Church in America became especially acute in the year 1890. Father Alexis Toth arrived in Minneapolis in that year to minister to the immigrants. Among his first tasks was to visit the local Roman Catholic bishop in order to receive canonical authority to undertake his ministry. The prelate, Archbishop John Ireland, was a hierarch who was deeply committed to the Americanization of all immigrants. At that time, he had little appreciation of the Eastern European immigrants, whose desire was to retain their religious traditions and not to be rapidly assimilated into the American society.[21]

The encounter between Father Alexis Toth and Archbishop John Ireland was of great importance. Difficulties began when Father Toth did not genuflect before the hierarch but only kissed his hand. When Archbishop Ireland learned that the priest was a Greek Catholic and that he was a widower, the bishop told Father Alexis that he had already written to Rome to protest the entrance of Greek Catholic priests into America. Furthermore, the archbishop refused to give Father Alexis permission to serve the Carpatho-Russians in Minneapolis.[22]

Father Alexis was a well-educated priest. Prior to his arrival in the United States, he had been the professor of canon law at the University of Presov. Believing that the decision of Archbishop Ireland was in opposition to the rights of Eastern-Rite Catholics and an insult to the Carpatho-Russians, Father Alexis began to organize a parish in Minneapolis without formal permission from the Roman Catholic hierarchy in the United States.[23]

When Archbishop Ireland instituted a lawsuit against Father Alexis and the Carpatho-Russian community, the devoted priest turned to the Orthodox Church. Father Alexis organized a committee and sent the members to San Francisco to speak with Bishop Vladimir (Sokolovsky) of the Russian Orthodox diocese of the Aleutian Islands and Alaska. Recognizing the desire of the Carpatho-Russians to return to the Orthodox Church of their ancestors, Bishop Vladimir traveled to Minneapolis and received Father Alexis Toth and the entire parish into the Russian Orthodox diocese on 25 March 1891. That day was not only the Festival of the Annunciation of Mary, the Mother of God, but also the First Sunday of Lent, which is known as the Sunday of Orthodoxy.

The action of Bishop Vladimir was formally recognized by the Holy Synod of the Church of Russia on 14 July 1892. A letter from Metropolitan Isidore of Novgorod and St. Petersburg stated: "The Ruling All Russian Holy Synod, becoming informed of the conversion re-uniting with the Holy Orthodox Church of the pastor and his faithful parishioners who emigrated from the Carpathian Mountains to

America, namely 361 Russian Uniates and their pastor, Father Alexis Toth, joyfully raising their prayers in thanks to the Lord God upon the blessed occasion impart Orthodox pastoral benediction upon the Reverend Toth and his parishioners, henceforth, Orthodox faithful."[24]

After his entrance into the Russian Orthodox diocese, Father Alexis Toth traveled throughout the northeastern United States to encourage the Carpatho-Russian clergy and laity to return to the Orthodox Church. Through the direct efforts of Father Alexis, about twenty Carpatho-Russian parishes, which contained about 29,000 faithful, entered the Orthodox Church. At the time of his death on 7 May 1909, Father Alexis Toth was eulogized as the "father" of Orthodoxy in America.[25]

This dramatic development caused the focus of the Russian Orthodox diocese of the Aleutian Islands and Alaska to shift from the Alaskan territory and San Francisco to the northeastern region of the United States. Under the leadership of Bishop Tikhon (Bellavin), the administrative center of the diocese was moved to New York City in 1905, chiefly because of the immigration and the return of the Carpatho-Russians to Orthodox Christianity. It has been estimated that as many as 250,000 Eastern Catholics who migrated from various parts of Eastern Europe entered the Russian Orthodox diocese by 1914. The unwillingness of the Vatican to recognize the legitimate concerns of the Carpatho-Russians accelerated this process. Indeed, the publication of the papal bull *Ea semper* in 1907 and its demand that Eastern Catholic clergy in North America be celibate only aggravated the difficult situation.[26]

The official United States government census figures reflect the dramatic development that occurred in the Russian Orthodox diocese. In the census of 1890, the diocese claimed to have 22 churches in Alaska and one in San Francisco.[27] In the census of 1906, the number of parishes had risen to 59.[28] Ten years later, in 1916, the diocese claimed to have 164 churches.[29] Perhaps as many as two-thirds of these parishes were located in the northeastern part of the United States and consisted of former Eastern Catholics.

ARCHBISHOP TIKHON

One of the most influential bishops of the Russian Orthodox Archdiocese during this period was Archbishop Tikhon (Bellavin), who assumed its leadership in September 1898. When he arrived in the country, Archbishop Tikhon was the only Orthodox bishop in the United States. In his capacity as head of the diocese of the Aleutians and Alaska, he was responsible not only for the Orthodox Christians of the Alaskan territory but also for those throughout the United States who were part of the Russian mission. This meant that his flock was multilingual and multinational. His jurisdiction stretched from the East Coast to the West Coast. It included both Native Americans in Alaska and many of the immigrants in the major cities of the East who had accepted the oversight of the Russian Orthodox diocese. This included many Serbian, Syrian, Albanian, Romanian, and Bulgarian immigrants, who also began to establish parishes during this period.[30]

Archbishop Tikhon was responsible for providing both structure and direction to the Russian Orthodox diocese at a very critical period in its development. In order to be closer to the new immigrants, he received permission to transfer the see of the diocese to New York in 1905. Upon his recommendation, the name of the see had been changed to the diocese of the Aleutian Islands and North America in 1900. It was raised to the status of an archdiocese in 1907. Under his leadership, St. Tikhon Monastery was established in South Canaan, Pennsylvania, and a seminary was established in Minneapolis for the training of priests, missionaries, and teachers. Archbishop Tikhon personally oversaw the construction of traditional, Russian-style church buildings in Chicago and New York. The Cathedral of St. Nicholas in New York, which is still standing today, was to be the center of the Russian Orthodox Archdiocese for decades to come.

Archbishop Tikhon also authorized the publication in 1906 of a *Service Book*, containing an English translation of the liturgy, Sacraments, and selected other prayer services. With the translation provided by Isabel Hapgood, this classic text became a valuable tool for the use of English in the liturgical services for decades.[31]

Archbishop Tikhon also had a vision for the developing church in America. He appears to have recognized that the Orthodox Church in the United States had the potential of becoming a truly indigenous church and not simply an extension of the Church of Russia. In 1905, he made a bold proposal for the creation of a unified American Church, which would have a number of diocesan bishops. These diocesan bishops would have specific responsibility for particular ethnic groups. Writing to the synod of the Church of Russia, he said:

The diocese of North America must be reorganized into an Exarchate of the Church of Russia. The diocese is not only multinational; it is composed of several Orthodox Churches which keep the unity of faith, but preserve their particularities in canonical structure, in liturgical rules, in parish life. These particularities are dear to them and can perfectly be tolerated on the pan-Orthodox scene. . . . It should be remembered, however, that life in the New World is different from that of the old; our Church must take this into consideration; a greater autonomy (or possibly autocephaly) should, therefore, be granted to the Church of America as compared with other metropolitan sees of the Russian Church.[32]

Archbishop Tikhon naturally assumed that the Church of Russia had jurisdiction over all Orthodox in America, a position that not all would accept even at that time. However, his bold proposal cannot be underestimated. It sought to create a single, united Orthodox Church that would be manifested in a united episcopacy. This united church would recognize its diverse membership and allow for differences in customs and practices of the various ethnic groups.

It would seem that Archbishop Tikhon had started to move in this direction when, in 1903, he requested that Father Innocent Pustynsky be consecrated in Russia as vicar for Alaska. A year later, Archbishop Tikhon and Bishop Innocent consecrated Father Raphael Hawaweeny as the bishop of Brooklyn, with special responsibility for the Arab Orthodox immigrants. Plans were also made to elect diocesan bishops who would serve the specific needs of Serbians and Albanians.[33]

Just prior to his departure from the United States, Archbishop Tikhon presided at the first All-American Council (Sobor) of the Russian Orthodox Archdiocese. Convened in Mayfield, Pennsylvania, in 1907, it brought together both clergy and lay representatives from the diocesan parishes, which then numbered about one hundred. The theme of the council was "How to Expand the Mission." While the council concerned itself with many practical matters, its structure and methodology were very significant. Under the leadership of Archbishop Tikhon, the council and its preparatory gatherings sought to establish a tradition of conciliarity that recognized the legitimate responsibilities of both the clergy and the laity.

Prior to leaving the United States to return to Russia in 1907, Archbishop Tikhon preached a sermon that emphasized the importance of the Orthodox mission in America:

Orthodox people must care for the dissemination of the Orthodox faith among the heterodox. Christ the Savior said that men lighting a lamp do not put it under a bushel but on a stand, and it gives light to all in the house (Mat 5:15). The light of Orthodoxy also is not lit for a small circle of people. No, the Orthodox faith is catholic. It remembers the commandment of its founder: "Go into all the world . . ." Mat: 28:19. It is our obligation to share our spiritual treasures, our truth, our light and our joy with those who do not have these gifts.[34]

Archbishop Tikhon left the United States because he had been elected the Archbishop of Iaroslav (1907–1914). After subsequently serving the see of Vilno (1914–1917), he was elected Metropolitan of Moscow. In the wake of World War I, he was elected to preside at the historic Church Council of 1917–1918. This council decided to restore the position of Patriarch of Moscow, which had been suppressed at the time of Peter the Great in 1700. With the Bolshevik revolution under way, at this council Tikhon was chosen by lot to become the new patriarch. Prior to his death in 1925, he steadfastly defended the church against the persecutions of the Bolsheviks. He was formally proclaimed a saint by the Church of Russia in 1990.[35]

OTHER ORTHODOX IMMIGRANTS

The rapid increase of immigrants from Greece, Carpatho-Russia, the Balkans, and the Middle East, which began toward the end of the nineteenth century, changed the character of the early parishes and all subsequent parishes established during the first half of the twentieth century. The Pan-Orthodox character of the early parishes was lost as various immigrant groups established parishes to serve their particular needs. As the Orthodox immigrants began to settle in the various cities of the United States, it became common for the parishes to be established along ethnic or linguistic lines. This phenomenon was commonplace not only among the Greeks and the Carpatho-Russians but also among the Serbians, Arabs, Bulgarians, Albanians, Romanians, and Ukrainians.

A parish serving Serbian immigrants was established in 1894 in Jackson, California.[36] At about the same time, a parish serving Arab immigrants came into existence in Brooklyn, New York, in 1895.[37] One for Bulgarians was established in 1907 in Madison, Wisconsin.[38] Another for Albanians was established in 1908 in Boston.[39] A parish for Romanian immigrants was established in 1904 in Cleveland, Ohio.[40] As the numbers of immigrants of these groups increased, other parishes were rapidly established in many of the larger cities.

The establishment of these ethnic parishes reflected the fact that each existed not only as a worshiping community but also as a center serving the cultural and social needs of the immigrants. In the midst of a new country, the immigrants found emotional support, assistance, and a part of their homeland within their churches. While these ethnic parishes served the immediate needs of the immigrants and their children, they did little to promote cooperation and unity among all the Orthodox.

Throughout the period of immigration up until 1921, the Russian Orthodox Archdiocese was the only Orthodox ecclesiastical jurisdiction and the Russian Orthodox bishop was the only resident hierarch in the United States. As a consequence, many Orthodox immigrants who were not of Russian background accepted the authority of the Russian bishop in the United States. This was especially true of the Serbs, Arabs, Albanians, and Romanians. In order to serve better the needs of these immigrants, the Russian Orthodox Archdiocese established a mission diocese with a bishop for Syrian immigrants in 1904. As we have noted, the first Orthodox bishop consecrated in the United States was Father Raphael Hawaweeny, a native of Damascus, Syria, who supervised the Arabic-speaking Orthodox for about twenty years.[41] Likewise, Father Stephen Dzubay was consecrated a bishop, in 1916, especially to serve the Carpatho-Russian immigrants.[42] Plans were also made to consecrate a bishop to serve the Serbian parishes, but this never materialized.

In much the same way that the Church of Russia and the Russian Empire acted as the protector of Orthodox Christianity throughout parts of Eastern Europe and the Middle East prior to the October revolution of 1917, so also the Russian Orthodox Archdiocese viewed itself as the protector of Orthodoxy in the United States. Given the cultural, ethnic, and historical associations of the Old World, it was somewhat natural that many Carpatho-Russian, Syrian, Serbian, Albanian, and Romanian immigrants would associate their parishes with the Russian Orthodox archdiocese.

The Greek immigrants did not follow the pattern that others did. Throughout the period of great immigration, there was very little contact between the Greek parishes and the Russian Orthodox Archdiocese. Although some authors have maintained that all Orthodox in America accepted the authority of the Russian bishop prior to 1921, there is not sufficient evidence to support this claim.[43] The vast majority of the Greek parishes were organized without any contact with the Russian bishops in America. When a parish of Greek immigrants needed a priest, the parish leaders generally appealed to the ecclesiastical authorities, either Athens or Constantinople.[44] Even the marriages of Greek immigrants in America often had to be approved by bishops in the homeland.[45]

Having said this, however, it must also be stated that there is evidence of limited cooperation between some Greek priests and the Russian Orthodox Archdiocese. In the years prior to World War I, at least three priests of Greek background appear to have served under the jurisdiction of the Russian bishop. These priests were Father Michael Andreades, Father Kallinikos Kanellos, and Father Theoklitos Triantafilidis. Each of these had studied in Russia and spoke Russian as well as Greek. In the early part of the twentieth century, these priests served parishes in the western part of the United States that were composed of both Greeks and Slavs.[46]

Some evidence also shows that a small number of Greek parishes turned to the Russian Orthodox Archdiocese for assistance prior to 1921. Specifically, the archives of the Russian Archdiocese contains letters from six Greek parishes that requested *antimencia* (altar cloths). Only one undated letter from this period was sent to the Russian Archdiocese from a Greek parish that was seeking a priest. These limited examples of Greek parishes that sought assistance from the Russian Orthodox Archdiocese are exceptions and not the norm.[47]

Indeed, evidence indicates that the Russian Orthodox diocese recognized that the Greek priests and Greek Orthodox parishes were not part of its jurisdiction. On the parish listings of the Russian Orthodox diocese for 1906, the Greek Orthodox parishes are not included. Furthermore, the document notes that in addition to the listed clergymen, "there are several Greek priests who are under the Metropolitan of Athens but who, so far as Episcopal Ministrations are concerned, call upon the Orthodox Archbishop of North America."[48] While this statement is ambiguous, it does indicate that the Russian Orthodox diocese recognized that the Greek priests in America were not fully under its jurisdiction. In this regard, it should also be noted that the Greek parishes were not listed among those belonging to the Russian Orthodox jurisdiction in lists published in 1911 and 1918.[49]

The Orthodox parishes of the late nineteenth and early twentieth centuries were, for the most part, ethnic communities. Most of the earliest Orthodox parishes in the continental United States served all Orthodox immigrants or merchants without regard for ethnic background. However, as immigration increased in the three decades before World War I, it became common for Orthodox parishes to be organized on an ethnic or linguistic basis. This practice reflected the fact that the parish was not only a worshiping community but also a center of social and cultural life. However, this practice did not contribute to a sense of Orthodox unity in America or Orthodox mission in America.

While the various immigrant groups professed the same Orthodox faith and generally followed the same liturgical practices, there was very little evidence of

Orthodox unity or cooperation. In the absence of a bishop whose authority was recognized by all Orthodox groups and a single unifying ecclesiastical structure, isolation among the Orthodox groups became commonplace. When compounded by linguistic barriers and cultural suspicion, this isolation frequently led to a type of de facto division among the Orthodox. This division among the Orthodox groups would become more acute in the period following World War I.

4
EARLY DIOCESAN DEVELOPMENTS

The Orthodox immigrants did not sever ties with their homeland. Although they lived in a new country, the immigrants were very much influenced by the political and ecclesiastical developments that occurred in their fatherlands during the late eighteenth and early nineteenth centuries. By means of ethnic newspapers, letters from relatives, and the reports of persons who recently arrived in America, the immigrants were kept informed of all the events that occurred in their homelands before, during, and after World War I.

Political differences in Greece following World War I spread to the United States and had a profound impact upon the Greek immigrants, as well as upon their ecclesiastical life. Similarly, the Bolshevik revolution of 1917 and the events that followed it had a momentous impact upon both the immigrants from Russia and other parts of Eastern Europe as well as the Russian Orthodox Archdiocese in America and the parishes associated with it. Having their roots in Eastern European politics, fratricidal disputes, parish divisions, and schisms became the principal characteristics of Orthodox Christianity in the United States in the two decades following the conclusion of World War I.

THE FOUNDING OF THE GREEK ORTHODOX ARCHDIOCESE

The formal organization of the Greek Orthodox parishes in the United States began at a time when the people of Greece were seriously divided between the followers of King Constantine I and the followers of Prime Minister Eleftherios Venizelos.[1] Following the assumption of power by Venizelos in 1917, Meletios

Metaxakis was elected Metropolitan of Athens. On 4 August 1918, the Holy Synod of the Church of Greece, under the presidency of Metropolitan Meletios, resolved to organize the Greek Orthodox parishes in America.[2]

Having great interest in the American situation, Metropolitan Meletios traveled to the United States in order to oversee personally the organization of the parishes. Accompanied by Bishop Alexander (Demoglou) of Rodostolou, Father Chrysostomos Papadopoulos, and Professor Amilkas Alevizatos of Athens, Metropolitan Meletios arrived in New York on 22 August 1918. Concerned with the need to establish a central ecclesiastical authority for the American parishes, Metropolitan Meletios began to meet immediately after his arrival with prominent clergy and laypersons. The metropolitan recognized that there was a great need for a bishop in the United States who could act with authority to bring unity and direction to the parishes, which at that time numbered about 140. Before leaving the United States on 29 October 1918, therefore, Metropolitan Meletios appointed Bishop Alexander of Rodostolou as the synodical representative.[3]

Bishop Alexander encountered severe difficulties from the very beginning of his administration. Although many Greek immigrants welcomed the presence of the bishop, others were firmly opposed to his leadership. This opposition was rooted in the struggle between the Royalists and the Venizelists, which divided not only the people of Greece but also the Greek immigrants in America. Both Metropolitan Meletios and Bishop Alexander were viewed by the Royalists as being closely associated with Venizelos and his republican political views. Therefore, the Royalists in America urged the priests to ignore the directives of the bishop, and they urged the faithful to disassociate themselves from priests who accepted the authority of the synodical representative.

Although Bishop Alexander had remained in the United States with the intention of uniting the Greek Orthodox parishes under his canonical authority, he rapidly discovered that many refused to accept his leadership. Politics, rather than canon law, had a greater influence upon the immigrants. A civil war among the Greek immigrants and division within the Greek Orthodox parishes had begun. This sad state of affairs would continue for about two decades.

The situation in the United States became even more acute following political changes in Greece. After the defeat of the Venizelos party in the election of 1 November 1920, the Royalists returned to power. Metropolitan Meletios was informed on 17 November 1920, in a letter from the minister of ecclesiastical affairs that Metropolitan Theokleitos was being restored to his see by royal order. Despite protests to Queen Olga and to the Ecumenical Patriarchate, Metropolitan Meletios was forced to vacate his residence. Still claiming to be the legitimate Metropolitan of Athens, he left Greece and traveled to the United States in February 1921. Without regard for the decisions of the new Holy Synod of the Church of Greece, Metropolitan Meletios and Bishop Alexander continued to try to organize the Greek Orthodox parishes in America.[4]

Despite the division between the Royalists and the Venizelists, which continued to deepen, and the opposition of the new Holy Synod of the Church of Greece,

Metropolitan Meletios and Bishop Alexander acted decisively to organize in a formal and legal manner the Greek Orthodox parishes in America. Through an encyclical dated 11 August 1921, Metropolitan Meletios called for the first Congress
of Clergy and Laity of the parishes in America. This historic congress, held in
New York on 13–15 September 1921, was the first time that clergy and lay representatives of the Greek Orthodox parishes from throughout the United States met
together. The most important action of the congress was the establishment of the
Greek Orthodox Archdiocese of North and South America.[5]

In order to give the new archdiocese a legal as well as an ecclesiastical authority, it was formally incorporated in the state of New York on 19 September 1921.
According to the document of incorporation, the purposes of the archdiocese
were:

To edify the religious and moral life of the Greek Orthodox Christians in North and South
America on the basis of Holy Scripture, the rules and canons of the Holy Apostles and of
the Seven Ecumenical Councils of the ancient undivided Church as they are or shall be actually interpreted by the Great Church of Christ in Constantinople and to exercise governing authority over and to maintain advisory relations with Greek Orthodox Churches
throughout North and South America and to maintain spiritual and advisory relations with
synods and other governing authorities of the said Church located elsewhere.[6]

New developments soon occurred in both America and Constantinople that further altered the direction of the Greek Orthodox Archdiocese. Less than two
months after the organization of the new archdiocese, Metropolitan Meletios was
elected Ecumenical Patriarch of Constantinople on 25 November 1921.[7] This dramatic turn of events was to have a monumental effect upon Orthodox Christianity
in America. Although Metropolitan Meletios was chosen to become patriarch at a
time when the Church of Constantinople was beset with many problems, he continued to have a profound concern for the Orthodox faithful in America. This is
very clearly evident in his enthronement speech, which was delivered in the patriarchal Church of St. George on 8 February 1922. After reflecting upon the state of
the Orthodox churches, the new patriarch spoke with much affection and with
much vision for the church in America:

I saw the largest and the best of the Orthodox Church in the diaspora, and I understood how
exalted the name of Orthodoxy could be, especially in the great country of the United States
of America, if more than two million Orthodox people there were united into the one
Church organization, an "American Orthodox Church."[8]

Less than a month after his enthronement, Meletios and the Holy Synod of the
church of Constantinople decided on 1 March 1922 to revoke the statement of
1908 that had placed the diaspora under temporary jurisdiction of the Church of
Greece. Two months later, a new statement issued by Patriarch Meletios and the
Holy Synod on 17 May 1922 canonically established the Orthodox Archdiocese of

North and South America as a province of the church of Constantinople. Bishop Alexander was subsequently appointed as the first archbishop.[9]

POLITICS AND SCHISM

The establishment of the archdiocese in 1921, the election of Metropolitan Meletios as Patriarch of Constantinople, and the decision to restore the American parishes to the jurisdiction of the Ecumenical Patriarchate did not immediately diminish the strife between the Royalists and the Venizelists in America. In fact, these great events may have contributed to further division.

Prior to these developments, the Holy Synod of the Church of Greece acted to establish its authority over the Greek Orthodox parishes in America and to diminish the authority of then-Metropolitan Meletios and Bishop Alexander. In 1921, the Holy Synod of the Church of Greece sent Metropolitan Germanos (Troianos) of Monemvasia and Lacedaemonos to be its exarch in the United States. The new exarch of the Church of Greece presented a serious challenge to the authority of Metropolitan Meletios and Bishop Alexander. Acting with the authority of both the Church of Greece and the government of Greece, Metropolitan Germanos sought to bring all priests and parishes under his authority.[10] His presence, however, only contributed to the division among the Greek Orthodox parishes. Metropolitan Germanos extended his authority over about fifty parishes during his brief stay in the United States.[11]

As a consequence of improved relations between the Patriarchate of Constantinople and the Church of Greece, Metropolitan Germanos was recalled in 1923. With his return to Greece, the formal division of the Greek Orthodox in America into two rival ecclesiastical jurisdictions should have come to an end. But it did not. The division between the Royalists and the Venizelists in the United States persisted and also continued to manifest itself in the parishes. Under the leadership of Royalists, a small number of parishes continued to oppose the authority of Archbishop Alexander and the three newly consecrated bishops of the archdiocese: Bishop Philaret (Ioannides) of Chicago, Bishop Joachim (Alexopoulos) of Boston, and Bishop Kallistos (Papageorgakopoulos) of San Francisco.[12]

The schismatic movement was reinvigorated with the arrival in the United States in 1923 of Metropolitan Vasilios (Komvopoulos) of Chaldea. A strong supporter of the Royalist cause, this hierarch refused to accept his recent appointment as Metropolitan of Chaldea. Upon arriving in the United States, the metropolitan went to Lowell, Massachusetts, where the representatives of thirteen Royalist parishes proclaimed him to be the head of the autocephalous metropolis of America and Canada. Although the Ecumenical Patriarchate deposed Vasilios on 10 May 1924, he continued his activity in the United States and was viewed by the Royalists as a martyred hero. His qualities as a preacher, liturgist, and administrator aided him in his struggle against the authority of the canonical archdiocese.[13]

The introduction of the new calendar (revised Julian) in 1923 further aggravated the division in America. Following the lead of its mother church and in harmony with the Church of Greece, the canonical archdiocese adopted the new calendar and abandoned the old Julian calendar, which was thirteen days "behind." This change, however, did not affect the manner of reckoning the date of Pascha (Easter). The rival metropolis under the leader of Metropolitan Vasilios retained the use of the old calendar. Thus, in addition to their political stance, the Royalist parishes also had an ecclesiastical issue to employ in their struggle against the archdiocese and patriarchate. The political views of the Royalists were merged with the religious views of the "old-calendarists," and the union led to the increase of hostility. Among the Slavic Orthodox, the old calendar (Julian) generally continued to be followed both in this country and abroad.[14]

The division among the Greek Orthodox parishes continued without resolution until 1930. On 9 April of that year, Patriarch Photios II of Constantinople, with the support of Archbishop Chrysostomos of Athens, appointed Metropolitan Damaskinos (Papandreou) of Corinth as exarch to America.[15] Having visited the United States in 1928 to collect the money for victims of the earthquake in Corinth, the metropolitan was well aware of the grave problems that afflicted the Greek Orthodox Archdiocese and its parishes. Following his arrival on 20 May 1930, Metropolitan Damaskinos began a series of meetings with clergy and laypersons. Being a highly respected hierarch who was admired for both his deep faith and his administrative ability, Metropolitan Damaskinos found support among many persons of both political persuasions. In accordance with his instructions, he formulated proposals to resolve the difficult situation and submitted these to the Ecumenical Patriarchate.

Based upon these recommendations, the Patriarchate, in cooperation with the Church of Greece, made two major decisions. First, Archbishop Alexander was relieved of his responsibilities. He was to be replaced by Metropolitan Athenagoras (Spirou) of Kerkyra, who was elected Archbishop of America on 13 August 1930. Second, all the bishops in America who had been involved in the dispute would be reassigned to new sees. Only Bishop Kallistos of San Francisco was permitted to remain in the United States to assist the new archbishop. While all the difficulties that afflicted the Greek Orthodox parishes in America were not resolved at once, these decisions provided a basis upon which reconciliation could take place.[16]

THE IMPACT OF THE RUSSIAN REVOLUTION

The Russian Orthodox Archdiocese in America was also gravely afflicted by difficulties resulting from the political developments occurring in Europe following World War I. As we have seen, in the four decades prior to the war, the Russian Orthodox Archdiocese underwent a period of remarkable growth as a result of immigration and the return of Carpatho-Russian immigrants to the Orthodox Church. In addition to the parishes of these immigrants, the archdiocese also included a small number of parishes composed of either Arab, Serbian, Romanian, Albanian, or Bulgarian immigrants. Having about one hundred parishes in the continental United States by 1917, the Russian Orthodox Archdiocese had also established a number of institutions. Among these were the Theological Seminary in Minneapolis (1905); Saint Tikhon Monastery in South Canaan, Pennsylvania (1906); and the Holy Annunciation College for Women in Brooklyn, New York (1915).[17]

Following the revolution of 1917, however, the Russian Orthodox Archdiocese in America was thrust into economic and administrative chaos. The victory of the Bolsheviks, the disestablishment of the church, and the persecution of Patriarch Tikhon and the other hierarchs of the canonical church were the principal events that had a profound impact upon the Russian Orthodox Archdiocese in America, its constituent parishes, and the immigrant faithful.

The stability that the archdiocese enjoyed prior to the revolution was rooted in the intimate relations that it had with both the imperial government and the Church of Russia. Following the revolution, the relationship with the state was severed, and the relationship with the patriarchate was strained and eventually broken. Without the financial support that had come from the old imperial government and without reliable communication with the Patriarchate of Moscow, the Russian Orthodox Archdiocese became afflicted with financial difficulties, internal dissension, and schism.[18]

Beginning during the war years, the voices of political dissent could be heard within the immigrant communities of the Russians in America. While most Russian Orthodox immigrants accepted the reality of the Russian monarchy and the relationship between the church and the imperial government, there was a small but vocal minority who publicly advocated socialistic principles. They also challenged the authority of the Russian Orthodox Archdiocese in America, which they viewed as the representative of the imperial government. The Russian Socialist Party, which was associated with the American Socialist Party, had chapters in most of the major cities of the United States where there was a sizable number of Russian immigrants. At its first convention in 1915, there were eighteen chapters with about 300 members. Within only two years, the membership had more than doubled in size. The meetings of the local chapters were usually held on Sunday morning and featured lecturers who spoke not only in favor of socialistic principles but also against the church. With the coming of the revolution of 1917, these dissidents became even more critical of the clergy and hierarchy of the Russian Orthodox Archdiocese in America.[19]

As a direct consequence of the Bolshevik victory in Russia, the Russian Orthodox Archdiocese in America was plunged into a twofold crisis of leadership and financial instability that was complicated by the activities of the political dissidents. On the eve of the revolution, Archbishop Evdokim (Meschersky), the primate of the archdiocese, left the United States to attend the All-Russian Council, which opened on 15 August 1917. Prior to his departure, the archbishop had entrusted the administration of the archdiocese to Bishop Alexander (Nemolovsky) of Canada. Following the council and the revolution, Archbishop Evdokim never returned to America. He subsequently joined the Living Church movement in 1922. When the report reached America that the archbishop would not return, a council of the Russian Orthodox Archdiocese was held on 12–15 February 1919 in Cleveland, Ohio. At this council, Bishop Alexander was formally elected the ruling archbishop of the archdiocese. However, his election was not confirmed by Patriarch Tikhon of Moscow until 27 August 1920.[20]

Despite his good intention, Archbishop Alexander was not able to bring harmony to the archdiocese, which was plagued by dissension and financial instability. Prior to the revolution, the Russian Orthodox Archdiocese in America had received its financial support from the imperial government. In the year 1916, for example, $550,000 was received of the $1 million that had been requested. With the Bolshevik victory, however, all financial aid from Russia ended. Moreover, by 1919, the archdiocese had a debt that exceeded $200,000. In an effort to reduce the debt and to pay clergy salaries, Archbishop Alexander weakened his position by making some poor financial decisions. He resorted to making additional loans and to mortgaging church property. Both of these actions were not approved by many laypersons and priests, who began to charge the archbishop with gross mismanagement.

Recognizing that the situation was beyond his control, Archbishop Alexander resigned his position on 7 June 1921 and turned over the administration of the archdiocese to Metropolitan Platon (Rozhdestvensky), who had recently returned to the United States as a refugee. Archbishop Alexander left America for Europe on 20 June 1920. After spending some time in Constantinople and on Mount Athos, he was appointed archbishop of Brussels and Belgium.[21]

The Third Council of the Russian Orthodox Archdiocese was held 5–9 November 1922 in Pittsburgh. Recognizing the decision of Archbishop Alexander, the delegates elected Metropolitan Platon as ruling hierarch of the archdiocese and invested him with the title Metropolitan of All America and Canada. Well known by many of the delegates, Metropolitan Platon had been archbishop of the archdiocese from 1907 to 1914. He became archbishop of Kishinev and Khotin in Russia in 1914 and was subsequently made Metropolitan of Kherson and Odessa. With the defeat of the White Army during the Russian civil war, Metropolitan Platon left Russian and went to Constantinople. There, he joined with other exiled bishops in establishing the Highest Russian Church Administration Abroad in 1920. He had returned to the United States initially to seek the support of the American government against the Bolsheviks.[22]

THE ESTABLISHMENT OF THE INDEPENDENT METROPOLIA

The authority of Metropolitan Platon was not recognized by all. Following the departure of Archbishop Alexander, Bishop Stephen (Dzubay) of Pittsburgh claimed that he was the rightful primate of the Russian Orthodox Archdiocese. He charged that Patriarch Tikhon had not formally approved the transfer of Metropolitan Platon to America. Indeed, there was no formal documentation of the appointment of Metropolitan Platon. However, most believed that Patriarch Tikhon had given his oral permission for the appointment of Metropolitan Platon through a representative of the Russian Orthodox Archdiocese who had been in Moscow in 1922. Bishop Stephen, however, did not accept this and became the leader of approximately sixty Carpatho-Russian parishes, which for a number of years had refused to recognize the authority of Metropolitan Platon.[23]

Another serious challenge to the authority of Metropolitan Platon came from the representatives of the Living Church movement in the United States. Beginning 1922–1923, a group of clergy sought to gain control of the Moscow Patriarchate with the covert support of the Soviet government. This schismatic group, which came to be known as the Renovated or Living Church, received the support of some bishops and began to introduce ecclesiastical reforms. Chief among these was the introduction of a married episcopacy. Hierarchs of the Living Church consecrated Father John Kedrovsky as their archbishop of America on 9 October 1923 in Moscow. He was a married priest from America and had been suspended in 1918 by Archbishop Alexander. Following his return to the United States, he became the leader of about twenty priests and a small number of faithful.[24]

With formal documentation from the Living Church synod in Moscow, Archbishop John Kedrovsky sought to take control of the Russian Orthodox parishes in the United States through the process of litigation. Although he was generally unsuccessful in his legal efforts, he did manage to gain control of the historic St. Nicholas Cathedral in New York City by a court decision in 1926. The control of the cathedral remained in the hands of his followers until 1943. This court decision was a critical blow to the authority and prestige of Metropolitan Platon.[25]

During the course of his struggle against the dissident cleric, Metropolitan Platon received a letter from Patriarch Tikhon dated 16 January 1924 that was to have great impact upon Russian Orthodoxy in the United States. The letter declared:

As we have data proving that the Metropolitan of North America has engaged in public acts of counterrevolution directed against the Soviet Power and of harmful consequences to the Orthodox Church, Metropolitan Platon will be dismissed from the government of the North American Diocese from the day on which this present decree is announced to him.

The choice of a candidate for the North American Hierarchical See will be the object of special discussion. It will be his duty personally to announce this decision to Metropolitan Platon and to take over from him all the Church property, governing the North American Diocese according to special instructions which will be given to him. Metropolitan Platon will be invited to come to Moscow to put himself at the disposal of the Patriarch.[26]

Not long after this decree was made public, the Fourth Council of the Russian Orthodox Archdiocese was held in Detroit 2–4 April 1924. The delegates were confronted with the serious dissension in the archdiocese, the threat of the Living Church movement, and the recent patriarchal decree. In the light of all of this, the delegates made two major decisions. First, the delegates reconfirmed the election of Metropolitan Platon as ruling hierarch of the archdiocese. Second, the delegates resolved "to declare the Russian Orthodox Church in America a self-governed Church so that it be governed by its own elected Archbishop by means of a Council of Bishops, a council of those elected by the clergy and laity, and periodic Councils of the entire American Church."[27] The delegates also stipulated that "spiritual contact and communion" with the Church of Russia should not be broken despite the decision to break administrative ties. From this time, the Russian Orthodox archdiocese of North America and the Aleutian Islands came to be known formally as the Russian Orthodox Greek Catholic Church or, simply, the Metropolia.[28]

The decision of the delegates at the council of 1924 to proclaim the Russian Orthodox Archdiocese to be autonomous was not an easy one. Yet, it was made by them with the belief that the Patriarchate of Moscow was not in a position to oversee the dioceses outside Russia at that time and with the hope that the action would strengthen the position of Metropolitan Platon against the activity of schismatic groups.

In order to substantiate their decision, the delegates based their action upon a decree issued by Patriarch Tikhon on 20 November 1920. This decree provided instruction for diocesan bishops to follow in the event that communication with the patriarchate was severed because of the Russian civil war. While the decree was not designed to deal with dioceses outside Russia, it became a basis for the dramatic action of the Metropolia.[29]

The council of 1924 helped to strengthen the position of Metropolitan Platon, but it did not prevent further divisions. Within ten years of the council, two significant events occurred.

First, the Russian Orthodox Synod Outside of Russia, also known as the Karlovtsy Synod or the Synod Abroad, established a rival diocese in the United States in 1927. Composed initially of about twenty parishes, this diocese was led by Archbishop Apollinary (Koshevoy), who had been at one time a vicar bishop of Metropolitan Platon. Made up of bishops who fled Russia after the civil war, the Karlovtsy Synod claimed jurisdiction over the entire Russian diaspora. Both in Western Europe and in America, this diocese attracted those Russians émigrés who were loyal to the monarchy and looked forward to the destruction of the Communist regime in the Soviet Union.

As a church organization, the Karlovtsy Synod Abroad was formally established by White Russian clergy and laity who fled their homeland in the wake of the Communist revolution and Russian civil war. In the company of thousands of refugees, some Russian bishops who had abandoned their dioceses in Russia fled to Constantinople in 1920. The Patriarchate of Constantinople provided assistance for these refugees in its schools, orphanages, and hospitals. On 20 December 1920, the patriarchate granted the Russian clergy limited canonical authority to minister to the refugees in the Archdiocese of Constantinople. Based upon this, the émigré bishops established an organization known as the Highest Ecclesiastical Administration of the Russian Church Abroad in Constantinople in 1921.[30]

Metropolitan Anthony (Khrapovitsky) of Kiev, the leader of the exile bishops, decided to move the organization to Sremsky-Karlovtsy in Serbia in 1921 at the invitation of the Patriarch of Serbia. On 18 August 1921, the Church of Serbia permitted the exile Russian clergy to establish their administration within the canonical boundaries of the Church of Serbia and under its supervision. At Sremski-Karlovtsy, the Russian exiles held a council in 1921. There they called for the restoration of the Romanov monarchy in Russia. They also urged the European nations to arm the exiles so that they could return to Russia and overthrow the Communists.[31]

Recognizing the extreme political character of the administration, the beleaguered Patriarch Tikhon of Moscow and the synod of the Church of Russia denounced the statements of the Karlovtsy Council and formally abolished the administration in a letter dated 22 April (5 May) 1922.[32]

The exile bishops accepted the decision, but they established a Temporary Episcopal Synod of the Russian Orthodox Church Abroad in 1922. This new organization was established on the basis of the 1920 decree of Patriarch Tikhon. As we have noted, this decree addressed the situation of dioceses in Russia that lost touch with the patriarchate during the civil war. The decree permitted the temporary association of neighboring diocesan bishops in Russia to deal with church affairs until normal communications were restored with the patriarchate. While the decree was not intended to apply to their situation, the exiled Russian bishops used this document to justify their new organization and to circumvent the earlier decision of Patriarch Tikhon.

In the period prior to his death, the beleaguered Patriarch Tikhon appears to have authored another document that opposed the activities of the émigré bishops. Known as the Last Testament, the document appeared after the death of Patriarch Tikhon on 25 March (7 April) 1925. Here, the patriarch clearly opposed the existence and action of the Karlovtsy Synod in no uncertain terms.[33]

The members of the Karlovtsy Synod refused to have any type of relationship with the Patriarchate of Moscow after 1927. They held that the official church in Russia had become a tool of the Communist regime. Thus, they forcefully affirmed the conviction that their jurisdiction was the authentic Russian Orthodox Church "in Exile."[34]

Second, Metropolitan Benjamin (Fedchenkov) came to the United States in 1933 as the exarch of the Moscow Patriarchate. After Metropolitan Platon refused to profess loyalty to the Soviet government as had been requested, Metropolitan Benjamin was appointed Archbishop of the Aleutian Islands and North America by Metropolitan Sergius, the acting *locum tenens* of the Patriarchate of Moscow, on 22 November 1933. This followed the formal suspension of Metropolitan Platon, which occurred on 16 August 1933. While only a few parishes initially joined the "exarchate" under Metropolitan Benjamin, he claimed to be the legal and canonical representative of the Patriarchate of Moscow. This diocese attracted those who believed that the Russian Orthodox Church in America had to maintain a canonical relationship with the Patriarchate of Moscow.[35]

By 1933, therefore, the Russian Orthodox in America were tragically divided. Four major Russian Orthodox jurisdictions claimed to be the rightful and legitimate successor of the Russian Orthodox Archdiocese that existed in America prior to the Russian revolution of 1917 and that traced its origin to the Alaskan mission. In terms of size, these were the Metropolia, the exarchate of the Moscow Patriarchate, the diocese of the Russian Orthodox Church Abroad, and the diocese associated with the Living Church movement. Each of these four jurisdictions had very different perspectives on the relationship of the Russian Orthodox Church in America to the Church in Russia.

THE ANTIOCHIAN ORTHODOX ARCHDIOCESE

The development of a separate jurisdiction for Arab Orthodox was accompanied by many peculiar features. As early as 1904, Bishop Raphael (Hawaweeny) had been consecrated to care for the Arab immigrants within the Russian Orthodox Archdiocese, a task begun as early as 1896. However, after 1915, the visiting Metropolitan Germanos (Shehadi) of Zahle in the Patriarchate of Antioch sought to draw the immigrants away from the Russian Orthodox Archdiocese. His followers, known as Antacky (pro-Antiochian), were opposed to the leadership of Bishop Aftimios (Ofiech), the successor of Bishop Raphael. They were known as Russy (pro-Russian). The former controlled about eighteen parishes, and the latter about forty.[36]

The Patriarchate of Antioch directly entered the situation in 1922, when it dispatched its first official observer, Metropolitan Gerasimos (Messara). He consecrated Archbishop Victor (Abo-Assaley) as the first bishop of the Syrian (Antiochian) Orthodox Archdiocese in 1924. Division among the Arab-speaking immigrants continued, however. In 1936, two rival groups of Russian bishops consecrated Archbishop Antony (Bashir) in New York and Archbishop Samuel (David) in Toledo, Ohio. The Patriarchate of Antioch eventually recognized both bishops and their parishes and permitted the two jurisdictions to function side by side. This situation remained in effect until a unified Antiochian Orthodox Christian Archdiocese was established in 1975.[37]

OTHER PARALLEL DIOCESES

The internal difficulties that afflicted the Greek Orthodox, Russian Orthodox, and Antiochian Orthodox in this country, combined with a growing sense of nationalism among the immigrants, had a profound impact upon the other Orthodox parishes and ethnic groups.

The Patriarchate of Constantinople claimed authority over the developing church in America on the basis of canon law and ancient ecclesiastical practices. However, the tremendous difficulties that the Greek immigrants experienced throughout the early decades of this century demanded the full attention of the patriarchate. This meant that the patriarchate was not in a position to deal with the various other Orthodox immigrant groups and to unite them into a single ecclesiastical province as had been envisioned by Patriarch Melitios in 1922.

As we have seen, the Russian Orthodox Archdiocese had made an attempt to gather the Serbian, Syrian, Romanian, Bulgarian, and Albanian immigrants and their parishes under its authority during the late nineteenth and early twentieth centuries. Leaders such as Archbishop Tikhon attempted to devise a creative plan that would recognize ethnic differences but also maintain administrative unity among the Orthodox undei the aegis of the Church of Russia.

However, the emphasis upon Russian nationalism and the attempts at Russification advocated by some leaders of the Russian Orthodox Archdiocese, such as Metropolitan Evdokim (Mischersky), combined with a sense of nationalism among the other immigrants, provided a basis for alienation between the Russian and non-Russian members of the archdiocese. This was further compounded by the difficulties that the Russian Orthodox Archdiocese experienced in the wake of the Russian revolution.

The Serbian parishes, which numbered about thirty-six, were organized into a diocese by the Patriarchate of Serbia in 1921. From 1920 to 1921, these parishes received leadership from Bishop Nikolaj (Velimirovich). Their first formal resident bishop was Mardarije (Uskokovich), who was assigned in 1927.[38]

The Romanians, with about forty parishes at the time, entered into a relationship with the Archbishop of Sibiu in Romania in 1923 and were organized into a diocese in 1930 by the Patriarchate of Bucharest. Bishop Polycarp (Morusca) was assigned to be the resident bishop in 1935.[39]

The Albanians, with three parishes, were organized into a diocese associated with the Church of Albania by Metropolitan Theophan (Noli) in 1932. As a priest, Father Noli had begun to organize the Albanian immigrants as early as 1908. Although he was elected a bishop in 1918, he was not consecrated until 1923 in Albania. Bishop Theofan permanently returned to the United States in 1931.[40]

The Bulgarians, with only five parishes, established a relationship with their mother church in 1922 and were finally organized into a diocese by the Church of Bulgaria in 1938. The diocese was led initially by Bishop Andrey (Velichky).[41]

Ukrainian immigrants, considering themselves ethnically and linguistically distinct from both Russians and Carpatho-Russians, organized parishes, especially after 1918. These Ukrainian immigrants came from Galicia, a non-Hungarian province of the Austrian-Hungarian Empire. When they arrived in America, most were Eastern-Rite Roman Catholics whose union with Rome dated from the Union of Brest in 1596. Like many of the Carpatho-Russians, a number of Ukrainians began to join the Russian Orthodox Archdiocese after their arrival in this country. Because of their growing sense of Ukrainian nationalism as well as the unwillingness of some Russian Orthodox leaders to recognize legitimate diversity in liturgical language and customs, the Ukrainian parishes gradually began to separate from the Russian Orthodox Archdiocese. In 1924, they organized an independent diocese under the leadership of Father John Theodorovich. He claimed to have been consecrated a bishop in Kiev. However, because of a question related to the status of those who consecrated him, Father John Theodorovich's ordination as a bishop was not recognized by other Orthodox churches. Because of this, the clergy and parishes associated with him had little contact with other Orthodox jurisdictions.[42]

The Ecumenical Patriarchate acted to establish a diocese for Ukrainian parishes and Carpatho-Russian parishes that left the Roman Catholic Church and entered Orthodoxy. The Ukrainian Orthodox Church in the United States, with about fifty parishes, was established in 1931. Under the jurisdiction of the Patriarchate of Constantinople, Father Bogdan Spilka was consecrated as its bishop in 1937.[43] The American Carpatho-Russian Orthodox Greek Catholic diocese was established in 1938 with Bishop Orestes (Chornock) as its bishop. At that time it contained about forty parishes.[44]

Writing in 1927, Archbishop Aftimios of Brooklyn emphasized the tragic consequences of the lack of jurisdictional unity when he said:

With a possible three million or even greater number of communicants residing in North America, the Holy Eastern Orthodox Catholic and Apostolic Church should be one of the major religious bodies in America. That it is not is due solely to the failure of its responsible leaders to come together as one Orthodox Catholic body for the organization of the Church in this country. . . . Though the Orthodox Church boasts a litany in her daily Divine Services beseeching God "for the peace of the Churches and the union of them all," she is herself in America the most outstanding example of the disastrous effects of disunion, disorder, secret strife, and open warfare that this country of divided and warring sects can offer.[45]

The concerns of Archbishop Aftimios and others led to an attempt to establish the Holy Eastern Orthodox Catholic and Apostolic Church in North America in 1927. Known popularly as the American Orthodox Catholic Church, this jurisdiction was designed initially to bring greater unity to a number of ethnic dioceses and to have special concern for Orthodox faithful born in America who were primarily English-speaking. Its organization had the formal support of Metropolitan Platon of the Russian Orthodox Archdiocese and the five other bishops of that jurisdiction. Much of the direction for the new jurisdiction came from Father Boris Burden and Father Michael Gelsinger. They had a genuine concern for making the Orthodox Church better known within American society. They were also concerned with the fact that many Orthodox young people were being attracted to the Roman Catholic Church and the Episcopal Church.

Despite the noble intentions of some of those involved in the new jurisdiction, it never received recognition from any of the mother churches. It also became afflicted with internal divisions. Metropolitan Platon of the Russian Orthodox Metropolia eventually distanced himself from the new organization. This led to serious tensions between him and Archbishop Aftimios.

In an effort to bolster the status of the new jurisdiction, Archbishop Aftimios began to consecrate others to the episcopacy. Father Sophronios Bashira was consecrated bishop of Los Angeles in 1928. Father Joseph Zuk was consecrated a bishop in 1932 and served about twelve Ukrainian parishes, which returned to Orthodoxy from Roman Catholicism. Father Ignatius Nichols was also consecrated bishop of Washington in 1932. He eventually disassociated himself from Archbishop Aftimios and became associated with other church groups claiming to be related to the Orthodox Church. After losing a court battle to Metropolitan Platon over control of his cathedral in Brooklyn in 1932, Archbishop Aftimios had few supporters. The plans for a unified church fell victim to the same tensions and conflicts that afflicted the ethnic dioceses in the 1930s.[46]

The difficulties attendant to the development of these parallel diocesan jurisdictions were great. With each wave of immigration, the disputes of the Old World often were manifested in the church life of the Orthodox in America. Although they were united in the same faith, the Orthodox were divided into numerous ecclesiastical jurisdictions. The establishment of these ethnic or even political dioceses, rather than genuine territorial dioceses, may have served the short-term needs of the immigrants. The practice, however, contravened traditional Orthodox polity and canon law.

These developments in America came a little more than fifty years after a historic council in Constantinople in 1872 dealt with very similar concerns. In the midst of the development of new regional autocephalous churches in the Balkans, this council condemned "ethnophylitism," sometimes translated as nationalism or tribalism, as a basis for the organization of the church. The council affirmed that the church in each place must be organized in such a manner that it includes all the believers in a particular region regardless of their ethnic or linguistic differences. A diocese or even a collection of dioceses by very definition, therefore, cannot be created to serve only a particular racial or ethnic group of believers to the exclusion of other believers. On the contrary, in order to reflect the gospel, which calls all to unity in Christ, a diocese must bring together all the believers in a given territory without regard to their specific particularities.[47]

The decision of this council simply reflected traditional Orthodox teachings regarding the church and its bishops. According to Orthodox canon law, it is expected that there be one bishop in each city or region, that this bishop serve all the Orthodox in his territory, that the bishops of a given province form a synod, and that one among them be recognized as the primate. As the head of a diocese, each bishop is meant to be a sign of unity.[48]

The period after World War I saw the Orthodox in America subdivided into a number of ecclesiastical jurisdictions. While these jurisdictions were structured as dioceses or archdioceses, each served a particular ethnic group. Although they were united in the same faith, they were tragically divided in a very real way. Clearly, there was an absence of true administrative unity, which should have reflected their unity in faith. From that time onward, the Orthodox appeared to give the impression that there was a variety of Orthodox denominations. Referring to this development, Father John Meyendorff says:

The multiplicity of jurisdictions is the fruit of the religious nationalism which was so widespread between the two World Wars. This nationalism found fertile ground in certain aspects of the American social structure. . . . In the case of the Orthodox, religious nationalism imported from Europe was superimposed on the American social strata. The result is that often the "Russian Orthodox" is thought to belong to a different denomination from the "Greek Orthodox."[49]

By 1933, there were at least twelve separate Orthodox jurisdictions in the United States. All claimed to profess the same Orthodox faith. But, there was very little contact or practical cooperation among them. This peculiar pattern of multiple and parallel ecclesiastical jurisdictions was alien to traditional Orthodox practice and contrary to canon law. However, the unparalleled immigration of Orthodox to America, combined with linguistic differences, cultural barriers, and Old World differences, led to the establishment of dioceses and archdioceses that gathered together the parishes serving the needs of particular ethnic groups. By 1933, the existence of parallel ethnic dioceses had become an unfortunate but characteristic feature of American Orthodoxy.

5
PROPOSALS FOR
JURISDICTIONAL
COOPERATION

The period of diocesan development was a time when the various Orthodox auto-cephalous churches of Europe and the Middle East sought to organize and unite their parishes into dioceses or archdioceses headed by a recognized bishop. This generally took place at a time when the American Orthodox were greatly influenced by political developments in the old countries. While the majority of the parishes responded to the initiates of the mother churches, some refused to accept these associations. By 1933, there existed at least twelve separate ecclesiastical jurisdictions serving, for the most part, the needs of particular ethnic groups. Some jurisdictions were associated with one of the autocephalous churches, and others were not. Although all the Orthodox claimed to profess the same faith and observe the same sacramental life, there were little regular contact and cooperation among them.

During the 1930s and 1940s a number of Orthodox leaders began to recognize the irregular status and the tragic consequences of the de facto disunity that afflicted the Orthodox in America. While there was no doctrinal issue dividing the various Orthodox jurisdictions, the role of language, politics, and Old World suspicions had provided a basis for estrangement. As a remedy for this situation, these leaders began to advocate the need for greater contacts among Orthodox clergy and laity of all jurisdictions, and they proposed a number of practical means for cooperation.

THE SEMINARY PROPOSAL

Archbishop Athenagoras (Spirou) arrived in New York on 24 February 1931 to take up his responsibilities as the new primate of the Greek Orthodox Archdiocese. Coming from the position as Metropolitan of Corfu, Athenagoras was selected by the Ecumenical Patriarchate and given the mandate to heal the bitter division of the Greek immigrants in America. The wounds between the Royalists and the Venizelists continued to afflict many parishes.[1]

The new Greek Orthodox archbishop quickly learned that the old disputes among the Greek immigrants would not be the only problem he would have to face. His attempts to heal divisions among the Greek Orthodox parishes would be greatly affected by the fact that there was little cooperation among the Orthodox jurisdictions. This lack of cooperation provided the basis for some serious difficulties involving parishes and clergy.

Slightly less that two years after his arrival, Archbishop Athenagoras had his authority challenged by Archbishop Apollinary (Koshevoy) of the Russian Orthodox Synod Abroad. The Russian Orthodox Synod Abroad claimed to have suspended Metropolitan Platon of the Russian Orthodox Archdiocese in 1927. A year earlier, Metropolitan Platon had rejected the authority of this synod of émigré bishops over the Russian diaspora. In order to challenge his authority, the Synod Abroad established a parallel jurisdiction in 1927 and appointed Bishop Apollinary as its head. While the extreme monarchial politics of this group and its scheme to unite all Russians outside the Soviet Union were repudiated by most of the members of the Russian Orthodox Metropolia in America at that time, a small number of parishes aligned themselves with Bishop Apollinary.

Bishop Apollinary also apparently envisioned the enlargement of his jurisdiction through the inclusion of Greek Orthodox parishes that opposed the leadership of Archbishop Athenagoras and the use of the new calendar (revised Gregorian) by the archdiocese. By 1932, Bishop Apollinary reportedly ordained to the priesthood three Greek immigrants. There was also some indication that the Russian Orthodox Synod Abroad (the Karlovtsy Synod) planned to consecrate a bishop to serve the needs of the dissident Greek Orthodox parishes. Bishop Apollinary's actions were based upon his view that the Greek Orthodox parishes were rightly under the jurisdiction of the Russian Orthodox Church in America since the days of the Alaskan mission.[2]

The initial difficulties between the Greek Orthodox Archdiocese and the Russian Orthodox Synod Abroad subsided following the death of Bishop Apollinary in 1933. Indeed, it would seem that the relationship between Archbishop Athenagoras and the new head of the Russian Orthodox Synod Abroad diocese, Archbishop Vitaly (Maximenko), was quite cordial. However, this did not end the interjurisdictional difficulties that were to afflict the ministry of Archbishop Athenagoras in particular and the cause of inter-Orthodox cooperation in general.[3]

A new schism among the Greek Orthodox erupted in 1934. Father Christopher Contogeorge, a critic of Athenagoras and a former priest of the archdiocese, was consecrated a bishop by Archbishop Sofronios (Bashira) and Archbishop Theophan (Noli) of the Albanian Orthodox diocese. Bishop Christopher Contogeorge then established a rival Greek Orthodox jurisdiction, known as the Archdiocese of America and Canada, initially headquartered in Philadelphia and subsequently in Lowell, Massachusetts. Challenging the leadership of Archbishop Athenagoras, this movement continued to attract a small number of Greek Orthodox parishes until it finally collapsed in 1955.[4]

Archbishop Athenagoras appears to have recognized the havoc that could easily result from the jurisdictional disunity in America. He saw that the efforts to heal schism among the Greek Orthodox and to reconcile dissident parishes could not be undertaken in isolation from the other Orthodox jurisdictions. Disunity, lack of understanding, and dissension could easily be employed by dissident clergy and laity.

Archbishop Athenagoras made a bold proposal in 1934 to establish an Orthodox theological seminary that would serve the needs of all the Orthodox jurisdictions in America. While pastoral schools and seminaries had been established for brief periods of time in the past, both by the Greek Orthodox Archdiocese and the Russian Orthodox Archdiocese, this was the first time that a proposal had been made to unite efforts on such an important venture. It was a masterful proposal to bring greater unity and cooperation to the major Orthodox jurisdictions.

From the earliest days of the development of Orthodoxy in North America, far-sighted leaders recognized the need to develop schools that would train future lay leaders and clergy for the church in America. Bishop Innocent had established a seminary in Sitka in 1858. Sometime about 1888, its limited activity was complemented by a school established in San Francisco. With the demise of these early institutions about the turn of the century, an attempt was made to establish a seminary in Minneapolis in 1905. This was subsequently transferred to Tenafly, New Jersey, in 1912. The seminary fell victim in 1923 to the administrative and economic chaos that shook the Russian-American church in the years following the Russian revolution of October 1917.[5]

Likewise, the Greek Orthodox Archdiocese had made an early attempt to establish a seminary. During his stay in the United States in 1921, Metropolitan Meletios was a forceful advocate for a seminary that would prepare future clergy to serve the needs of the church in America. Under the leadership of Meletios, Saint Athanasius Seminary formally opened on 4 November 1921 in Astoria, New York. Despite the critical need for such an educational institution, the seminary closed in 1923. Its demise perhaps resulted from two major factors. First, the archdiocese was still too weak to provide the necessary financial and administrative support, chiefly because of the continuing struggle between the Royalists and the Venizelists. Second, it appears that many of the immigrant clergy were opposed to the concept of a local seminary. They may have feared the development of a cadre of new clergy who possessed a better education and who were better able to serve the needs of the developing American church.[6]

The proposal of Archbishop Athenagoras for an Orthodox seminary, therefore, must be understood against the background of this history. This was not the first time that there had been a call for a seminary. It was, however, the first time that a proposal had been made for a seminary that would truly serve the needs of all the Orthodox jurisdictions in America.

During 1934, an interjurisdictional organization committee met to discuss the development of the plan that had also received the preliminary approval of Metropolitan Platon of the Russian Orthodox Archdiocese. It was proposed that the school be located in Pomfret, Connecticut, on a large estate that the Greek Orthodox Archdiocese had recently purchased. The organizational committee recommended that the seminary receive students from all the jurisdictions and, likewise, that the faculty reflect the many jurisdictions. English was to be the language of instruction. Greek and Church Slavonic would be used in the liturgical services. It was also recommended that the seminary be a graduate-level institution accepting young men who already possessed an undergraduate degree. The plans referred to the school as the General Orthodox Theological Seminary.[7]

The proposal fell victim to the changing situation of the Russian Orthodox jurisdictions. During the period in which the plans were being formalized, Metropolitan Platon died on 30 April 1934. He was succeeded by one of his vicars, Bishop Theophilus (Pashkovsky). With these significant changes, an opportunity arose for a reconciliation between the Russian Orthodox archdiocese, generally known then as the Metropolia, and the Russian Orthodox Synod Abroad. Metropolitan Theophilus traveled to Serbia in November of the same year to participate in a conference of Russian bishops from the Russian diaspora. At that conference, a plan was established to unite the Russian Orthodox Church Outside of Russia.

When Metropolitan Theophilus returned to the United States, he met with the four other bishops of the Metropolia and two bishops of the jurisdiction of the Karlovtsy Synod Abroad. These bishops agreed to the plan and sent an encyclical to the faithful declaring that the division of the Russian Orthodox Church in America had come to an end. This accord essentially subordinated the Metropolia to the authority of the Council of Bishops of the Russian Orthodox Synod Abroad, then headquartered in Sremsky-Karlovtsy, Serbia. The president of this synod was Metropolitan Anthony (Khrapovitsky), formerly of Kiev and Galicia. This plan remained in effect until 1946.[8]

With his new relationship with the Karlovtsy Synod, Metropolitan Theophilus refused to proceed with plans to establish the Pan-Orthodox Seminary. Indeed, it appears that the proposal had been discussed in Serbia by the Russian bishops and had been disapproved. This led Metropolitan Theophilus to initiate plans to establish his own seminary.[9]

When Archbishop Athenagoras learned that the Metropolia had rejected the cooperative proposal and was proceeding to establish its own seminary, he had no other alternative than to proceed with his own plans. Archbishop Athenagoras presided over the opening of Holy Cross Theological School on 5 October 1937 in Pomfret, Connecticut.[10]

Nearly a year later, on 3 October 1938, Metropolitan Theophilus opened St. Vladimir's Seminary in New York City. Another institution, known as a pastoral school, was also opened on 24 October 1938 at St. Tikhon Monastery in New Canaan, Pennsylvania. The fact that the Metropolia opened two schools at the same time appears to reflect an unresolved division between those who wanted a pastoral school and those who wanted a more advanced theological seminary somewhat equivalent to the academies of old Russia.[11]

With the establishment of these schools, an important chapter in Orthodox theological education in America began. The opening of these schools indicated that the leadership of both the Greek Orthodox Archdiocese and the Russian Orthodox Metropolia recognized the need to provide education here in America for future clergy and laity who would serve the developing church in this country. However, at the same time, an important opportunity for interjurisdictional cooperation was lost. The two schools would serve the particular needs of each jurisdiction and would not be able to bring about a greater sense of unity and common mission among the future clergy.

THE COUNCIL OF BISHOPS PROPOSAL

Archbishop Athenagoras was not alone in the desire for greater cooperation among the Orthodox in America. The primate of the Greek Orthodox Archdiocese found a friend and a committed ally in the person of Metropolitan Antony (Bashir), who became the head of the Syrian (Antiochian) Orthodox Archdiocese in 1936. Following his appointment by the Patriarchate of Antioch, Metropolitan Antony worked vigorously for the eradication of divisions among the Arab Orthodox immigrants. For about two decades, they had been divided between those who favored association with the Russian Orthodox in America and those who favored direct association with the Patriarchate of Antioch. During his thirty-year tenure as head of the Syrian (Antiochian) Orthodox Archdiocese, Metropolitan Antony was a forceful advocate of the use of the English language in liturgical services. He also graciously welcomed into his archdiocese persons who had been raised in other religious traditions but who were attracted to the Orthodox Church. Like Archbishop Athenagoras, Metropolitan Antony also seems to have realized that divisions among his own flock could not be healed without giving attention to the larger issue of the lack of concrete cooperation among all the Orthodox.

Shortly after becoming head of his archdiocese, Metropolitan Antony joined with Archbishop Athenagoras in proposing the establishment of a Conference of Orthodox Bishops. This was a bold proposal that reflected an idea that had been discussed by individual Orthodox leaders for decades. With the support and approval of Archbishop Athenagoras, Metropolitan Antony wrote a letter to Metropolitan Theophilus on 2 October 1937, in which the proposal was presented. Antony and Athenagoras envisioned a conference that would bring together at least once a year the canonical heads of the various Orthodox jurisdictions in America. The essential purpose of the conference was "to work together for the establishment of order and respect for Orthodox laws and traditions among the various Orthodox Churches."[12]

Clearly, the proposal was a bold and significant one aimed at increasing harmony and cooperation among the Orthodox jurisdictions, beginning with their heads. Despite its merits, however, Metropolitan Theophilus refused to accept the proposal. His continued association with the Karlovtsy Synod Abroad appears to have prevented collaboration. Nonetheless, this rejection did not deter Metropolitan Antony and Archbishop Athenagoras. As we shall see, the proposal subsequently provided the basis for the establishment of a cooperative association of bishops in 1943.

THE MAGAZINE PROPOSAL

Archbishop Athenagoras was persistent in his desire to find ways of increasing Orthodox cooperation in America. While the earlier proposals for the Pan-Orthodox Seminary and a conference of bishops were rejected by Metropolitan Theophilus, the head of the Greek Orthodox Archdiocese once again made another dramatic proposal in a letter dated 27 March 1941. Archbishop Athenagoras expressed grave concern in this letter over the fact that the jurisdictional divisions among the Orthodox in America prevented their church from being a valuable witness in American society.

It should be remembered that, as Europe began to be engulfed in war, the Orthodox in America were divided into at least about twelve separate jurisdictions. Some of these had direct links with an autocephalous Orthodox Church in Europe or the Middle East. Others, most notably the Metropolia, had no direct link with a mother church and considered themselves autonomous. Some followed the new calendar, while others followed the old calendar. In addition, the language barriers, cultural and political hostilities, and geographical isolation tended to contribute to the isolation of the heads of the various Orthodox jurisdictions. These divisions gave the impression that the Orthodox Church in the United States was a sadly divided body with no common witness in the society.

With this tragic reality of disunity in mind, Archbishop Athenagoras said in his letter to Metropolitan Theophilus:

Our Church, although she is the Orthodox Church of Christ and although our Christian faithful have exceeded the five million mark, is still, officially, "the forgotten Church in America." Clergy and faithful are not sufficiently known to each other. We have made no effort to make our Orthodox Church and the immense treasure of her dogma, her moral teachings, history, traditions and rituals known to the American government, churches of other denominations, intellectuals, and to the American public in general. We do not have the means to defend our Faith against any kind of proselytism.[13]

To assist the Orthodox in making their faith better known and to defend the church's faithful against forms of proselytism, Archbishop Athenagoras made another creative proposal for pan-Orthodox cooperation. He suggested to Metropolitan Theophilus that the jurisdictions join to establish and to publish a magazine that would be dedicated to the propagation of the Orthodox faith.

A number of the jurisdictions had already begun to publish their own newspaper or journal. Beginning about 1908, the Metropolia began publishing the *Russian-American Orthodox Messenger* in Russian and subsequently in English. Likewise, the Greek Orthodox Archdiocese briefly published the weekly *Ecclesi-*

astical Herald between 1921 and 1923. It was succeeded in 1934 with *The Orthodox Observer.* Both were published in Greek. Despite the existence of these periodicals, Archbishop Athenagoras recommended that the new publication be the official organ of all the Orthodox jurisdictions in America. He proposed that it be published in English, that the editorial board be made up of clergy and laity of the various jurisdictions, and that the sponsoring jurisdictions assume the cost of financing the magazine.[14]

THE FEDERATION

As in the case of the earlier proposals, there is no record of any positive response from Metropolitan Theophilus. However, the initiatives taken by both Archbishop Athenagoras and Metropolitan Antony began to bear some fruit. During the period of World War II, a movement was inaugurated to have Orthodox Christianity formally recognized as a major faith in the United States. This movement was actually inaugurated in order to ensure that Orthodox members of the armed forces would receive their proper religious designation and to assure that Orthodox chaplains receive the same recognition as those of the other recognized religions.

To strengthen the Orthodox position in this matter, the proposal for the Conference of Orthodox Bishops was revived. With the approval of their respective bishops, Father Michael Gelsinger of the Syrian Orthodox Archdiocese, Father Boris Burden of the Russian Orthodox Patriarchal jurisdiction, and Attorney George Phillies of the Greek Orthodox Archdiocese drafted a plan for what was called the Federated Orthodox Greek Catholic Primary Jurisdictions in America. This was designed to be an association of four jurisdictions led by their presiding hierarchs. The four primary jurisdictions that composed the federation were the Greek Orthodox under Archbishop Athenagoras, the Syrian (Antiochian) Orthodox under Metropolitan Antony, the Russian Orthodox patriarchal under Metropolitan Benjamin (Fedchenkov), and the Serbian Orthodox under Bishop Dionysius. Also participating in the work of the federation were Bishop Bogdan (Spilka) of the Ukrainian Orthodox diocese and Bishop Orestes (Chornock) of the Carpatho-Russian Orthodox diocese. Both of these jurisdictions were associated with the Patriarchate of Constantinople.[15]

The federation gained major recognition when its existence was formally recognized in a bill passed by the New York State legislature and signed into law with some degree of fanfare by Governor Thomas E. Dewey on 25 March 1943. This was followed by an Orthodox Service of Thanksgiving held in the Senate chamber. The service was led by the four presiding Orthodox bishops. This event, which was widely publicized, appears to have been the beginning of a process whereby various state legislatures and agencies of the federal government began to identify Orthodox Christianity as a major faith in the United States in the following decades.[16]

At the time of the signing of the bill, Governor Dewey spoke about the significance of the occasion. Although his words may have exaggerated somewhat the actual situation of the Orthodox, they provide us with an indication of the hope that many saw in the new organization. The governor said:

In the Old World, their jurisdictions differed only in languages and in the nationalities of their parishioners. Transported to the New World, their worshippers came to realize that even those superficial differences were erased by their common language. In short they were no longer Greek, Russian, Syrian or Serbian but American. Hence, the union resulting in the "Federated Orthodox Greek Catholic Primary Jurisdictions in America" . . . the Church which shall be known in the future as the American Orthodox Church.[17]

The federation became a legal corporation on 7 October 1943. The Articles of Incorporation state that the primary purpose of the federation was "to secure unity of action and effort in all matters which are of common concern to Orthodox Greek Catholic jurisdictions in America." It is also interesting to note that the articles stated that the federation would establish and maintain a theological school and would also establish committees to address problems and concerns from a Pan-Orthodox perspective.[18]

A Eucharistic Liturgy on 22 August 1943 solemnly marked the formal establishment of the federation. The Liturgy was held in the civic auditorium in Buffalo, New York, because the space in the local Orthodox churches was limited. The liturgy was led by Archbishop Athenagoras, Metropolitan Antony, and Bishop Bogdan. For many, the liturgy was an important sign that the Orthodox had entered upon a new phase of cooperation.

The federation had two major weaknesses, which ultimately contributed to its becoming inactive by 1945. The first weakness was that membership in the federation was limited. It included only those jurisdictions that had direct canonical links to the Patriarchates of Constantinople, Antioch, Moscow, and Serbia. While the Romanian Orthodox diocese and the Bulgarian Orthodox diocese were technically eligible for membership in the federation, internal difficulties apparently prevented their participation.

Because of the insistence of Metropolitan Benjamin, full membership in the federation was restricted to those hierarchs who had a canonical relationship with an autocephalous church. Consequently, Metropolitan Theophilus of the Russian Orthodox Metropolia was not invited to participate in the federation. This is explained because Metropolitan Benjamin considered the Metropolia to be in a state of schism from the Church of Russia. The fact that Metropolitan Theophilus had chosen to ignore invitations to cooperate with other hierarchs since 1935 must have contributed to the decision of Archbishop Athenagoras and Metropolitan Antony to accept the rather strict position of Metropolitan Benjamin. However, the Metropolia was the largest of the Russian Orthodox jurisdictions in America. The fact that it was excluded meant that the federation did not represent a sizable number of Orthodox clergy and laity.

The second major factor that contributed to the dissolution of the federation centered upon its administrative leadership. Attorney George E. Phillies had been active from the beginning in the organization of the federation, so active that he acquired the title of chancellor of the federation. Difficulties arose, however, when it became common knowledge that Phillies not only belonged to the Greek Orthodox Archdiocese but also was actively involved in a Protestant Episcopal parish in the Buffalo area. While serving as the administrative head of the federation, Phillies apparently saw nothing wrong with continuing his association with the local Episcopal parish.[19]

Metropolitan Benjamin viewed the position of Phillies as a clear violation of Orthodox Church polity. From his perspective, it was simply impossible for an Orthodox Christian to be also a member of a Protestant parish. Upon the insistence of Metropolitan Benjamin, the other hierarchs met and came to an agreement regarding the leadership of the federation. They agreed that there was no lay head of the federation, that the bishops were to exercise the leadership of the federation, and that it is not permissible for an Orthodox Christian to be a member or a communicant of another church.[20]

Apparently, this agreement did not resolve the crisis. When Phillies refused to renounce his participation in the Episcopal parish, Metropolitan Benjamin publicly announced that the attorney was no longer the chancellor of the federation. By the end of 1944, Bishop Dionysios and Metropolitan Benjamin withdrew their active support of the federation.[21]

The debate over the position of Phillies reflected a deeper question regarding the relationship of the Orthodox Church to other Christian groups in general and the Episcopal Church in particular. Early Orthodox leaders in America had sought to establish close relationships with the leaders of the Protestant Episcopal Church. At the international level, the Orthodox and the Anglicans had been involved in contacts and informal theological dialogue from the late nineteenth century, and these became more intense during the 1930s. These cordial relations and discussions appear to have been reflected in the positive attitude toward the American Episcopalians that can be seen especially in the ministry of both Archbishop Tikhon and Metropolitan Meletios.

However, most Orthodox leaders were quick to point out that the cordial relationships between the Orthodox and the Episcopalians did not imply that there was an agreement in faith between the two churches. Indeed, despite their desire for recognition and, at times, financial assistance from the Episcopalians, knowledgeable Orthodox representatives were careful to avoid accepting a fundamental equality between the Orthodox Church and other Christian groups. At the same time, however, there is evidence that some Orthodox faithful were encouraged by some leaders to attend Episcopal parishes in those parts of the country where Orthodox parishes had not been established. These diverse perspectives must have created confusion in the minds of some Orthodox and Episcopalians. The difficulties involving Phillies clearly reflect this.

This relationship between Orthodox and other Christians was a major issue that did not receive sufficient attention in the United States during the 1930s and 1940s. Yet, it could not be long ignored. This was especially true as Orthodox clergy and laity began to emerge from the isolation of the old immigrant communities and become more involved in the larger society. In the United States Orthodox would find themselves in direct and constant contact with Roman Catholics and Protestants in a manner that was rare in the Old World at that time.

Despite its lofty goals, therefore, the federation could not endure major difficulties related to its membership and its leadership. Both Archbishop Athenagoras and Metropolitan Antony continued to support the principles of the federation with the hope that it could be reorganized. However, the difficulties that afflicted the federation were compounded by developments within a number of Orthodox jurisdictions during the postwar years. Among these developments was the election of Archbishop Athenagoras as Ecumenical Patriarch of Constantinople on 1 November 1948.[22]

Although the federation had a limited existence, its significance cannot be diminished. It was the first formal association of Orthodox bishops in the United States. The establishment of the federation was an indication that the old barriers of language, politics, and cultural suspicion could be overcome and that issues of common concern could be addressed. Bringing together in a consultative body the primates of six jurisdictions, the federation was an important association that indicated a growing recognition of the critical need for cooperation and the common resolution of problems. As we shall see, the federation provided a historical precedent for the establishment of the Standing Conference of Canonical Orthodox Bishops in America (SCOBA) in 1960. The federation gave a sign that cooperation among Orthodox at the local level was not only possible but also greatly desirable.

Moreover, as we shall see in the next chapter, the changing political situation in parts of Eastern Europe would once again affect a number of the Orthodox jurisdictions in America. While some Orthodox in America moved toward greater unity in the postwar years, others became more divided over political developments in Eastern Europe.

6
THE CHALLENGE
OF THE OLD WORLD

The period from about 1945 to about 1965 was one of slow but gradual transition for the Orthodox Church in the United States. Yet, it was a transition marked by two major characteristics, which appear to be in opposition. First, the political changes in Eastern Europe and the Soviet Union occurring during and after World War II not only affected the condition of the Orthodox Church in that part of the world but also had a profound impact upon a number of the Orthodox jurisdictions in this country. Differences in the evaluation of the political and ecclesiastical situations in the old country frequently led to further divisions among the Orthodox in this country.

The second characteristic of this period of transition was the gradual development of the Orthodox Church from one comprising chiefly immigrants to one comprising persons born in this country and nurtured by its educational system. Although this process had been actually taking place from at least the 1920s, it appears to have become more pronounced in the postwar period. While migration of Orthodox from the Balkans, Russia, and the Middle East by no means ceased, the quotas imposed by the government in the 1920s assured that the numbers of the earlier period would never be repeated.

The changing character of church membership in the postwar period, in turn, provided greater stability for the development of parishes and diocesan institutions for the larger Orthodox jurisdictions, especially the Greek Orthodox Archdiocese, the Russian Orthodox Metropolia, and the Antiochian Orthodox Archdiocese. While cultural differences and Old World rivalries did not cease to affect the members of the various jurisdictions, there was evidence of a greater interest in forms of Orthodox cooperation that would bring together the clergy and laity of the various jurisdictions, especially at the local level. There were also some important indications that Orthodox theologians were in a better position to express their distinctive teachings within ecumenical forums.

THE RUSSIAN ORTHODOX DIOCESES

The Russian Orthodox parishes and diocesan administrations in the United States were greatly affected by both political and ecclesiastical developments in the Soviet Union that began as early as 1939. From that year, the threat of war began to provide a basis for a new relationship between the church and the Communist government. This dramatic change brought to an end the overt persecution of the church by the state that had begun in 1917. Antireligious activities were abruptly terminated and the services of the church and its hierarchs were accepted by the government as the country entered into battle with the Nazis. From the perspective of the church, what was at stake was not a political system but the motherland itself. The most obvious expression of this modus vivendi was that the Soviet government permitted the election of Metropolitan Sergius (Stragorodsky) as patriarch in 1943 and Metropolitan Alexis (Simansky) as patriarch in 1945. This concordat between the church and the Soviet government would have an affect not only upon the place of Orthodoxy in the Soviet Union but also upon Orthodox Christianity throughout the world.[1]

Patriarch Alexis of Moscow initiated a concerted effort to strengthen the position of the church in the Soviet Union and to increase the activities of the Church of Russia within the affairs of world Orthodoxy almost immediately after his installation in 1945. Closely related with these goals was his desire to reconcile the dioceses and paradiocesan administrations of the Russian Orthodox in Western Europe, America, and the Far East that had separated from the patriarchate in the period following the death of Patriarch Tikhon in 1925. The Moscow patriarchate clearly recognized that the newfound and limited freedom of the church in Russia could be greatly damaged by the ecclesiastical dissidents in Europe, America, and the Far East. Likewise, the Moscow patriarchate recognized that the attempt to assert its position within world Orthodoxy would be weakened by the existence of Russian Orthodox dioceses in the so-called diaspora that were not in full communion with their mother church.[2]

The Russian Orthodox Synod Outside of Russia, the Karlovtsy Synod Abroad, presented the Moscow Patriarchate with its greatest opposition. As we have noted, this body united the Russian Orthodox jurisdictions in Europe, America, and the Far East in 1937. The concordat between the church in Russia and the Soviet government was not well received by most of the bishops of the Synod Abroad. Following the election of Patriarch Sergius 1943, the bishops of the Synod Abroad met in Vienna on 8–13 October 1943. Under the leadership of Metropolitan Anastasy (Gribanovsky), formerly of Kishinev, the eight bishops authored a resolution that denounced the election of the new patriarch and opposed the new relationship between the church and state in the Soviet Union. In a portion of their harshly worded statement, the bishops of the Synod Abroad said:

The election of Metropolitan Sergius to the throne of Patriarch of Moscow and All Russia is an act that is not only uncanonical, not even religious, but rather political and elicited by the interests of the Soviet Communist party authorities and their leader-dictator, Stalin. . . . The election of a Patriarch and the convocation of the Synod is necessary to Stalin and his party as a means of political propaganda. The Patriarch is only a toy in his hands.[3]

While many Russian Orthodox in Western Europe and America were less critical of the developments in the Soviet Union, the Synod Abroad clung to its official position even after the subsequent election of Patriarch Alexis in 1945. The Synod Abroad refused to acknowledge the legitimacy of the official church in Russia and continued to view its bishops as "pseudobishops" who were the instruments of the Communist government.

Some of the members of the Synod Abroad also looked upon the Hitler regime quite differently than did the Russians in the Soviet Union. Many Russian exiles looked to German National Socialism as an adversary to Soviet Communism. In 1938, for example, Metropolitan Anastasy of the Synod Abroad wrote a letter to Adolph Hitler to thank him for assistance given for the construction of the Russian Orthodox cathedral in Berlin. A portion of the letter states:

We see a special providence in the fact that precisely now when in our homeland churches and shrines are being destroyed and desecrated, this church is founded and built. Together with many other omens, the construction of this church strengthens our hopes that an end is approaching for our long-suffering country. He who manages destiny will send us a leader and that leader will raise up our land and give it once more national greatness, just as He sent you for the German people.[4]

Shortly after the close of the war in Europe, Patriarch Alexis sent a letter on 10 August 1945 to the leaders of the Synod Abroad. The letter reviewed from the perspective of the Moscow Patriarchate the development of the Synod Abroad. References were made to both Patriarch Tikhon and Patriarch Sergius, who repudiated the activities of the Synod Abroad. Adding his voice to theirs, Patriarch Alexis stated that the Synod Abroad existed in clear violation of the canons of the church that dealt with organization and polity. He referred to the Synod Abroad as a "Renegade Assembly" that had done great damage to the church. In spite of this, however, the patriarch appealed to the leaders of the Synod Abroad to repent of their sins and reestablish a canonical relationship with their mother church.[5]

Responding indirectly to the appeal of the patriarch, Metropolitan Anastasy, the presiding hierarch of the Synod Abroad, wrote a letter to the Russian Orthodox faithful in January 1946. This letter reviewed the Synod Abroad's own understanding of its development. The metropolitan claimed that the Synod Abroad was organized as a result of a directive given by Patriarch Tikhon in 1920. Having said this, Metropolitan Anastasy affirmed that the Synod Abroad could not unite itself with the Patriarchate of Moscow because its bishops have collaborated with the atheistic government. "Having linked their fate with the government which has never ceased to proclaim its atheism," he said, "the clergy have lost their power to preach the truth. To please the government, even the highest and most responsible of the bishops are not ashamed to propagate the manifest untruth that there was never any religious persecution in Russia." Metropolitan Anastasy concluded his letter by stating that any ecclesiastical actions taken by the Moscow Patriarchate against the Synod Abroad would be considered without authority.[6]

In the United States, the Russian Orthodox Metropolia began to take a more conciliatory position with regard to the Patriarchate of Moscow as early as 1943. In that year, a majority of the Metropolia bishops voted to commemorate in the liturgical services the new patriarch of Moscow. An official delegation from the Metropolia went to Moscow in 1945 at the time when a council was being held to elect a new patriarch. Although the American delegation was not permitted to participate in the deliberations, its members did meet privately with Patriarch Alexis after his election. These developments occurred in spite of the fact that the Metropolia was still officially associated with the Synod Abroad.[7]

These conciliatory actions of the leaders of the Metropolia enabled the Patriarchate of Moscow to issue a decree on 14 February 1945, that stipulated the conditions by which the Metropolia could be reconciled to its mother church. The essential portion of the decree indicated that the primate of the Metropolia would have to be approved by the patriarchate and that the bishops of the Metropolia would have to abstain from political activities directed against the government of the USSR. Naturally, reconciliation would also mean that the Metropolia would have to disassociate itself from the Synod Abroad.

Indications from both sides seemed to show a genuine willingness for reconciliation. Representing the Patriarchate of Moscow, Archbishop Alexis of Yaroslav and Rostov came to the United States in September 1945 and met with leaders of the Metropolia in order to work toward reconciliation. A series of meetings took place with both clergy and laity. However, no agreement could be reached. For the representatives of the Metropolia, the critical issue appears to have been the degree of autonomy that the church in America would enjoy.[8]

A significant statement on the status of the Russian Orthodox Church in America was published on 18 October 1946 in the Russian language newspaper *Novoye Russkoye Slovo* in New York. Popularly known as the Letter of the Five Professors, the document analyzed the position of the Metropolia and proposed a course of action. The authors recognized that the difficult position of the Metropolia was determined by two major facts. First, it had broken its ties with the Patriarchate of Moscow in 1933 and was viewed by the mother church as being in schism. Second, the Metropolia had subordinated itself to the Synod Abroad in 1937.[9]

Since the time of this affiliation, the authors also noted that significant changes had taken place in the relationship between church and state in the Soviet Union. A new relationship had developed during the war that led to the election of new patriarchs in 1943 and 1945.

Also of importance is the fact that the authors of the Letter of the Five Professors noted that significant developments had taken place with regard to the

Synod Abroad. In advance of a Communist victory in Yugoslavia, the Synod Abroad moved its headquarters to Munich, Germany, in 1944. While centered in Serbia, the Synod Abroad had maintained some form of canonical association with the Church of Serbia. However, according to the Letter of the Five Professors, the synod lost the blessing and protection of the Church of Serbia when it moved its headquarters to Germany. Because of this move, the professors declared that the Synod Abroad "lost ties with the universal Church." The professors then continued:

Subordinating ourselves to this Synod, our Church (the Metropolia) in substance subordinates itself to a group of bishops who really have no jurisdiction themselves. Because of this, some people are inclined to speak only of our cooperation with the Synod. This term "cooperation," however, is not correct because the acts of 1936–1937 definitely subjected our Church under the Synod Abroad.[10]

Claiming that the existence of the Synod Abroad had no basis in the canonical tradition and that it was not recognized formally by any autocephalous church, the professors recommended that the Metropolia formally break its ties with the Synod Abroad and work to establish full communion with the Patriarchate of Moscow. Such a new relationship, they argued, should recognize a broad autonomy for the Metropolia that "would remove all influences of the Soviet government, direct or indirect, on our church."[11]

The authors of the letter recognized the need for a canonical relationship to exist between the Metropolia and the Patriarchate. But, they also recognized the need to keep the Metropolia free from political influence coming from the Communist government in the Soviet Union.

The Seventh Council of the Metropolia, bringing together clergy and laity from the parishes, was held on 26–29 November 1946 in Cleveland. The majority of the delegates agreed with the general positions expressed by the Letter of the Five Professors. They voted overwhelmingly in favor of a historic resolution that requested Patriarch Alexis of Moscow to unite the Metropolia to his fold and to be its spiritual head upon the conditions that the Metropolia retain its autonomous status and the right of self-government. In the same resolution, the delegates stated that the relationship between the Metropolia and the Synod Abroad was terminated. Finally, the delegates affirmed that the Metropolia would remain a self-governing church even if the Patriarchate failed to accept the conditions of reconciliation.[12]

While this resolution was approved by a majority of the delegates, the bishops of the Metropolia were deeply divided over the issues. No agreement could be reached among them in Cleveland. Over the next twelve months, it became clear that four bishops were in favor of the resolution, and four were opposed. Metropolitan Theophilus led those who accepted the resolution, and Archbishop Vitaly (Maximenko) led those who refused to accept it. Eventually, Archbishop Vitaly and the three other bishops left the Metropolia and reestablished a jurisdiction of the Synod Abroad in North America. About fifty parishes eventually left the

Metropolia and accepted their authority. The Metropolia retained about 200 parishes.[13]

Despite these developments, negotiations between the bishops of the Metropolia and the Moscow Patriarchate did not end in a formal agreement. Metropolitan Gregory (Chukov) of Leningrad came to this country on 17 July 1947 and began a series of meetings with Metropolitan Theophilus and other leaders of the Metropolia over the course of two months. The negotiations were suspended when it became clear that the Moscow Patriarchate would not recognize the conditions for reconciliation established by the Cleveland council.[14]

As a consequence, Patriarch Alexis issued a decree on 16 December 1947 that suspended Metropolitan Theophilus and the other bishops of the Metropolia. Essentially, the Moscow Patriarchate reaffirmed that the Metropolia was in a state of schism. At the same time, the Patriarchate appointed Archbishop Markary (Ilinsky), a bishop formally part of the Metropolia, as its Archbishop of New York and Exarch of the Moscow Patriarchate. With only a few exceptions, however, the clergy and faithful of the Metropolia continued to recognize the authority of Metropolitan Theophilus, who was in his thirteenth year as primate. While it eventually gained legal right to the historic St. Nicholas Cathedral in New York, the exarchate headed by Archbishop Makary acquired no more than ten parishes throughout the country.[15]

The development of the Russian Orthodox jurisdictions in the United States was further affected when the bishops of the Synod Abroad transferred their headquarters to New York in 1950. The Synod Abroad had moved from Sremski-Karlovtsy, Yugoslavia, to Munich, Germany, in 1944. The new move to the United States in 1950 coincided with the migration to this country of thousands of Russian émigrés from Eastern Europe and the Far East in the years following the close of the war. As the war in Europe came to a close, Russian bishops, clergy, and laity who were ardent opponents of Communism hid in isolated areas of Austria, Bohemia, and Bavaria. There, they carefully calculated their activities so that they would come under American and not Soviet jurisdiction when the war ended. For many, it was their second escape from Communism. It is understandable, therefore, that these displaced persons looked to America as the land where they could not only practice their faith but also maintain their political views without the fear of Communist advance.

The majority of these Russian exiles became associated with parishes of the Synod Abroad when they came to America, thus breathing new life into this jurisdiction. During the 1950s, the Synod Abroad claimed to have eighty-one parishes which served 55,000 members. The new exiles were not attracted to the parishes of the Exarchate of the Moscow Patriarchate because of its affiliation with the official church in Russia. Likewise, the exiles were generally not attracted to parishes of the Metropolia. The reasons for this varied. First, most of the Metropolia parishes had a strong Carpatho-Russian character, which was unacceptable to the new immigrants. Second, the Metropolia was on record as recognizing the Patriarch of Moscow, although there were no formal ties to the Church of Russia. Finally, the majority of the Metropolia parishes were composed primarily of American-born members whose attitude differed greatly from that of the new émigrés.[16]

The three Russian Orthodox jurisdictions were deeply divided over issues related to the legitimacy of the church in Russia and the mission of Orthodox in America. It was only to be expected that tremendous rivalry developed. In many places, members of parishes became divided in their allegiances. Civil courts frequently had to determine which party owned parish property. As the cold war heated up, and McCarthyism began to flare, the loyalty of many Russian Americans was questioned because they recognized authority of the official church in Russia and the position of the Moscow Patriarchate. These accusations were aggravated by the anti-Communistic rhetoric of many of the newly arrived displaced persons. The division among the Russian Orthodox jurisdictions and the tragic war of words that was carried on did very little to contribute to the witness of Orthodoxy during this period.

The three Russian Orthodox jurisdictions were not the only ones to be affected by European political and ecclesiastical developments in the postwar period. The smaller Romanian, Serbian, Bulgarian, Albanian, and Ukrainian dioceses also were divided over political and ecclesiastical events in Eastern Europe.

THE ROMANIAN ORTHODOX DIOCESES

The Romanian diocese was the first to experience a division rooted in the political developments in the motherland. A Communist-dominated government came into existence as early as 1945, although King Michael did not abdicate until 1947. In the wake of these changes, a number of those who were associated with the earlier government and who were strongly anti-Communistic fled the country and eventually made their way to the United States.

A Romanian diocese had been established in the United States in 1932. Bishop Polycarp (Morusca) arrived from Romania to serve as head of this diocese in 1935, which came to be known as the Romanian Orthodox Missionary Episcopate. On the eve of the war, Bishop Polycarp returned to Romania in 1939 with the intention of providing a personal report to the synod of the Church of Romania on his activity. Although he continued to maintain some contact with his diocese in America, Bishop Polycarp was never permitted to return to the United States. This fact, together with the political changes in Romania, gradually thrust the diocese into a crisis. A candidate to replace Bishop Polycarp was proposed by the Patriarchate of Bucharest in 1947. However, because of the new Communist regime in Romania, many of the newly arrived Romanian émigrés were suspicious of the potential dangers inherent in the church-state relationship there.

A congress of clergy and lay delegates met in Detroit in 1950. At this meeting, Father Andrei Modolvan was elected to serve as bishop. His election was approved by the Patriarchate, and he was consecrated on 12 November 1950, in Sibiu, Romania. When Bishop Andrei returned to this country, he immediately began to encounter opposition, especially from those émigrés who had left Romania with the

Communist takeover. They claimed that the official church in Romania had compromised itself because of its relationships with the government. Because of this, they challenged the legitimate authority of Bishop Andrei.

Representing the majority of parishes, the opponents of Bishop Andrei convened a congress in July 1951 in Chicago. They declared that the parishes that they represented were completely autonomous from the Church of Romania, and they established a new diocesan jurisdiction independent from the authority of Bishop Andrei. It was titled the Romanian Orthodox Episcopate of America. At the same congress, Viorel Trifa was selected to be a bishop. Since Bishop Polycarp was still alive in Romania and viewed as a political prisoner of its Communist regime, the bishop-elect was at first proposed to be a vicar bishop. A former political activist, he had arrived in the United States in 1950 and became an ardent critic of both political and ecclesiastical developments in Romania.

Viorel Trifa was consecrated a bishop by bishops of the Ukrainian Orthodox Church in the United States in 1952. At that time, he took the name Bishop Valarian. Many of the other Orthodox jurisdictions in America viewed the development of this diocese as irregular and the consecration of Bishop Valarian as questionable. Following the death of Bishop Polycarp in Romania in 1958, Bishop Valarian Trifa was recognized by his diocese as its formal head, and he began to seek closer relationships with the Russian Orthodox Metropolia. In 1960, he was once again consecrated a bishop by bishops of the Metropolia, and his diocese began an affiliation with the Metropolia. The diocese consisted then of about thirty parishes.

Bishop Andrei died in 1963. Three years later, a diocesan congress with representatives from about twelve parishes that remained under the jurisdiction of the Patriarchate of Bucharest elected Father Victorin Ursache as the new bishop. With approval of the Patriarchate of Bucharest, he was consecrated in August of that year in Windsor, Ontario. Archbishop Iakovos of the Greek Orthodox Archdiocese was the presiding hierarch.[17]

THE BULGARIAN ORTHODOX DIOCESES

Political developments in Bulgaria in the period following World War II also had an effect upon the Bulgarian Orthodox diocese in the United States. The synod of the Church of Bulgaria had acted in 1922 to establish a mission to unite the several parishes that had come into existence. Not until 1938, however, was a diocese formally established. Bishop Andrei (Petkov) came to this country in the same year to head the new diocese. With the outbreak of war, Bishop Andrei returned to Bulgaria.

In the wake of the Communist victory in Bulgaria, Bishop Andrei returned to this country in 1945 and identified himself with anti-Communistic factions. Two years later, in 1947, he led his diocese to a formal break with the Church of Bulgaria. At a meeting of clergy and lay representatives in 1947, it was resolved that the diocese was an inseparable part of the Bulgarian Orthodox Church. However, the delegates declared that as long as the Communist regime existed in Bulgaria, they would not accept decisions from the synod of the Church of Bulgaria but would maintain only a spiritual relationship.[18]

In response to this decision, the Church of Bulgaria refused to accept the actions of the assembly and dismissed Bishop Andrei from his duties as bishop. For the most part, however, the Bulgarian Americans were solidly behind their bishop and firmly opposed to the Communist government in Bulgaria. Under the leadership of Bishop Andrei, his diocese remained in a state of formal separation from the mother church from 1947 to 1962. During this period Bishop Andrei made some overtures to the Russian Orthodox Metropolia to establish a relationship with it. However, no agreement could be reached.

Finally, in 1962 the division ended. The Church of Bulgaria formally recognized Bishop Andrei and his diocese. This reconciliation, however, led to a new division. At a diocesan assembly in Detroit in 1963, the leaders of eighteen parishes charged Bishop Andrei with violating the provisions of the diocesan reorganization in 1947. Claiming that the official church in Bulgaria was a tool of the Communist government, the representatives of these parishes proceeded to establish a new diocese and to elect Father Kyrill Yonchev as their bishop. He was consecrated a bishop in 1964 by bishops of the Russian Orthodox Synod Outside of Russia.[19]

THE SERBIAN ORTHODOX DIOCESES

Division among the Serbian Orthodox in America in the postwar period also reflected political developments in Yugoslavia. The Church of Serbia acted to establish its own diocese in this country in 1921. Five years later, Father Mardarje Uskokovich was consecrated as its first bishop. Following the death of the bishop in 1935, the diocese was directed from Yugoslavia until 1940, when Bishop Dionisije was dispatched to this country to take charge of the diocesan administration. With the postwar political developments in Yugoslavia, Bishop Dionisije became more and more vocal in his opposition to the Communist government, although he claimed to remain faithful to the official church in Serbia.

The Church of Serbia acted to reorganize its diocesan administration in the United States in 1963. At that time, it divided the single diocese into three dioceses. Each diocese was designed to contain no more than twenty parishes each. In the midst of this reorganization, Bishop Dionisije was accused of financial mismanagement and removed from authority by the synod of the Church of Serbia. Three new bishops were appointed to lead the dioceses.[20]

Representatives from a majority of the parishes refused to accept the removal of Bishop Dionisije and the ecclesiastical reorganization effected by the Church of Serbia. These representatives believed that the actions were based upon political motivations. As a result of this, the representatives established their own independent diocese, with Bishop Dionisije as its head. They declared that this diocese was completely autonomous and free from the official church in Serbia as long as Yugoslavia is under Communist control. In subsequent letters to other Orthodox

Church leaders, Bishop Dionisije claimed that the actions taken against him were a direct result of his anti-Communistic position.[21]

The division led to a series of lawsuits involving the authority of the Church of Serbia over its administration in this country and property rights. The Supreme Court of Illinois at first decided a case in favor of the Bishop Dionisije faction. It ruled that he had been improperly removed from his position and that the diocesan reorganization was invalid. However, in 1976 the United States Supreme Court reversed the decision. The High Court determined that civil courts must accept the rulings of duly constituted religious bodies when they adjudicate disputes over internal discipline and government. This decision was seen as a landmark one for churches with a hierarchical form of internal government.[22]

Although Bishop Dionisije lost the court case, about fifty Serbian Orthodox parishes continued to accept his leadership. From time to time, he sought to align his diocese with such bodies as the Ukrainian Autocephalous Orthodox Church and the Patriarchate of Alexandria. This was done because most of the larger Orthodox jurisdictions in this country failed to recognize this independent Serbian Orthodox diocese.[23]

THE ALBANIAN ORTHODOX DIOCESES

Both political and ecclesiastical developments in Albania also stand behind a further division of Albanian Orthodox Christians in America in the postwar period. The Russian Orthodox Archdiocese set about to organize the handful of Albanian parishes in 1908, when Theophan Noli was ordained a priest. Father Noli was a forceful advocate of the use of Albanian in the liturgical services for the Albanian immigrants whom he served, especially in Boston. In 1918 he became the administrator of the Albanian Orthodox Mission in America, which continued to maintain a tenuous relationship with the Russian Orthodox Archdiocese. Father Noli returned to Albania and served in the Albanian Parliament from 1921 to 1924. During this period, he participated in a synod in 1923 that declared the Church of Albania to be autocephalous. Father Noli was ordained a bishop in the same year. The Patriarchate of Constantinople did not formally recognize the autocephalous status and continued to claim jurisdiction over the church in Albania until 1937.

Soon after becoming a bishop, Theophan Noli was elected premier. However, after serving for about six months, he was banished from Albania in the midst of a political upheaval. After spending eight years in Germany, Bishop Theophan was finally admitted to the United States in 1932, where he resumed leadership of the Albanian Orthodox diocese. He devoted much of his time to translating liturgical books into both Albanian and English. He also became an advocate of Pan-Orthodox cooperation.[24]

The Patriarchate of Constantinople granted autocephaly to the Church of Albania in 1937 and recognized Archbishop Christopher (Kissi) as its primate. Through the intrigues of the Communist government, Archbishop Christopher was deposed, imprisoned, and replaced as primate by Archbishop Paisi (Vodica) in 1949. The Patriarchate of Constantinople refused to recognize the uncanonical removal of Archbishop Christopher as primate and continued to recognize his authority. Consisting of twelve parishes, the Albanian Orthodox Diocese in America under Archbishop Theophan, however, recognized the new primate and sought to develop a relationship with him.

Chiefly as a result of this difference, a small number of clergy and laity withdrew from the diocese and sought to come under the jurisdiction of the Patriarchate of Constantinople. In response to their petition, the Patriarchate sent Bishop Mark (Lipa) to the United States in 1950 to serve these parishes. An administration serving no more than three parishes was established in 1956.[25]

UKRAINIAN ORTHODOX DIOCESES

A new wave of political refugees from Ukraine arrived in the United States especially during the period between 1949 and 1955. Among these were clergy and laity who had established Ukrainian Orthodox Church organizations either in Ukraine or in Western Europe during World War II or in the wake of the war. At the time of their arrival, there were already in existence in the United States two separate Ukrainian Orthodox dioceses. One of these, led by Metropolitan Bohdan (Shpilka), was under the jurisdiction of the Ecumenical Patriarchate. It contained about twenty parishes. The other jurisdiction, known as the Ukrainian Orthodox Church of the United States, was led by Archbishop Mstyslaw (Skrypnyk) and contained about one hundred parishes. The clergy of this jurisdiction generally did not receive recognition from other Orthodox in America because of canonical questions associated with its origin in the Ukraine in 1921 and the manner by which its first bishops were ordained. [26]

These new Ukrainian immigrants of the early 1950s generally preferred to remain a part of the church organizations with which they had been associated in Europe. These organizations were essentially transferred to the United States after having been organized in refugee centers of Europe in the years after the war. The Ukrainian Autocephalous Orthodox Church in the United States was established in this country in 1950 under the leadership of Archbishop Hrihoriy (Osiychuk). About twenty parishes constituted this jurisdiction. The Holy Ukrainian Autocephalic Church in Exile was established in this country in 1954 under the leadership of Metropolitan Polycarp (Sikorsky). About ten parishes constituted this jurisdiction. The life of both of these jurisdictions has been characterized by extreme Ukrainian nationalism and a general unwillingness to become involved in Pan-Orthodox cooperation or witness.[27]

The postwar period was one in which new divisions arose among some of the Orthodox jurisdictions in the United States. As was the case in the period following World War I, political developments during the course of World War II and in its wake had a profound impact upon the Orthodox Church in the Soviet Union and other parts of Eastern Europe.

The political and ecclesiastical developments in the Soviet Union and the Balkans also had a profound impact upon the Orthodox faithful of Russian, Romanian, Bulgarian, Serbian, Albanian, and Ukrainian backgrounds in the United States.

Many Orthodox in America sought to maintain canonical ties to their mother church in spite of the latter's association with Communistic governments. Other Orthodox in America, especially newly arrived political exiles, came to believe that canonical ties with the mother church had to be broken because of perceived political involvement in the latter's administrative affairs. The divisions that afflicted many Orthodox dioceses in America reflected not only ecclesiastical concerns but also political ideologies.

During the period following World War II, divisions within many Orthodox jurisdictions were aggravated by the political and nationalistic ideologies of newly arrived émigrés who were strongly anti-Communist. As we have seen, the diocesan divisions usually reflected divergent political perspectives. The new émigrés had little concern for the unity of Orthodoxy in America or for the witness of the Orthodox faith in this society. On the contrary, they frequently viewed their diocese and their parishes as political associations that existed not only to maintain ethnic traditions but also to challenge the authority of the government and the church in Communist-controlled lands. Often with little real knowledge of the mission and purpose of the church, persons with specific political ideologies sought to use particular dioceses in order to advance their political and ethnic creeds.

7
THE CHALLENGE
OF THE NEW WORLD

The political developments in the Soviet Union and the Balkans, as well as ethnic rivalries, continued to have a profound impact upon certain elements of the Orthodox in America in the period following World War II. Yet, at the same time, both external and internal factors were also forcing many within the Orthodox Church in the United States to move beyond these divisive tendencies and to take more seriously the pastoral needs of the younger generations, as well as its missionary responsibilities within the wider society. The changes in demographics, the need for new avenues for religious education, the need for liturgical renewal, and the dialogue with the Christian West were powerful challenges that could not be easily ignored. Despite the presence of divisive tendencies, many Orthodox boldly sought to address these challenges.

A CHANGING MEMBERSHIP

The various immigrant groups who were related to the Orthodox Church had a number of characteristics in common with other immigrant groups in the United States during the late nineteenth and early twentieth centuries. The immigrants in most major cities formed an insulated subculture. Within this subculture, the language of the fatherland was spoken, and the ethnic customs were preserved. While the immigrants usually had jobs outside their ethnic neighborhood, their social contact with the wider society was limited. They lived in their own "society" and seldom had much contact with persons from other ethnic backgrounds. As a result of this, interethnic marriage outside one's ethnic group was uncommon and generally frowned upon.

For the Orthodox immigrants of the various ethnic backgrounds, the parish church was central to their subculture. Normally, the parish church was at the geographical heart of their neighborhood. The immigrants could easily walk to the church for the liturgical services not only on Sunday and feast days but also at other times. The music, ritual, and especially the language of worship not only nurtured their spiritual development but also heightened their emotional contact with the Old World.

In addition to preserving the Orthodox faith, the parish church was also viewed by the immigrants as an important place where the language of their former homeland was preserved and taught. The religion and language of the Old World were inextricably linked in the minds of the immigrants. It was not uncommon, therefore, that the immigrants sought to organize, from the 1920s onward, afternoon schools to teach their children the language and culture of the old country and to counter the inevitable movement toward acculturation. During the 1930s and 1940s, these afternoon schools could be found in the parishes of nearly all the Orthodox immigrant groups. In some major cities, especially in the postwar period, modest attempts were even made to establish and maintain parochial schools.[1]

Especially during the postwar period, three powerful factors contributed to the gradual transformation of the Orthodox Church in the United States from an immigrant church to a more indigenous church composed primarily of persons born and educated in this country. The first factor was the decrease in immigration. The immigration laws passed in the 1920s placed greater restrictions on immigration from the Balkans, Russia, and the Middle East. The massive immigration of Orthodox Christians that took place in the late nineteenth and early twentieth centuries would never be repeated. During the period between 1930 and 1960, the influx was more measured and contained. Indeed, each Orthodox jurisdiction was affected somewhat differently by this fact. Migration of Russians and Carpatho-Russians during this period was quite meager. On the other hand, certain jurisdictions, such as the Greek Orthodox, continued to receive a steady flow of immigrants into the urban parishes. As we noted in the previous chapter, a number of displaced persons who came to America as political refugees had an impact upon some of the smaller jurisdictions.

The second factor was the changing membership of the Orthodox parish. After the period of World War II, it was clear that the composition of most Orthodox parishes had begun to change radically. With the decrease in immigration, the majority of the parishes of the larger and older jurisdictions were composed primarily of Orthodox Christians born in this country, nurtured by its educational institutions, and far more acclimated to the wider society. To be sure, the majority of these were the sons and daughters of the immigrants. Yet, these new generations were not as acquainted with the language, culture, and politics of the old country as were their parents and grandparents. While generally treasuring their cultural inheritance, the new generation of Orthodox Christians were Americans who saw themselves neither as immigrants nor as strangers in a foreign land.

The divisions that afflicted many parishes and a number of jurisdictions in the wake of World War II reflect a subtle conflict between those Orthodox who were born and raised in this country and those who were newly arrived. The former had less interest in the political developments in Eastern Europe and generally sought to maintain canonical ties between their diocese and the mother church. The immigrants of the post–World War II period, however, were generally strongly opposed to the Communist governments and the official church in their homelands. Together with speaking against Communism, they also sought to separate the American dioceses from association with the mother churches.[2]

The third factor was the suburbanization of the parish. In the years after 1950, the majority of the Orthodox parishes established in the United States were in the suburbs. In some cases, there were newly created parishes. In other cases, parishes relocated their church buildings from the inner city to the suburbs. This development reflected the fact that the majority of the Orthodox had themselves left the inner city and had moved to the suburbs. While the inner-city parishes continued to attract those newly arrived immigrants, the suburban parish served the needs of very different types of Orthodox parishioners. Some were the children or grandchildren of the immigrants. Some had come to Orthodoxy after being raised in other Christian traditions. Some were the non-Orthodox spouses of Orthodox. Indeed, it was becoming increasingly common for Orthodox to marry outside their ethnic group. While this had been frowned upon in earlier times, it was becoming increasingly common from the 1950s onward.[3]

These factors led to some important developments in Orthodox parish life. During this period, the use of English in the liturgical services began to increase. Religious education programs for children and classes for adults became more popular. Clergy were expected to be not only better educated but also more sensitive to the pastoral needs of parishioners who were less homogeneous and increasingly more educated and more affluent.

There is no doubt that the changing character of membership in Orthodox parishes created a tension that affected Orthodox in America from that time onward. This tension essentially centered upon the degree of adaptation that Orthodoxy had to undergo in order to serve the new generations of parishioners, to engage in missionary activity, and to be a forceful witness in American society.

On one hand, some advocated little, if any, adaptation. They felt that the ancient liturgical language and the myriad of ethnic customs were essential to the Orthodox faith. For them, ethnicity and religion were intimately related and could not be easily separated, and the distinctiveness of Orthodoxy was in its external characteristics that were inherited from the old country. Moreover, they believed that the church had a responsibility to preserve the language, customs, and folkways of the old country. Placing much emphasis upon the ethnic character of their parish and diocese, these persons were not able to make a distinction between the unchanging affirmations of the Orthodox faith and those changeable characteristics of the church throughout the ages.[4]

Others affirmed that the Orthodox Church in this country was not a church in exile but one destined to provide a distinctive witness in this society. These persons recognized that, in the past, Orthodoxy had penetrated a wide variety of cultures and Christianized a wide variety of peoples precisely because of its ability to preach the faith in a manner that was meaningful and understandable. While not altering the ancient faith, the church throughout the ages had always adapted its liturgical language to suit the needs of new populations. They affirmed that the church had never been bound to a particular language or culture; rather, the church had sought to use every language for the propagation of the gospel and to transform every culture with its message.[5]

At both the level of the local parish and the level of the national church, each jurisdiction responded somewhat differently to this tension. It was clear that it was a tension rooted in the maturation of Orthodox Christianity in this country that could not be easily ignored.

Father Georges Florovsky spoke boldly to the Orthodox about their obligation to share their faith with others:

Now let us be frank and outspoken. Have you really fulfilled your obligation? Your spiritual obligation to your American home and nation? Have you brought into the common treasury of American civilization all your treasures which you have inherited from your forefathers and ancestors? Have you taught Americans of other descriptions to know the Orthodox Church? Have you taught them to understand the pure Orthodox Faith? . . . Have you not rather kept your traditions to yourselves? . . . Have you not regarded it rather as something which belonged only to Russians, or else to Greeks, to Romanians, to Albanians and does not belong to other nations, to people with other national backgrounds? Have you done what was your first responsibility?[6]

RELIGIOUS EDUCATION AND YOUTH MINISTRY

One of the principal areas where the changing membership and its concerns became manifest, especially between 1945 and 1960, was religious education and ministry to youth. Following some practical patterns established by Roman Catholics and Protestants, most of the Orthodox jurisdictions greatly increased the formal attention given to nurturing the young in the teachings of the church and keeping the youth involved in church-related activities.

From as early as the 1930s, there are signs of interest in developing programs for the religious education of young people. About 1932, for example, the Greek Orthodox Archdiocese established a Department of Sunday Schools. This department encouraged the development of parish Sunday schools and eventually published some religious education texts in Greek. Sponsored by the Syrian (Antiochian) Orthodox Archdiocese, Father Michael Gelsinger wrote a *Handbook for Orthodox Sunday Schools* in 1938. It contained a small catechism and selected Bible verses. The Russian Orthodox Metropolia in 1935 appointed an Educational Council in order to encourage and standardize Sunday school instruction in the parishes. This led to the publication in Washington, D.C., of a series of leaflets known as *The Orthodox Sunday School*, which contained a discussion theme and Scripture reading for each Sunday class.[7]

Although this series was published in English, this was an exception to the rule. The limited religious education pamphlets and texts published in the period between 1930 and 1950 and used in the parishes were usually not written in English. During this period especially, those Sunday schools or afternoon schools that existed in local parishes normally had the dual tasks of imparting religious instruction and teaching the language and customs of the old country.

It was difficult for many Orthodox clergy and laity, especially those born elsewhere, to recognize the distinctive importance of religious education and the need to teach classes for children in English. As early as 1926, however, Bishop Joachim (Alexopoulos), the Greek Orthodox bishop of Boston, could see the direction that the church would have to take. In a rather insightful observation, he said:

We place the Sunday Schools in the series of priorities since we regard them to be greater in significance than the Greek Schools, as regards the desired purpose of molding character and preserving religious and ethnic conscience over a period of time, because we fear, whatever measure is taken to perfect the Greek School, the children will not be able to speak Greek fluently and satisfactorily, as they will speak and feel about English, which will become for them a living language while Greek will be forgotten and difficult, as it has already started in our day.[8]

Between 1950 and 1960, the movement among the Orthodox for sound and substantial religious education programs took on a greater importance. The Tenth Clergy-Laity Congress of the Greek Orthodox Archdiocese in 1950 formally authorized the establishment of a Sunday school curriculum in English. At the Twelfth Clergy-Laity Congress in 1954, a formal program for the administration of Sunday schools was approved. Similarly, the Russian Orthodox Metropolia established the Metropolitan Council Sunday School Committee in 1951, which led to a new series of Sunday school texts. At about the same time, the Syrian (Antiochian) Orthodox Archdiocese and the Carpatho-Russian diocese began the publication of their own religious education materials.

The work of religious educators in the various jurisdictions began to be coordinated in 1954 by Sophie Koulomzin, a distinguished Orthodox educator and a person greatly responsible for conveying to others the importance of Orthodox religious education. She was the first person to teach a course on religious education at St. Vladimir's Seminary in 1956. The religious educators who informally became associated with Koulomzin included Father Michael and Mary Gelsinger of the Antiochian Orthodox Archdiocese, Xenaphon Diamond of the Greek Orthodox Archdiocese, Father John Kivko of the Russian Orthodox Metropolia, and Father Vasile Hategan of the Romanian Orthodox Episcopate.[9]

A conference of about twenty-five Orthodox religious educators was held in 1956 in Valley Cottage, New York. The representatives of the seven Orthodox jurisdictions present decided to formally establish the Orthodox Christian Education Commission. The aims of the commission were "to find an Orthodox approach to the readily adapted Protestant pattern of Sunday Schools . . . , to relate Orthodox teachings to the American situation and particularly to new approaches to education, and perhaps most significant, to seek to create an inter-Orthodox forum for the exchange of ideas, problems, and practical solutions for the educational needs of Orthodox parishes and dioceses."[10]

During the first decade of its existence, the commission was responsible for publishing a bulletin that promoted research and the exchange of information in the field of Orthodox religious education. The commission also sponsored yearly conferences devoted to specific themes related to religious education and youth ministry. The early work of the commission did much to sketch the fundamental principles of an Orthodox approach to religious education in this country.

Despite the many accomplishments of the commission during its first decade of existence, it was unable to sponsor a unified curriculum for the Orthodox religious education of youth designed to be used by all the jurisdictions. Each of the major jurisdictions continued to publish and promote its own materials. The commission was able to provide its members with valuable advice and guidance in the areas of religious formation and educational psychology. Certainly, this contribution cannot be underestimated. Yet, the leaders of the various jurisdictions were simply not at a point where they could recognize the value of a unified curriculum. They could not see that a unified curriculum not only could embody the best approach to Orthodox religious formation but also could contribute to the establishment of greater unity among the Orthodox in America.

However, the significance of the commission must not be underestimated. Its work was, from the beginning, Pan-Orthodox in its composition, its scope, and its concerns. It did much to establish new relationships among clergy and laity from the various jurisdictions who were concerned especially with the religious formation of young people. While it did not establish a unified curriculum, it did a great deal to promote Pan-Orthodox cooperation and consultation. Indeed, it was a grassroots organization that did much to indicate that Orthodox from various jurisdictions had a great deal in common despite their past differences and their past isolation. Constance Tarasar, a distinguished Orthodox educator in her own right, said: "The very idea of bringing together Orthodox pastors and teachers from various nationalities and jurisdictions was, in itself, a relatively new idea, and the actual foundation and development of the Commission became the first successful cooperative Pan-Orthodox project on a national scale."[11]

Closely related to these developments in the area of religious education were a number of Pan-Orthodox endeavors in the area of specialized ministry to teenagers and college students. In 1950, the Orthodox Christian Fellowship was established at Columbia University in New York by Father Georges Florovsky. This expression of pastoral ministry was designed to serve all the Orthodox students at that university regardless of jurisdictional affiliation. This fellowship became the model for similar associations established by Orthodox clergy and laity at a number of colleges and universities throughout the country in the 1950s.[12]

During the same period, a number of the jurisdictions acted to establish national organizations designed to serve the specialized needs of teenagers. The Council of Eastern Orthodox Youth Leaders was established in 1954. Its principal aim was to bring together on a regular basis the leaders of the numerous jurisdictional youth organizations. The council was designed to create a forum for contact and cooperation among all Orthodox youth and their leaders. During the same year, a Pan-Orthodox Committee was established to oversee the development of an Orthodox award for deserving Boy Scouts. Like the Orthodox Christian Education Commission, these organizations were essentially grassroots in nature. Yet, they did much to bring together Orthodox from a variety of jurisdictions and to encourage pan-Orthodox cooperation.[13]

Despite these noble accomplishments, little formal attention was given to the development of programs for adult religious education and faith formation during this period. This was a critical failure that would have profound consequences. In the period after World War II, most Orthodox young adults who were born in this country were furthering their education and were in constant contact with other Americans of different religious backgrounds. Yet, most Orthodox young adults were sadly limited when it came to understanding and expressing their faith. Many had been taught to understand the church chiefly as an ethnic community. Few had developed a genuine appreciation of the doctrinal and ethical teachings of the Orthodox Church. Few heard sermons that they could truly understand. Fewer understood the meaning of the church's ritual.

Many church leaders appear to have ignored these facts. Yet, these difficult facts led some farsighted clergy to begin to pay more attention to the importance of adult religious education and worship. As a result, there was an increase in the number of books and pamphlets in English designed to provide explanation of the teachings, customs, and traditions of the Orthodox Church. It is interesting to note that Archbishop Michael of the Greek Orthodox Archdiocese published his study entitled *The Orthodox Church* in 1952. About the same time, Metropolitan Antony (Bashir) of the Antiochian Orthodox Archdiocese published his study entitled *Studies in the Greek Orthodox Church.* Father George Mastrantonis, a pioneer in the writing of books and pamphlets for American Orthodox readers, published his *What Is the Eastern Orthodox Church?* in 1956. Father Timothy Andrews in 1953 provided a comprehensive bibliography of the growing number of books and pamphlets.[14]

This period saw the publication of a number of prayer books, often bilingual, that contained the text of the liturgy of St. John Chrysostom. Within the Greek Orthodox Archdiocese, no less that four such bilingual versions of the liturgy appeared between 1948 and 1955. While three of these were prepared by parish priests, one was published by the seminary press in 1950 and received the official sanction of the archdiocese. In addition to these prayer books, a number of guides to the liturgical services began to appear.[15]

It should be remembered that, for nearly all of the jurisdictions, the Eucharist Liturgy was celebrated in their own particular liturgical language. The most common were Greek, Church Slavonic, and Arabic. Other languages, such as Albanian, Romanian, and Ukrainian, were used by particular jurisdictions. During this period, English was beginning to be used in some degree by some clergy in certain jurisdictions, but by no means all.

Metropolitan Antony (Bashir), an early proponent of the use of English in liturgical services, expressed forcefully his view in 1957 when he said:

While we must still minister to many who remember the ways and customs of another land, it is our policy to make the Church in the United States an American Church. In my own Archdiocese, under my administration, we have pioneered in the introduction of English in our services and sermons. From the beginning of my ministry, I began printing English service books, and the training of English speaking priests. We are tied to no sacred language; we recognize all tongues as the creation of God, and employ them in worship. We have no desire to perpetuate anything but the Gospel of Christ, and that we can do as effectively in English as in any other tongue.[16]

Not all the leaders of the Orthodox Church in the United States would have stated the case for the liturgical use of English as strongly as Metropolitan Antony did in 1957. While many recognized the pastoral and missionary imperative to introduce the greater use of English into the liturgical services, others emphasized the historic value and cultural significance of the more ancient liturgical languages. Many clergy and laypersons viewed the use of English as an abandonment of ethnic concerns. The language question was by no means resolved between 1950 and 1960. Indeed, it continued to affect all the Orthodox jurisdictions in the United States.

Despite the controversies that erupted, the 1950s saw a growing use of English in liturgical services. Often, it was used first at Pan-Orthodox vesper services or Divine Liturgies that brought together clergy and laity from a number of jurisdictions. During the 1950s, these services were often held in conjunction with retreats and conferences. In addition, the first Sunday of Lent, known as the Sunday of Orthodoxy, became a significant day on which clergy and laity from various jurisdictions in a particular city would gather together for the celebration of vespers. These Pan-Orthodox services of worship and prayer did much to bring the Orthodox closer together in professing the same faith and in enabling them to move beyond differences.

EARLY ECUMENICAL WITNESS

The entrance of some American Orthodox clergy and laity into the activities of the National Council of Churches and the World Council of Churches provided them with an opportunity not only to cooperate with Western Christians in social activities and theological dialogue but also to work together in providing a unified Orthodox witness.

The participation of American Orthodox theologians in ecumenical organizations and conferences became more pronounced and more formal especially after 1950. We have taken note of some early positive contacts between Orthodox and Western Christians. While in California, Father John Veniaminov visited Roman Catholic missions about the year 1836. In the early decades of the twentieth century, both Metropolitan Meletios of the Greek Orthodox Archdiocese and Archbishop Tikhon of the Russian Orthodox Archdiocese sought to maintain cordial relationships with bishops in the Protestant Episcopal Church. An Anglican-Orthodox Fellowship was established in the United States in 1934 and served as the American counterpart to the more famous Fellowship of Sts. Sergius and Alban, begun in England in 1928. Both organizations reflected the conviction held by many at the time that Anglicanism and Orthodoxy had much in common and that these points of agreement deserved greater study.

These early attempts at building positive relationships and establishing opportunities for dialogue were frequently damaged, however, by covert and overt attempts by some Protestants to bring Orthodox Christians into their fold and also by the harsh reaction of some Roman Catholics to the entrance of Eastern-Rite Catholics into the Orthodox Church. The mutual respect and understanding that would later become part of the ecumenical movement were not always central to the relationship among Christian groups in America in the early decades of this century.

The National Council of Churches of Christ in the U.S.A. was founded in 1950. As a cooperative ecumenical association, it initially reflected a merger of the earlier Evangelical Alliance, founded in 1867, and the Federal Council of Churches of Christ, founded in 1908. Although the new council was dominated by Protestant denominations and Protestant perspectives from the beginning, it was viewed by some as an American counterpart to the World Council of Churches, which was established in 1948.

Within the first few years of the establishment of the National Council of Churches, a number of Orthodox jurisdictions formally became members. These included the Syrian Orthodox Archdiocese, the Russian Orthodox Greek Catholic Church (the Metropolia), the Romanian Orthodox Episcopate, the Ukrainian Orthodox diocese, and the Greek Orthodox Archdiocese. Between 1954 and 1958, Father Georges Florovsky served as one of the vice presidents of the council.[17]

The participation of Father Florovsky and other Orthodox in the early work of the council certainly brought to it theological perspectives that were distinctive. Yet, the Orthodox frequently found themselves in meetings with Western Christians who had little or no appreciation of the history and teachings of the Christian East. Because of this, the Orthodox frequently found themselves engaged in theological deliberations that were dominated by Protestant perspectives. While the Orthodox were full members of the council, their impact upon its work during its early years was minimal.[18]

The Second Assembly of the World Council of Churches, held in Evanston, Illinois, in 15–31 August 1954, provided a number of American Orthodox theologians with a valuable opportunity for active participation. At the First Assembly of the World Council of Churches in Amsterdam in 1948, there was a total of eighteen Orthodox delegates present. None of these came from America. At the Evanston assembly, there were twenty-eight Orthodox delegates present. Of this number, nine were from America. In addition, there were two consultants and eight accredited visitors from the Orthodox jurisdictions in America. Because of this, a number of American Orthodox took a very active part in the activities of the assembly. Father Georges Florovsky, for example, delivered one of the major addresses, and Archbishop Michael of the Greek Orthodox Archdiocese was elected one of the copresidents of the council.[19]

Speaking of the importance of Orthodox participation in the Evanston assembly, Archbishop Michael said:

Did our participation in Evanston result in gain or loss? Beyond all doubt, in gain and even very great gain, prodigious for the prestige of our Mother, the ancient and most holy Orthodox Church. We were not there without being noticed. We did not mingle with the other representatives so as to lose our own color and to become agreeable to them. We were not afraid to proclaim to those present the whole truth on the subject of the faith of the Church.[20]

Another significant ecumenical conference occurred only a few years later in 1957: the North American Study Conference on Faith and Order held at Oberlin, Ohio. Jointly sponsored by the National Council of Churches and the World Council of Churches, the conference was devoted to the theme "The Nature of the Unity We Seek." Of the over 200 delegates, only 10 were American Orthodox, representing four jurisdictions. Despite their small number, the Orthodox contributed to the work of the conference, which came in the wake of the Evanston assembly.[21]

The Orthodox delegates presented the conference with a brief but very significant commentary on the theme. This statement remains one of the most cogent and precise articulations of the Orthodox Church in ecumenical conferences.[22] A portion of the statement says:

"The Unity We Seek" is for us a given unity which has never been lost and, as a Divine gift and essential mark of Christian existence, could not have been lost. The unity of the Church of Christ is for us a unity in the historical Church, in the fullness of faith, in the fullness of continuous sacramental life. For us this unity is embodied in the Orthodox Church which kept, *catholikos* (fully) and *anelleipos* (flawless), both the integrity of the apostolic faith and the integrity of the apostolic order.[23]

The early activity of the National Council of Churches, as well as the Evanston assembly of the World Council of Churches (WCC), provided the Orthodox participants from America with valuable opportunities to present the teachings of their church and to enter into theological dialogue with Western Christians. Although the Orthodox presence in North America dated from 1794, the opportunities for genuine dialogue between Orthodox and Western Christians in this country had been minimal prior to the 1950s. While these new encounters were not without their difficulties, the presence of the Orthodox clearly reflected their desire to acquaint the delegates from the Western Christian traditions with the distinctive faith perspectives of the Christian East.

For the American Orthodox, this period marked their fledgling steps into the arena of inter-Christian dialogue, a movement that would become much more pronounced in subsequent decades. In these early ecumenical meetings, the Orthodox delegates demonstrated that the presence of the Orthodox Church and the distinctive character of its teachings could no longer be ignored in inter-Christian dialogues in the United States.

These ecumenical organizations and conferences also provided the Orthodox delegates from the various jurisdictions with the opportunity to have greater direct contact with each other. Faced with the challenge of presenting the Orthodox faith to Western Christians, the Orthodox delegates recognized the need to cooperate with each other and to present a united Orthodox witness that transcended the differences of ethnic languages and cultures as well as Old World rivalries. The jurisdictional divisions did not prevent the Orthodox from affirming their common faith and presenting it in a unified manner.[24]

Closely related to the unified Orthodox ecumenical witness was a drive to have the Orthodox Christianity better recognized as a major faith. This movement had its origin in the work of the old federation and was associated at first with the movement to have Orthodox military personal during World War II receive their appropriate religious designation. During the period after the war, committees of Orthodox clergy and laypersons organized to have state governments and federal agencies grant the same recognition to the Orthodox faith that had been given to others. Throughout the 1950s and into the early 1960s a number of states and governmental agencies passed resolutions that designated Orthodox Christianity as a major faith insofar as this could be done legally.[25]

The concern expressed by so many Orthodox over this issue was an important sign that they were looking for greater recognition from the wider society. In earlier decades, the Orthodox were concerned primarily with survival in an environment that was seen as hostile. Bolstered by movements toward greater cooperation and unity as well as the presence of Orthodox theologians in high-level ecumenical forums, many Orthodox had now come to believe that the Orthodox faith deserved to be recognized as one of the major religious traditions in American society.

Throughout the period following the close of World War II, there was a demonstrable increase in contacts and cooperative activities among the members of the various Orthodox jurisdictions in America. As a consequence of ethnic and political differences, divisions continued to afflict many parishes and many dioceses. Yet, there was a growing recognition that all the Orthodox shared the same faith. Indeed, among many there was a growing recognition that the Orthodox Church had a distinctive witness to make in American society. With joint liturgical services and joint educational projects and through unified participation in ecumenical gatherings, the representatives of the major Orthodox jurisdictions began, in some measure, to overcome the isolation from one another that had generally characterized the Orthodox in America for decades. At the same time, the American Orthodox began to recognize, in some measure, their responsibility to all Christians and to the society in which they lived.

8
TOWARD GREATER
UNITY AND WITNESS

The quest for greater administrative unity among the Orthodox jurisdictions in America found concrete expression in the establishment of the Standing Conference of Canonical Orthodox Bishops in America (SCOBA) in 1960. Building upon the tradition of the earlier federation, SCOBA began to oversee the various inter-Orthodox activities and to coordinate ecumenical witness, which was born during the 1950s. It also became the focal point of efforts to establish a Provincial Synod of Orthodox Bishops, which would better serve the needs of Orthodox faithful and better reflect the organizational principles of Orthodox ecclesiology.[1]

THE ESTABLISHMENT OF SCOBA

About two years after his arrival in this country to become head of the Greek Orthodox Archdiocese in 1949, Archbishop Michael (Constantinides) convened a meeting of Orthodox bishops on 12 March 1952. Participating in this historic gathering were Metropolitan Anthony (Bashir) of the Syrian (Antiochian) Orthodox Archdiocese, Metropolitan Leonty (Turkevich) of the Russian Orthodox Greek Catholic Church (Metropolia), Metropolitan Anastasy (Gribanovsky) of the Russian Orthodox Synod Abroad, Metropolitan Markary (Illinsky) of the Exarchate of the Patriarchate of Moscow, Bishop Orestes (Chornak) of the Carpatho-Russian Orthodox Greek Catholic diocese, and Bishop Bogdan (Spilka) of the Ukrainian Orthodox diocese. The latter two jurisdictions were dioceses of the Ecumenical Patriarchate, like the Greek Orthodox Archdiocese.[2]

The meeting was significant if only because the heads of the three Russian Orthodox jurisdictions met together. There were intense rivalry and disputes between these jurisdictions resulting from divergent claims of authority in America and very different understanding of the authority of the Patriarchate of Moscow. The Exarchate was directly responsible to the Moscow Patriarchate. The Metropolia was in formal schism from the Moscow Patriarchate since 1924 but open to some form of mutual recognition. The Synod Abroad had only recently established its headquarters in New York as hundreds of its members came to the United States fleeing from further Communist advances in the Balkans and the Far East. The Synod Abroad was composed of Russian exiles who were staunch monarchists and who claimed that the Moscow Patriarchate had no authority because of cooperation with the Communist government. In addition to these significant differences, each jurisdiction saw itself as the rightful and canonical continuation of the old Alaskan mission.

At this historic meeting in New York, the bishops resolved to establish a consultative body. Like the federation that proceeded it, this body was meant to deal with common issues that affected the Orthodox in America. Since it was only a voluntary association, it was not meant to have any formal or canonical character. Unlike the federation, however, membership in this voluntary association was not restricted only to those primates who had a direct canonical association with an autocephalous church.

Despite the resolution of the meeting, no formal association of bishops came into existence. While this was a period of increased cooperation at the grassroots level, it would appear that the growing rivalry between the three Russian Orthodox jurisdictions precluded the development of a formal association of bishops. Indeed, among many of the Russian Orthodox hierarchs in America, there was little concern for cooperation at this time. Each of these jurisdictions was concerned with affirming its distinctive characteristics and attracting parishioners.[3]

A new phase in the development of greater conciliarity among the Orthodox in America began in 1960. SCOBA came into existence under the leadership of Archbishop Iakovos (Coucousis), the newly elected primate of the Greek Orthodox archdiocese.

Archbishop Iakovos was no stranger to the church in America. Born in Turkey and educated at the famous Patriarchal Theological School of Halki, he came to America in 1939 to serve on the faculty of the Holy Cross Greek Orthodox School of Theology. He later served as the pastor of the Annunciation Cathedral in Boston from 1942 to 1954. During these years, he became well aware of the difficulties that affected Orthodoxy in America and the unique opportunities for its development. Prior to his election to head the Greek Orthodox Archdiocese in 1959, he served for five years as the representative of the Patriarchate of Constantinople to the World Council of Churches.

Slightly more than a year after his arrival in the United States, Archbishop Iakovos set in motion a new proposal for a conference of Orthodox bishops. At his invitation, the representatives of eleven jurisdictions met on 15 March 1960 at the headquarters of the Greek Orthodox archdiocese in New York City. The ten bishops and one priest who were the official representatives of their respective jurisdictions resolved to establish a Standing Episcopal Conference. Archbishop Iakovos became its president.[4]

At the fifth meeting of the eleven presiding bishops, a formal constitution for SCOBA was approved. Although the conference did not contain representatives from every jurisdiction, it was certainly far more representative than the earlier federation. Like the earlier federation, however, the conference remained a voluntary association of the presiding bishops. Yet, the establishment of the conference was seen as a very significant expression of conciliarity that could lead to more formal unity.[5]

During the first decade of its existence, the conference became a very important forum in which the bishops, as well as the theological and pastoral staff, could meet regularly to deal with issues of common concern. Moreover, during the early years of its existence, the conference brought under its aegis a number of Pan-Orthodox committees and activities that had been established at the grassroots level in previous years. The conference also began to oversee and coordinate a unified Orthodox witness in ecumenical gatherings.[6]

Archbishop Iakovos spoke about the early accomplishments of SCOBA and its potential:

The cooperation of the Orthodox Churches within the Standing Conference has borne fruits: i.e., the body of the Orthodox Armed Forces chaplains, the pan-Orthodox Committee on Scouting, the Office of Campus Ministry for the benefit of our university students, the Ecumenical Relations Commission, and the Religious Education Publishing Commission. If this cooperation continues with the same sincerity toward our Orthodox faithful in America, perhaps it will have as its result one day the blessing of the Mother Churches to change the Standing Conference into a pan-Orthodox provincial synod, under the aegis of the Ecumenical Patriarchate. Such a provincial synod will contribute immeasurably to the perpetuation and growth of Orthodoxy in the United States.[7]

The establishment and early development of the conference took place at a time when the Orthodox Church throughout the world was also reaffirming its conciliar tradition. The most concrete expression of this renewed conciliarity was the four Pan-Orthodox conferences held between 1961 and 1968. At the invitation of the Ecumenical Patriarchate, representatives from the autocephalous and autonomous churches sent their representatives to these gatherings, which were held in Rhodes in 1961, 1963, and 1964 and at Chambésy (Geneva) in 1968.[8]

The most important result of these gatherings was that the age-old principle of conciliarity had been reaffirmed. Throughout the nineteenth and early twentieth centuries, political developments and wars had made it very difficult for the representatives of the regional Orthodox churches to meet together and to address common concerns. These conferences provided the opportunity for bishops and theologians from the various regional churches to meet one another and to begin to develop a consensus on critical issues affecting the entire church.

Two themes received the greatest attention in these conferences. First, the representatives resolved to begin the process of convening a Great and Holy Council, which would someday gather together Orthodox bishops and theologians from throughout the world. The term *ecumenical council* was carefully avoided. But in the minds of many, this gathering would certainly have the potential of being received as one. In order to prepare for this council, the conferences eventually settled upon ten topics, which would be examined in preconciliar meetings.[9]

Second, the conferences approved the presence of the Orthodox Church in ecumenical dialogue designed to restore the visible unity of Christians. This decision led directly to greater Orthodox involvement in the World Council of Churches. It also led to the establishment of bilateral theological consultations between the Orthodox and Oriental Orthodox churches, the Anglican Church, the Reformed Churches, the Roman Catholic Church, and the Lutheran Church.[10]

The renewal of Orthodox conciliarity at the worldwide level was very well received by SCOBA. There was a strong feeling that the breakdown of isolation among the Orthodox at the worldwide level could only help strengthen Orthodox unity in America. From its very inception, SCOBA became, in the words of Father John Meyendorff, "a symbol and a hope for all those who were consciously working towards a united Orthodoxy in America in accordance with the Orthodox understanding of the church and in agreement with the holy canons."[11]

ECUMENICAL WITNESS AND DIALOGUE

The Standing Conference took very seriously the challenge of Orthodox involvement in ecumenical witness and dialogue. The fact that Orthodox Christians in America lived, worked, and studied in such close proximity with Roman Catholics and Protestants was a reality that could not be ignored. The Orthodox in America were not living in religious ghettos insulated from other Christians. Unlike their counterparts in other parts of the world, the Orthodox in America were confronted with the tragedy of Christian disunity on a daily basis.

From the beginning of the twentieth century, there had been opportunities for formal dialogue between Orthodox and Protestants. The historic encyclical of the Patriarchate of Constantinople in 1920 called for the establishment of a Fellowship of Churches that would lead to greater understanding and dialogue. This proposal found a measure of fulfillment with the establishment of the World Council of Churches in 1948. The Orthodox churches of Constantinople, Alexandria, Antioch, Jerusalem, Cyprus, and Greece were among the founding members. Two American Orthodox jurisdictions, the Russian Orthodox Metropolia and the Syrian Orthodox Archdiocese, also held independent memberships.[12]

The contemporary ecumenical movement entered a dramatic period of development in the 1960s. The Orthodox Church of Russia began to adopt a more moderate position regarding dialogue with the Christian West. This was signaled dramatically by its entrance into the WCC in 1961. The Orthodox churches of Serbia, Romania, Bulgaria, Poland, Czechoslovakia, and Finland also joined the WCC in subsequent years. This meant that all the regional autocephalous and autonomous Orthodox churches were members of the WCC by 1966.[13]

At the Second Vatican Council (1963–1965), the Roman Catholic Church became more attuned to the need for dialogue with the other Christian churches and especially with the Orthodox Church. The historic meeting between Patriarch Athenagoras of Constantinople and Pope Paul VI in Jerusalem in 1964 was a significant sign of this new relationship. The historic lifting of the anathemas of 1054 between Constantinople and Rome in 1965 gave some the impression that the centuries-old schism was about to end.[14]

Especially significant about this new phase in ecumenical relations was that these developments were not simply affecting the clerics and theologians. Especially in America, the laity was becoming interested in the movement to overcome prejudices, to understand differences, and to work for Christian reconciliation.

SCOBA responded in a number of significant ways to the emerging ecumenical movement and to some of the issues being raised in the American context. First, a statement entitled "The Discipline of Holy Communion" was issued by SCOBA on 22 January 1965. In this pastoral statement, the SCOBA bishops stated that they "viewed with satisfaction the progress in mutual understanding that is leading the separated Christian bodies closer to each other in faith and life." With this in mind, the bishops urged the faithful to understand these historic developments and to become "instruments of peace and reconciliation."[15]

At the same time, the bishops clearly stated that developments in the ecumenical movement did not mean that Orthodox Christians were free to participate in the sacramental life of other churches. The bishops reaffirmed the Orthodox position that the Eucharist is not principally the means toward unity but rather primarily the expression of communion with the church and the acceptance of its teachings. In their concluding words, the bishops said:

The Standing Conference would at this time remind the children of the Church as they pray, study and work for Christian reunion that the Eucharistic Mystery is the end of our unity not the means to that end; and that, therefore, decisions reached by Christian bodies outside the Orthodox Church have no significance of validity for the Orthodox Church or her members.[16]

Second, SCOBA approved on 12 October 1966, and subsequently published, a document entitled *Guidelines for Orthodox Christians in Ecumenical Relations*. This document was a clear result of the recognition that the Orthodox position on ecumenical witness and dialogue had to be given greater amplification. The primary purpose of this text, therefore, was to provide the clergy and laity of the eleven jurisdictions of SCOBA with concrete guidance for their participation in ecumenical gatherings. The document sought to express the principles of Orthodox involvement in the quest for Christian reconciliation that were not only rooted in the Orthodox understanding of the church but also responsive to the demands of a society that was religiously pluralistic.

This brief text could not answer every question that was being raised at a time when relationships among the Christian churches were undergoing dramatic changes. Yet, this document does have an important historic significance. It was the first attempt by Orthodox bishops and theologians to deal in a formal manner with some of the doctrinal and practical issues associated with issues of Christian reconciliation.[17]

The Standing Conference also authorized the establishment, and oversaw the activity, of a number of committees of theologians to meet with their counterparts from other Christian churches in the United States. Theological consultations were established with the Episcopal Church in 1962, the Roman Catholic Church in 1966, the Lutheran Churches in 1968, and the Reformed Churches in 1968. With varying degrees of fruitfulness, these consultations examined points of doctrinal differences and agreement. Despite the inherent difficulties in such endeavors, the establishment of these consultations has remained one of the most significant accomplishments of SCOBA.[18]

Father John Meyendorff expressed some of the Orthodox concern over their involvement in the ecumenical movement:

There will certainly be no Christian unity outside Orthodoxy: the uninterrupted, organic tradition of united Christianity is authentically preserved in the Orthodox Church. And it is our responsibility to make this truth to be accepted as a relevant challenge in the ecumenical movement. Unfortunately, Orthodox thought in this matter is too often polarized between two equally wrong positions: "open" relativism and "closed" fanaticism. The first accepts the naive Protestant idea that it is sufficient to forget about "doctrines" and practice "love" to secure unity. The second fails to accept the authentically Christian values of the West, which Orthodoxy simply cannot reject, if it wants to be faithful to the fullness of Christian truth.

Between these two positions—which are both unfaithful to the present Orthodox reality—lies the road of a conscious and sober participation in the ecumenical movement, implying no compromise, but much love and understanding. This road is the right one, not simply because it is the "middle road," but mainly because it reflects the truly catholic spirit of the Orthodox faith.[19]

AN OPPOSING PERSPECTIVE

While SCOBA was the national church body that brought together the primates and other leaders of the major Orthodox jurisdictions in the United States, there were a small number of other jurisdictions claiming to be Orthodox who were not part of the conference. These other jurisdictions generally did not accept the Orthodox conciliar developments and the expressions of Orthodox ecumenical witness that were supported by SCOBA.

The Russian Orthodox Synod Abroad was one such jurisdiction. Popularly known as the Karlovtsy Synod or the Synod Abroad, it had been invited to send a representative to the organizational meeting in 1960 that led to the establishment of SCOBA. Although the Synod Abroad had a representative at Pan-Orthodox meetings in 1952 and 1959, it refused to participate in the meetings that led to the birth of SCOBA.

As we have already noted, the Synod Abroad established a diocese in the United States in 1927. A tentative unity was established between the Synod Abroad and the Metropolia in America between 1935 and 1946. Aligning themselves with the Nazi opposition to Communism, the leadership of the Synod Abroad moved their headquarters to Berlin in 1945. Five years later, in 1950, the headquarters was again moved to New York City in conjunction with the migration of thousands of Russian Orthodox from Eastern Europe and the Far East. With a slight increase of parishes in the United States, the Synod Abroad continued to see itself as the Russian Orthodox "church in exile," having the responsibility of preserving not only the Orthodox faith but also Russian language and culture until the day when Russia would be freed of Communism and its faithful could return to their homeland.

The initial reason for the Synod Abroad's aversion to the developing conciliarity in America was its repudiation of the activity of the Patriarchate of Moscow. The Synod Abroad refused to recognize the legitimate authority of the Patriarchate of Moscow and its clergy since 1926. Never abandoning its allegiance to the old Russian monarchy, the Synod Abroad claimed that the Patriarchate was thoroughly controlled by the Communists after the death of Patriarch Tikhon in 1925.[20]

The Synod Abroad made the bold claim that it was the free and legitimate Russian Orthodox Church in exile. With this declaration, the Synod Abroad consistently opposed those Orthodox conciliar movements both in America and worldwide in which the Patriarchate of Moscow had representatives. Referring to the representative of the Patriarchate of Moscow, Metropolitan Anastasy of the Synod Abroad said:

We must avoid as a pestilence every kind of contact with them. You know that these people with thoroughly buried consciences will never cease from waging war on us, although they constantly change their methods of warfare. At times they openly attack us and at times they utilize a circumventing maneuver in order to conceal their true purpose. Often they appear as angels of light, in order to delude even the chosen ones if possible.[21]

Within the American context, therefore, the Synod Abroad would not be a part of any organization at which there was a representative of the Exarchate of the Patriarchate of Moscow. In refusing the invitation to the meeting of 15 March 1960, Metropolitan Anastasy, the primate of the Synod Abroad, said that neither he nor any other bishop of theirs would sit at the same table with the representatives of the Patriarchate of Moscow.[22]

This perspective of the Synod Abroad was also reflected in its view of the Pan-Orthodox Conference in Rhodes in 1961. Because a delegation from the Patriarchate of Moscow was present, members of the Synod Abroad began to question the very authenticity of this and subsequent Pan-Orthodox gatherings. Referring to the first Rhodes conference, one member of the Synod Abroad declared that it was "a gathering even more shameful, for the primacy of the Soviets garbed in Church vestments was recognized in a free Orthodox milieu. And through this, a question mark arose over all of free Orthodoxy with regards to its gracefulness, whether it still remained in Christ or had already gone over to the anitchrist."[23]

In addition to being a vocal opponent to the authority and the activities of the Patriarchate of Moscow, the Synod Abroad took a number of actions that reflected its anti-Communistic political ideology and its unwillingness to contribute to greater Orthodox unity in America. Throughout the late 1950s and 1960s, the Synod Abroad received from the Russian Orthodox Metropolia the parishes that refused to commemorate at liturgical services the Patriarch of Moscow. Likewise, in 1958 the Synod Abroad accepted a group of anti-Communistic, immigrant clergy and laity from the Romanian Orthodox Episcopate. A few years later, in 1963, the Synod Abroad accepted a like-minded group clergy and laity from the Bulgarian Orthodox diocese. In this case, the Synod Abroad even consecrated Father Kyril Yonchev as a bishop and established a new diocese especially for those staunchly anti-Communistic Bulgarian Orthodox immigrants who repudiated the authority of the Patriarchate of Bulgaria.[24]

The Synod Abroad also became a vocal opponent of Orthodox participation in ecumenical dialogues and organizations. This position appears to have become more acute after the conciliar decisions of the Pan-Orthodox conferences of 1961 and 1963 and especially after the entrance of the Patriarchate of Moscow into the World Council of Churches in 1961.

The Orthodox Church both at the worldwide level and in the United States viewed ecumenical witness as an expression of the mission of the church. However, one of the bishops of the Synod Abroad viewed ecumenical witness as "a path which leads to the embrace of godless communism and prepares for the kingdom of the anti-Christ." He declared that those Orthodox who participate in ecumenical forums "mutilate the teachings concerning the Church of Christ and adjust it to the demands of the current mode."[25]

Between 1965 and 1969, Metropolitan Philaret (Voznessensky), who became primate of the Synod Abroad in 1964, wrote four public letters of protest that opposed the conciliar movement in Orthodoxy as well as Orthodox ecumenical witness. These letters not only further isolated the Synod Abroad from world Orthodoxy but also depicted the Synod Abroad as the "remnant" in which the faith is held in purity free from all forms of modernism, Communism, and ecumenism. Because of this, some in the Synod Abroad viewed it as "the only Orthodox Church remaining in America and the entire world whose hierarchy stands fully behind traditional Orthodoxy and against the approaching union."[26]

During this same period especially, the Synod Abroad became a haven for those clergy and laity of other Orthodox jurisdictions in America who opposed Orthodox ecumenical witness. Certainly, the Synod Abroad continued to maintain a strongly Russian identity and character. However, because of its opposition to developments in the Orthodox world, it began to attract persons who were not of

Russian background but who were opposed to the policies articulated by the auto-cephalous churches and by those jurisdictions that were part of SCOBA. On this trend, one member of the Synod Abroad said:

It is through no intention of its own that the Russian Orthodox Church Outside of Russia has become, in these critical times for world Orthodoxy, a veritable beacon and haven for Orthodox clergy and faithful of all nationalities who strive to learn and preach the truths of Orthodox Christianity in harmony with a fully Orthodox hierarchy. . . . Whole Orthodox Churches are being led by a hundred forms of worldly influence into forgetfulness of Or-thodoxy and into outright apostasy; and Orthodox bishops in every Church and jurisdiction are either taking the lead in this suicidal movement or maintaining what has now surely be-come a traitorous silence.[27]

These extreme sentiments were to be expressed in the publications and tracts produced in many quarters of the Synod Abroad. In somewhat less of an extreme manner, the views were more formally expressed by the Council of Bishops of the Synod Abroad in their meeting in Montreal in 1971. There, the bishops formally repudiated the developments in the Patriarchate of Moscow. They also declared that ecumenism "was a heresy against the dogma of the Church." Although the Synod Abroad represented less than fifty parishes and perhaps less than 1,000 parishioners in the United States, the words of their bishops only further alienated this body from other Orthodox both in this country and throughout the world.[28]

PROPOSALS FOR A PROVINCIAL SYNOD

Throughout the first decade of its existence, it was obvious that SCOBA had be-come an important vehicle for common witness and limited cooperation among the jurisdictions that voluntarily became members. It had far outlived its prede-cessor. It was viewed by many as an important expression of Orthodox unity in the United States. Despite the vocal opposition of some smaller groups, such as the Synod Abroad, SCOBA expressed the concern for greater unity and the desire for ecumenical witness that the vast majority of Orthodox in America affirmed.

However, there always had been a serious defect in the organizational status of SCOBA. The conference began as, and had always remained, a voluntary associa-tion of bishops who were related to particular jurisdictions. Each presiding hier-arch had maintained his own ultimate autonomy in relationship to other SCOBA bishops. Each jurisdiction had maintained its own distinct independence and char-acteristic features. Finally, most of the jurisdictions associated with SCOBA had been actually provinces of mother churches in Europe or the Middle East. This meant that the pastoral needs of the Orthodox in America had sometimes come into conflict with policies of the various mother churches.

All this shows that SCOBA was simply a consultative body. It had never had any genuine authority over and above the jurisdictions that constituted it. Any decision that it made ultimately had to be approved by each of the jurisdictions and in some cases by the mother churches. Indeed, this is the fundamental reason SCOBA could not deal with the critical organizational challenges that confronted American Orthodoxy. Paradoxically, SCOBA was in a better position to cultivate a common ecumenical witness than it was to deal with serious issues of division within American Orthodoxy.

From its beginning, SCOBA was not able to gather together regularly all the Orthodox bishops in America for any type of consultation. According to its constitution, membership in the Standing Conference was limited to one bishop from each jurisdiction. Normally, this would be the presiding bishop of each jurisdiction.

SCOBA was never able to establish a national association of clergy. While SCOBA was able to foster some clergy associations at regional and local levels, it was simply not able to bring about any genuine sense of common witness and common support among the Orthodox clergy as a whole. Indeed, throughout most of their histories, the various seminaries and graduate schools of theology have been primarily concerned with preparing future clergy to serve the particular needs of persons in particular jurisdictions. Only recently have the two graduate schools of theology begun to take more seriously their obligation to rise above narrow interests and to serve the greater needs of the Orthodox in America.

SCOBA was never able to bring together clergy and laity from all the jurisdictions to discuss common concerns and to fashion common resolutions. Each of the particular jurisdictions has had its own national gathering of delegates that met either annually, biannually, or triennially. There has been no serious and consistent attempt to establish any contact among the delegates to these jurisdictional gatherings.

SCOBA was always hard-pressed to deal effectively with points of differences between jurisdictions. Relationships between the jurisdictions had frequently been strained when a parish or a clergyman sought to move from one ecclesiastical body to another. Relationships had also been strained when differences arose over the qualifications for ordination, the requirements for marriage, and the manner in which new parishes are established. SCOBA had little ability to adjudicate differences or to provide guidelines for relationships among the jurisdictions.

Finally, SCOBA was not able truly to speak and act in the name of the Orthodox Church in the United States. For all practical purposes, SCOBA was not able to express the position or the view of Orthodox Christianity in relationship to other religious bodies, to ecumenical bodies, to charitable agencies, or to governmental agencies. This has been painfully evident on many occasions.

Father John Meyendorff expressed with clarity the need for Orthodox unity in America when he wrote in 1968:

We must be united. The nationalistic feelings which currently separate the Orthodox Church in America into a dozen or more jurisdictions is sinful, uncanonical and impractical for further progress. It is sinful because it is contrary to Christian love. It is uncanonical because it contradicts the clearest statements of the Ecumenical Councils: "That there not be two bishops in one city (First Ecumenical Council, canon 8). It is impractical for the obvious reason that a unified Church of some 3,000,000 communicants would be much more able to face the problems we face now in our individual jurisdictions.[29]

From the time of SCOBA's formation, there were movements to alter its fundamental consultative character and transform it into a genuine provincial synod of bishops. This provincial synod would have to have all the characteristic dignity and authority accorded to it by Orthodox canon law. It would also have to have the recognition of the autocephalous churches acting with the leadership of the Ecumenical Patriarchate. This synod of bishops not only could be an effective, canonical expression of full Orthodox unity in this country but also could be a positive force to guide the development of unifying structures at the regional and local levels.

Even at the first planning meeting for the new conference in 1960, a memorandum was presented by Metropolitan Antony (Bashir) that emphasized the need to form a genuine synod of bishops and not simply a consultative body. "Our failure to form one united jurisdiction in America," said the Metropolitan, "is a constant reproach as well as an absolute violation of the sacred canons and must be corrected. This can be done by forming an American Synod composed of the chief hierarchs of each national jurisdiction who shall retain their present autonomy in internal matters, but act together in common issues, and plan a corporate union at the earliest opportunity."[30] While he had been one of the founders of the earlier federation, Metropolitan Antony clearly recognized that the success of a new organization depended upon it being a genuine synod.

At the eleventh regular meeting of SCOBA on 22 January 1965, the Commission on Unity presented a bold report that reviewed the reasons it was desirable to change the fundamental character of SCOBA. The report also affirmed that greater unity does not preclude legitimate diversity in practices, customs, and languages. The report recognized that the unification of the jurisdictions could not be achieved immediately. Rather, there must be a gradual unification by degrees. The first degree would be the canonical unification of the Orthodox episcopate in America.

The report then proposed that the Standing Conference petition all the autocephalous churches to be recognized as "the Holy Synod of the Orthodox Church in America." The proposal stated that this synod would achieve a high degree of coordination by having authority to approve all episcopal consecrations, to be a court of appeal for bishops, to establish ecumenical policy, to oversee inter-Orthodox chaplaincies, and to be responsible for communications with other Orthodox churches. The proposal stated that the Exarch of the Ecumenical Patriarchate would serve as the president of the synod and that each national jurisdiction would be represented by one bishop.[31]

The proposal was formally opposed by the Russian Orthodox Patriarchal Exarch and the bishop of the Bulgarian Orthodox jurisdiction. However, the proposal passed with the approval of six representatives. Then, SCOBA adopted unanimously the following recommendation: "The report of the Ad Hoc Commission [will] be submitted to the Mother Churches by the respective hierarchs, accompanied by a personal letter of explanation, and a request for blessing and action and that the Chairman submit the Report to the Ecumenical Patriarchate with an additional request, signed by the Chairman and the Secretary, that it be placed on the agenda of the next Pan-Orthodox Conference at Rhodes."[32]

Subsequent meetings of SCOBA in 1965 and 1966 considered the responses that gradually came from some of the autocephalous churches. While not opposing the proposal in principle, the Ecumenical Patriarchate requested further study of the American situation. It subsequently indicated its willingness to approve the establishment of a provincial synod. The Church of Antioch believed that the topic should be placed on the agenda of the Pan-Orthodox Conference. Strong negative reaction, however, came from the Church of Russia and the Church of Serbia. It was clear that on the worldwide level, there was no clear consensus coming from the autocephalous churches regarding developments in America.[33]

A more modest proposal was offered by SCOBA on 9 May 1968. A majority of the hierarchs voted to send three representatives to the forthcoming Pan-Orthodox Conference scheduled for Chambesy (Geneva). The task of the delegation would be to initiate discussion among the representatives of the autocephalous churches on the topic of forming a united church in America. Within five months, however, the Ecumenical Patriarchate informed Archbishop Iakovos, the chairman of SCOBA, that the subject of Orthodoxy in America could not be placed on the agenda because its topics had already been determined.[34]

Once again, at the 18 May 1968 meeting of SCOBA, the representatives approved an appeal to the organizers of the Pan-Orthodox Conference and authorized Archbishop Iakovos to write letters directly to the heads of the autocephalous churches regarding the situation of Orthodoxy in America. After noting a number of reasons greater unity is desirable, the Appeal to the Pan-Orthodox Conference says:

All of us and all our faithful priests and people are aware of this pressing need as we are hampered in all of our common efforts by divisions not of our own making which stand as unavoidable obstacles to our spiritual and ecclesiastical welfare and progress. We cannot overstate the seriousness of our need for some early canonical solution to our jurisdictional confusion which is unprecedented in the history of our Orthodox Church and in absolute violation of its well known structure. . . .

Therefore, we respectfully request that an immediate canonical basis be formed with the agreement of the Autocephalous Churches for the creation of one Orthodox Church in America which will provide for the pastoral care of the several cultural and national entities in America, and guarantee the common witness and mission of Orthodoxy to the West.[35]

It is difficult to determine all the reasons that prevented the mother churches from responding favorably to the request from SCOBA. But, two reasons seem to predominate during this period. First, many of the mother churches were simply reluctant to relinquish any authority over their particular dioceses. Despite the clear witness of the traditional principles of ecclesiology, many of the mother churches believed that their dioceses were made up of "their people," and they had legitimate authority to care for them. The mother church was usually unwilling, therefore, to lose the support that came from the daughter diocese in America. Second, there often was no clear consensus within the jurisdiction itself. Within each jurisdiction, some argued for greater unity. Yet, the movement toward greater unity was opposed either overtly or covertly by others who preferred to maintain the distinctive character of their jurisdiction.

Despite these conflicting views, significant attempts to express better the unity of the Orthodox Church in the United States found a valuable expression in the work of the Standing Conference of Canonical Orthodox Bishops, especially between 1960 and 1970. As a consultative body bringing together the heads of eleven jurisdictions, SCOBA became a significant association that began to oversee and direct many of the grassroots Pan-Orthodox organizations that had come into existence. At a time when the ecumenical movement was gaining momentum in the United States, SCOBA was instrumental in organizing and directing a unified Orthodox witness.

Moreover, the various appeals of SCOBA to the autocephalous churches were a sure sign that the Orthodox in the United States were on the threshold of a new period of witness and mission that would be best served by a provincial synod of bishops. This synod would bring together all the canonical Orthodox bishops in this country. Such a body would better serve the needs of the Orthodox faithful and better reflect the principles of Orthodox ecclesiology. Although preliminary efforts did not meet with complete success at the time, they did help to bring greater attention to the situation of the Orthodox in the United States.

9
AN ERA OF TRANSITIONS

The year 1970 marked the beginning of two major controversies that profoundly affected the development of the Orthodox Church in the United States and marked a transition to a new stage of growth. The Russian Orthodox Metropolia was granted autocephalous status by the Patriarchate of Moscow in 1970. This meant that the Metropolia, from then on, known as the Orthodox Church in America, had been given recognition to be a fully independent, self-governing local church. This dramatic decision, however, was not recognized by all. During the same period, the Greek Orthodox Archdiocese became embroiled in discussions over greater use of vernacular languages in worship. While both issues created much discord lasting well over a decade, they were expressions of deeper concerns over the permanent witness and mission of Orthodox Christianity in the United States.

THE AUTOCEPHALY QUESTION

The position and status of the Russian Orthodox Metropolia were dramatically altered by the political and ecclesiastical developments in the Soviet Union, especially after the death of Patriarch Tikhon in 1925. The October revolution of 1917 not only affected the relationship between church and state in the Soviet Union but also dealt a profound blow to the Russian Orthodox communities in the United States and Western Europe. The loss of financial support, combined with crisis in leadership and schisms, shook the Russian Orthodox Church in America throughout the 1920s. Under the leadership of Metropolitan Platon (Rozdestvensky), the Metropolia in 1924 declared itself to be "temporally autonomous" from its mother church, the Patriarchate of Moscow. This action was taken chiefly because many in America felt that communication with the official church in the Soviet Union was unreliable. Moreover, by 1933, the leaders of the Russian Orthodox Metropolia were refusing to give any pledge of loyalty to the government in the Soviet Union.[1]

When attempts to reconcile the Metropolia to its mother church failed, the Holy Synod of the Patriarchate of Moscow, led by the acting locum tenens of the Patriarchate, Metropolitan Sergius, declared on January 5, 1935, that the Metropolia was schismatic. Despite this bold action, the majority of the clergy and laity of the Metropolia's approximately 250 parishes remained faithful to the leadership of Metropolitan Platon.[2]

In the period following World War II, there were attempts to reconcile the Metropolia with the Moscow Patriarchate. While the Metropolia recognized the "spiritual authority" of the Patriarch of Moscow and commemorated him in liturgical services, no formal reconciliation took place. In fact, the Patriarchate of Moscow reaffirmed its interdict upon the Metropolia in 1947.[3]

This means that from 1935 to 1970, the Metropolia was in a state of formal schism from its mother church. Given the difficult situation for the church in the Soviet Union, however, the Patriarchate of Moscow was not in a position to press its concerns. At the same time, the Metropolia continued to have a type of de facto recognition from the Patriarchate of Constantinople and its Archdiocese in America. As early as 1930, the Metropolia received its sacramental chrism from the Patriarchate of Constantinople by means of the archdiocese.[4] More recently, evidence of the close relationship can be seen in the episcopal ordination of Father Theodosius Lazar as the Metropolia's bishop of Alaska on 6 May 1967. In addition to four bishops of the Metropolia, two bishops of the Patriarchate of Constantinople's American jurisdictions participated in the ordination.[5]

Some leaders in the Metropolia during the late 1950s and early 1960s proposed that it formally petition to enter into communion with the Patriarchate of Constantinople. Based upon canon law and ecclesiastical practice, the Patriarchate affirmed jurisdiction over the developing church in America. However, the Patriarchate was not always in a position to act upon its claims. Some in the Metropolia believed that its irregular status could be cleared through formalizing the informal relationship that had developed with Constantinople since 1924.[6]

Perhaps recognizing these tendencies in the Metropolia, the Patriarchate of Moscow began in 1966 to intensify its opposition to those Russian Orthodox jurisdictions in America and Europe that were not in communion with the Church of Russia. As part of this opposition, the Patriarchate of Moscow asked other autocephalous churches to cease contact with those jurisdictions that it considered schismatic. The principal jurisdictions with which the Moscow Patriarchate was concerned were the Metropolia, the Synod Abroad, and Russian Orthodox exarchate of Western Europe, which had entered into formal communion with the Patriarchate of Constantinople 1931. Clearly, what was at stake were the Pan-Orthodox conciliarity and cooperation at the highest level, which had been growing since the first Pan-Orthodox Conference of 1961.[7]

The Metropolia found itself in a very difficult situation. Metropolitan Ireney (Bekish), the primate of the Metropolia (1965–1968), addressed a Christmas message to all Orthodox patriarchs in 1965–1966. In this letter, the Metropolitan affirmed that the Metropolia simply could not return to the jurisdiction of the Patriarchate of Moscow. He said that "the existence of two very different and often contradictory social structures in America and Russia, and the fundamental distrust we have toward any instruction issued from communist countries, make the submission to the Moscow Patriarchate virtually inconceivable." In order to support this position further, the Metropolitan noted that church canons disapprove of structures "in which the Christians of one country are submitted to ecclesiastical authority of another state. Even when the political relations between the two states are normal and friendly, the Church which is under the authority of foreign leadership is suspected of being 'alien.' "[8]

Father Alexander Schmemann, the dean of St. Vladimir's Theological Seminary, traveled in May 1966 to the Ecumenical Patriarchate in Constantinople as the envoy of the bishops of the Metropolia. There, he met with Patriarch Athenagoras. This was the same person who had served as archbishop of the Greek Orthodox Archdiocese in America from 1931 to 1948. Although he was well aware of the situation in America, the Patriarch apparently did not envision the possibility of the Metropolia coming into communion with Constantinople at that time. In fact, Constantinople had only recently relinquished its relationship with the Russian Orthodox Archdiocese of Western Europe. Father Schmemann reported that the Patriarch urged him to encourage the Metropolia to be reconciled with its mother church.[9]

Metropolitan Ireney planned his own journey to Constantinople and to the other patriarchates in 1967 in order to plead the cause of the Metropolia. However, this plan was thwarted when Patriarch Alexis of Moscow wrote to the heads of the autocephalous churches and urged them not to permit Metropolitan Ireney to officiate at liturgical services in their respective jurisdictions.[10]

Against the backdrop of these events, new contacts were established between the Metropolia and the Patriarchate of Moscow. While attending the assembly of the World Council of Churches in Uppsala, Sweden, in 1968, three representatives of the Metropolia met with Metropolitan Nikodim (Rostov) of the Moscow Patriarchate. At this meeting the Patriarchate broached the topic of autocephaly and, thus, clearly went beyond previous positions regarding the potential status of the Metropolia. Subsequent meetings of representatives from both quarters were held in New York, Geneva, and Tokyo in 1969. Following additional meetings, the final agreement was signed in New York on 31 March 1970 by Metropolitan Nikodim and Metropolitan Ireney. Central to the agreement was a request from the Metropolia to the Patriarchate of Moscow to be recognized formally as an autocephalous church.[11]

The Patriarchate of Moscow lifted its interdiction against the Metropolia on 8 April 1970, which had been in effect since 1935 and reaffirmed in 1947. This action marked the formal end of the schism. On 10 April 1970, the Patriarchate formally issued the Tome of Autocephaly for the "Orthodox Church in America." This document affirmed that the Patriarchate of Moscow recognized the former Metropolia as one of the self-governing Orthodox churches. It also noted that the exarchate of the Patriarchate of Moscow was abolished, although individual clergy and parishes could choose to remain directly under the Moscow Patriarchate. Finally, it called upon the other autocephalous churches to recognize the new status of the Metropolia as the autocephalous Orthodox Church in America.[12]

The grant of autocephaly was formally announced at the All-American Council of the Metropolia held on 20–22 November 1970, in South Canaan, Pennsylvania. At this meeting the representatives formally changed the name of their jurisdiction from the Russian Orthodox Greek Catholic Church in North America to the Orthodox Church in America.[13]

In a Message to All Orthodox Christians in America, the council addressed the theme of greater unity. A portion of the message says:

We have the same faith, the same Tradition, the same hope, the same mission. We should then constitute one Church, visibly, organically, fully. Such is the requirement of our Orthodox Faith and we know that always and everywhere the Orthodox Church has existed as one Church. There can, therefore, be no excuse for our jurisdictional divisions, alienation from one another, and parochialism. The removal of such divisions and the organic unity of all Orthodox in America is the goal of our Church and we invite you to become part of the unity.[14]

While there were indications at least as early as 1965 that autocephaly could be granted to the Metropolia by the Moscow Patriarchate, the actual event set off a new storm of controversy. In a certain sense, the Metropolia had been acting as a de facto autocephalous jurisdiction since 1927, although it was viewed as schismatic by the Patriarchate of Moscow. Thus, by 1970 it seems that the leaders of the Metropolia would not be content with any lesser status, such as autonomy, which would still subordinate the jurisdiction to the Patriarchate of Moscow. The fact that the Patriarchate of Moscow agreed to the granting of autocephaly did regularize the Metropolia in the eyes of its mother church. However, the action did not lead immediately to the resolution of the multiple jurisdictional situation in America. Indeed, the situation appears to have become more complex.

During the first years of its existence, the new Orthodox Church in America took a number of important actions. First, on 9 August 1970, clergy and laity gathered in Kodiak, Alaska, for the solemn services at which the missionary monk Herman of Spruce Island was proclaimed a saint, the first formally recognized in North America.[15]

Second, the Orthodox Church in America received two other jurisdictions. The Albanian Orthodox Archdiocese under Bishop Stephen (Lasko) became a diocese within the Orthodox Church in America in 1971. This jurisdiction had been associated with the Church of Albania prior to its liquidation by the Communist government.[16] The Bulgarian Orthodox diocese under Bishop Kyril (Ionchev) became part of the Orthodox Church in America in 1976. This jurisdiction had been part of the Russian Orthodox Church Outside of Russia since 1964.[17] These two jurisdictions essentially followed the example of the Romanian Orthodox Episcopate, which had become part of the old Metropolia in 1960.[18] In agreeing to accept these jurisdictions, the new Orthodox Church in America permitted them to maintain a high degree of autonomy and to maintain their identity as ethnic dioceses.

Finally, at the Fifth All-American Council in 1977, the retiring Metropolitan Ireney was succeeded by Bishop Theodosius (Lazor). The new Metropolitan was the first American-born primate of any jurisdiction. The election of the young former bishop of Alaska was viewed as a further sign of the growing indigenous character of the Orthodox Church generally.

THE PAN-ORTHODOX CRISIS

The granting of autocephaly to the former Metropolia by the Patriarchate of Moscow led to discussions within the entire Orthodox world over a number of topics. Chief among these was the topic of how autocephaly is properly granted. Closely associated with this were questions related to the canonical authority of the Patriarchate of Constantinople and the canonical authority of other autocephalous churches. Indeed, it seems that the peculiar situation of Orthodoxy in America became the backdrop against which interpretations of history and canon law were discussed.[19]

Father Alexander Schmemann, one of the leading advocates of autocephaly at the time, spoke of the debate that followed its granting:

The storm provoked by the "autocephaly" of the Orthodox Church in America is probably one of the most meaningful crises in several centuries of Orthodox ecclesiastical history. Or rather it could become meaningful if those who are involved in it were to accept it as a unique opportunity for facing and solving an ecclesiastical confusion which for too long a time was simply ignored by the Orthodox. For if America all of a sudden has become the focus of Orthodox attention and passions, it is because the situation of Orthodoxy here, being the most obvious result of confusion, was bound to reveal sooner or later the true nature and scope of, indeed, a Pan-Orthodox crisis.[20]

The most significant documents dealing with these issues are the four letters exchanged between the Patriarchate of Constantinople and the Patriarchate of Moscow during the years 1970–1971. Even before autocephaly was granted, the patriarchate of Constantinople indicated that it would not recognize this new status for the Metropolia. Yet, these letters provide some insight into the points of agreement and the points of disagreement that characterized the discussions at the time. As can be expected, the letters also reflect some of the emotions of the moment as well as some underdeveloped historical perspectives.[21]

There are important points of agreement between Constantinople and Moscow regarding the situation in America. First, both agree to the restoration of normal canonical relations between Moscow and the Metropolia. Here, there is a clear recognition that the Metropolia had been in a peculiar situation since 1924.

Second, both Constantinople and Moscow agree on the crucial principle that only one unified Orthodox Church can properly exist in any country. They recognize that canon law demands the unity of a territorial jurisdiction. This point is especially important because it opposes those who promote the multiplicity of jurisdictions in America in order to propagate ethnicity or political ideologies.

Third, both Constantinople and Moscow agree that only an Ecumenical Council will finally confirm the development of a united church in America. Both recognize the importance of the process of preparation for the Great and Holy Council, which is examining a number of themes, including diaspora and autocephaly.

Finally, both Constantinople and Moscow agree that the Ecumenical Patriarchate of Constantinople has a primacy of rank and honor in the church. This affirmation clearly opposes those who believed that Moscow was making an attempt to usurp the rightful place of Constantinople within the Orthodox Church.[22]

Of course, the four letters also express some serious points of disagreement. First, Constantinople affirms that autocephaly is properly recognized only by an ecumenical council. Until such a council is held, however, Constantinople claims that it has the right to designate a local church to be autocephalous. Moscow, on the other hand, affirms that each autocephalous church has the right to grant canonical independence to one of its parts.

Second, there is disagreement over the development of Orthodoxy in America. Moscow appears to claim canonical authority over the church in America in virtue of the fact that it established the Alaskan mission in 1794. Constantinople does not recognize the absolute right of Moscow over the developing church in America. Constantinople does recognize the reality of overlapping jurisdictions in America, which have created an extraordinary and irregular situation. While not abandoning its own canonical privileges, Constantinople indicates that a clear resolution to the situation cannot come about without the agreement of the various Orthodox churches.[23]

The action of the Patriarchate of Moscow in granting autocephalous status to the Metropolia/Orthodox Church in America was subsequently recognized by the autocephalous churches of Georgia, Bulgaria, and Poland.[24]

The action of the Patriarchate of Moscow has not been formally recognized by the autocephalous churches of Constantinople, Alexandria, Antioch, Jerusalem, Serbia, Romania, Cyprus, and Greece. These churches have not broken communion with the Metropolia/Orthodox Church in America. They view the Metropolia/Orthodox Church in America as a jurisdiction that is no longer in a state of schism from its mother church.[25]

THE LANGUAGE QUESTION

At the very same time that the controversy over autocephaly was developing, the Greek Orthodox Archdiocese, the largest of the American jurisdictions, also was shaken by debate regarding the use of a fifth-century form of Greek as the principal language of liturgical services. By 1970, English had certainly become the principal language of the vast majority of Greek Orthodox faithful. Most of these were second-, third-, or fourth-generation Americans with some Greek ancestry. Others had entered the Archdiocese after having been raised in different religious traditions. Since the 1950s, English had become the principal language of religious education. By the early 1960s, English was the principal language of administrative meetings. In 1964, the Archdiocesan Clergy-Laity Congress formerly recommended that certain prayers, the Creed, and the Scripture lessons be read in both English and Greek in the Eucharistic Liturgy. This action sanctioned a practice that was already in place in many parishes.[26]

After serving as primate of the vast Archdiocese for more than a decade, Archbishop Iakovos was well aware of the diversity of its membership, as well as the pastoral needs of his flock. Therefore, in planning for the 1970 Clergy-Laity Congress, the Archbishop himself courageously proposed a reevaluation of the Archdiocese's position on the use of the vernacular in liturgical services:

During the 1970–1980 decade, it will be necessary for us to face the language problem under more demanding and critical circumstances. The two present American-born generations, mixed marriages, the indigenousation of our Church, the educational level of our children, the limited Greek academic preparation of our priests—all these shall demand that our Church proceed in a logical and imperative re-evaluation of our known position in terms of language.[27]

Even before the more than 1,000 delegates convened in New York for the twentieth Clergy-Laity Congress, the cautious, pastoral approach to the language issue expressed by Archbishop Iakovos came under attack by extremists. These persons claimed that the greater use of English would be a threat to the perpetuation of the Greek language and culture in America.

The archbishop did not bow to the pressures of the extremists. In his keynote address to the congress, he reaffirmed his conviction that greater use of English in the liturgical services was necessary. Furthermore, he proposed the production of a new translation of the liturgy that would contribute to more active participation by the faithful. In his response to the extremists, the archbishop consistently affirmed his own devotion to Greek ideals, culture, and language. Yet, he also affirmed that the Orthodox Christians of Greek descent had a profound obligation to share their faith and their religious heritage with the rest of America:

I believe that our Church, without ceasing to be racially rooted in Greece and religiously in Phanar (the Ecumenical Patriarchate), must accept the fact that America is the place in which God has intended it to grow and bring many more into its fold; and that it has an obligation, without compromising in matters of faith, to adapt itself to the existing conditions and needs, changing in the final analysis even the language, but never its spirit or ethos.[28]

Under the leadership of the archbishop, the majority of the delegates at the Clergy-Laity Congress subsequently approved the report of the Committee on Liturgical and Linguistic Renewal. This report recognized that people in the vast Archdiocese of North and South America speak a number of vernacular languages, such as Greek, English, French, Spanish, and Portuguese. It also affirmed that it is important in the Orthodox tradition that the faith, teaching, and liturgies of the church be transmitted to the faithful in the vernacular language. With this in mind, the report recommended that "the Archdiocese permit the use of the vernacular language as needed in Church services in accordance with the judgement of the parish priest in consultation with the bishop."[29]

There is no doubt that the modest decision of the Clergy-Laity Congress regarding the use of the vernacular in worship was wholeheartedly approved not only by the delegates in New York but also by the vast majority of pastors and parishioners throughout the Archdiocese. In reality, the decision simply reflected the fact that the vernacular was already being used in one degree or another in many parishes. Moreover, the decision also reflected the deeper reality that the vast majority of parishes of the Archdiocese were serving Americans of diverse cultural and ethnic backgrounds.

However, a small but vocal minority criticized the decision of the congress and, in some cases, even distorted its intent. This opposition was led by the Greek language press in the United States, and it was generally supported by the press in Greece. An organization devoted to the "preservation of the Greek language and the Greek Orthodox Church" issued a manifesto that not only rejected the decision of the congress but also called for the replacement of the archbishop. Comprising primarily persons who had opposed the policies of the archbishop for some time, this organization appealed especially to the emotions of recent immigrants. Even the military government of Greece expressed its concern over rumors that the Archdiocese was going to abolish the use of Greek in the liturgical services.[30]

With the controversy heating up, the synod of the Ecumenical Patriarchate met on 31 August 1970 to discuss the resolutions of the congress. Since the Archdiocese is an ecclesiastical province of the Patriarchate of Constantinople, all decisions had to be approved by the patriarch and the synod of bishops.

Following the synod's deliberation, Patriarch Athenagoras addressed a letter to Archbishop Iakovos and one to the clergy and laity of the Archdiocese. Having served as archbishop in America from 1931 to 1948, Patriarch Athenagoras, the president of the synod, had a firsthand understanding of the developing church in America. Well aware of difficulties inherent in the American situation, Patriarch Athenagoras was intent upon preventing any schism in the Archdiocese similar to what he had experienced in the 1930s and 1940s. Both his letters, therefore, commended the leadership of the archbishop and deplored the misunderstandings created by the congress's decision. With regard to the language question, the Patriarch diplomatically affirmed that "the Greek language is and will remain the basic and preeminent liturgical language of the Greek Orthodox Archdiocese of America."[31]

The words of the Patriarch were certainly designed to end any divisive movement within the Archdiocese, even a movement of a small but vocal minority. He knew very well that the use of English would not only continue but also increase. While they rejected the resolution of the Clergy-Laity Congress, the Patriarch and the synod did not forbid the greater use of the vernacular where appropriate. Such a course of action would have been unthinkable, given the fact the Orthodox tradition has consistently emphasized the value of local languages for the teaching of the faith and for the liturgical services.

The divisive tendencies of some within the Archdiocese and outside it were dramatically aggravated again in 1975. With Archbishop Iakovos still the victim of unscrupulous attacks both in the United States and in Greece, the Patriarchate of Alexandria sent a bishop to the United States as its designated exarch. The presence of this bishop was a direct challenge to the legitimate authority of Archbishop Iakovos. Metropolitan Methodios (Fouyas) of Askoum conducted a number of meetings with defrocked bishops and priests. His attention appears to have been to establish a jurisdiction that would contain the clergy and laity who opposed the policies of Archbishop Iakovos.[32]

The Patriarchate of Constantinople formally condemned the action of the Church of Alexandria. In insisting that the exarch be withdrawn, Constantinople reaffirmed its canonical authority over the Orthodox in the diaspora. The Patriarchate of Alexandria eventually agreed to the request of Constantinople and withdrew its bishop.[33]

Despite their immediate negative consequences, all these unfortunate developments appear to have led to some serious reflection about the status, composition, and governance of the Archdiocese. After much discussion both within the Archdiocese and within the Patriarchate of Constantinople, a new organizational charter was approved in 1977. This charter divided the Archdiocese into ten dioceses led by a local bishop. These bishops would meet in synod under the presidency of the archbishop. It is most interesting that the new charter declared that the Archdiocese "serves all Orthodox living in the western hemisphere." In this broadened mission statement, there is no direct reference either to ethnic background or to language usage. Despite the difficulties over language, which the Archdiocese continued to experience, the words of the charter clearly indicated a more inclusive vision was developing in the Archdiocese.[34]

THE CHALLENGE TO SCOBA

The debate over autocephaly, the language controversy, and the question of the relationship of the Patriarchate of Constantinople to the church in America were serious issues. These issues troubled not only the various jurisdictions in America but also the various Orthodox churches throughout the world. In the United States, however, the discussions had a chilling effect upon Pan-Orthodox cooperation. In the period between 1970 and 1990, the underlying tensions manifested themselves in the relationship among clergy of the various jurisdictions, in the relationships among the theological schools, and, to some degree, in the work of the grassroots inter-Orthodox organizations. These tensions were fueled by the extreme views coming from partisans on all sides of the discussions.

Although the Greek Orthodox Archdiocese and the Orthodox Church in America/the Russian Orthodox Metropolia were the two jurisdictions most acutely affected by the controversies, all the jurisdictions were touched by their consequences. Indeed, in the two decades between 1970 and 1990, the thrust toward greater unity appeared to yield to a reaffirmation of jurisdictional distinctiveness.

As one might expect, the organization most seriously damaged by the new situation was the Standing Conference of Canonical Bishops. The bishops of SCOBA continued to meet, usually on a yearly basis throughout the period between 1970 and 1990. Yet, there were some notable changes in both the composition and the concerns of SCOBA. The Orthodox Church in America/Metropolia decided not to be represented by its primate. Rather, one of the other diocesan bishops became its SCOBA representative. Many saw this decision as an indication that it had diminished its interest in SCOBA. At the same time, discussions within SCOBA centered primarily upon the development of a new constitution that would somehow take into account the new status of the Orthodox Church in America/Metropolia. Finally, the thrust toward greater Orthodox unity and a provincial synod, which had dominated the agenda of SCOBA from 1965 to 1970, was virtually lost.

In an attempt to strengthen the role of Archbishop Iakovos and his influence as chairman of SCOBA, the Patriarchate of Constantinople designated him as "Patriarchal Exarch Plenipotentiary" in December 1970. He was designated as the person "with the right to preside over consultations and meetings of the Orthodox Canonical Bishops in America for the purpose of commonly examining, deliberating upon, and regulating questions both of specific and inter-Orthodox nature that may on occasion arise in your ecclesiastical life."[35] This authorization, however, appears to have done little to revive the weakened SCOBA. The difficulties that the Archdiocese experienced left Archbishop Iakovos with little time or energy to devote to the cause of Orthodox unity.

A number of significant events during the period between 1970 and 1990 seemed to bear witness to the inability of SCOBA to function even as a consultative body.

First, Metropolitan Philip (Saliba) of the Antiochian Orthodox Christian Archdiocese proposed the establishment of a Bilateral Commission, which would bring together representatives from his jurisdiction and the Orthodox Church in America/Metropolia. At its first meeting on 3 March 1981, the commission affirmed that both jurisdictions desired the establishment of one self-governing church in America under the leadership of one synod of bishops. This commission led to greater cooperation between these two jurisdictions in the areas of religious education, theological education, and missions.[36]

Elected to head the Antiochian Archdiocese in 1966, Metropolitan Philip had become a strong spokesman for greater Orthodox unity. As the leader of the third largest Orthodox jurisdiction in America, he often appeared to present moderate positions in the midst of the discussions about both autocephaly and language. Undoubtedly, one of his greatest contributions was his ability to heal the division among the Syrian Orthodox in 1975. Together with Archbishop Michael (Shaheen), head of the diocese of Toledo, Metropolitan Philip brought together the two jurisdictions, which had been divided since 1934. Canonically associated with the Patriarchate of Antioch, the unified jurisdiction came to be known as the Antiochian Orthodox Christian Archdiocese. This change of name placed less emphasis upon ethnic considerations and fully emphasized the Archdiocese's relationship with the Patriarchate of Antioch.[37]

Second, the tragic inability of SCOBA to take more seriously the actions of some jurisdictional leaders subtly to oppose greater unity was highlighted very forcefully in a joint Lenten Encyclical published in 1989 by Metropolitan Theodosius of the Orthodox Church in America/Metropolia and Metropolitan Philip. In affirming the need for greater unity, the two bishops said:

It is no secret that Orthodox jurisdictions in this Western hemisphere have developed attitudes and positions which have become an excuse to circumvent unity. Sometimes the excuse is the difference in liturgical style, sometimes language, sometimes ethnic traditions; these excuses cannot be accepted as valid reasons to divide the One True Church. Indeed, such variations have always had their place within the common Orthodox Tradition. They must—and easily can—be maintained within a unified Church. It is when they are used as divisive arguments that they serve as excuses to maintain the status quo in which we have buried ourselves over these years. We can wait no longer![38]

Finally, the weakened position of SCOBA was also evident in its inability to respond decisively to the movement of hundreds of former evangelical Christians into the Orthodox Church.

Beginning as early as 1968, a number of evangelical Protestant pastors, many of whom were once associated with Campus Crusade for Christ, began to discuss together their movement toward the Orthodox Church. Formal contacts with various representatives of three Orthodox jurisdictions began in 1977. These discussions raised a number of questions related to Orthodox doctrine, liturgical practices, and polity. Finally, after much discussion in various quarters, the Antiochian Orthodox Christian Archdiocese unilaterally acted in 1987 to chrismate and to ordain the former evangelical clergy and to receive through chrismation about 2,000 believers gathered in about ten parishes. While most Orthodox leaders joyously welcomed the former evangelicals into the Orthodox Church, the manner in which they were received sparked new discussions and some measure of controversy.

As an organization, SCOBA had only a minor role in these momentous developments. As early as 1981, Reverend Peter Gillquist, the leader of the evangelical pastors, wrote to Archbishop Iakovos, the chairman of SCOBA, requesting guidance. While the matter was referred to the SCOBA Ecumenical Commission, no firm direction materialized. The evangelicals then had no other choice but to deal separately with particular jurisdictions. Clearly, the process of receiving the former evangelicals could have been smoother if SCOBA has been in a position to speak and to act in the name of the Orthodox Church. Throughout the entire process, however, SCOBA was able to provide only limited guidance.[39]

THE NATURE OF THE CHURCH

All of these historic controversies and events of the period between 1970 and 1990 shook the Orthodox Church in the United States and raised serious questions about its identity and mission in this country. Although the Russian Orthodox Metropolia and the Greek Orthodox Archdiocese were the two jurisdictions that were the most profoundly affected by the controversies, all of the Orthodox jurisdictions were struggling with the same fundamental issue, although perhaps less publicly. This issue was the nature of the Orthodox Church in the United States.

For generations, it had become common for the Orthodox in America to view themselves as part of a diaspora. The Orthodox immigrants who came to the United States since the late nineteenth century were seen as people who had been dispersed from their homeland. In some cases they even viewed themselves and their children as exiles who found themselves in a wilderness that could never really be home. There was always going to be a longing for another place, which, of course, always appeared to be a better place.

The understanding of the Orthodox Church in this country was also colored by this perspective from the late nineteenth century. Each jurisdiction came to see itself as an extension of the mother church in this country. The fundamental purpose of the jurisdiction was to care for "its people." This meant that a high priority was placed upon the preservation of the Old World language and culture. Far from being a church serving the people of this country, the Orthodox Church came to be seen as a diaspora church in which each particular jurisdiction was serving the needs of a particular ethnic group. It is no wonder that each jurisdiction often seemed to depict itself as a particular denomination. Indeed, some even appeared to have the characteristics of a sect.

The immediate consequences of this ethnocentric way of viewing the jurisdiction were threefold. First, movements toward greater unity of the jurisdictions were not encouraged, especially by those who saw their jurisdiction as an instrument designed to preserve a particular ethnic language or culture. The thrusts toward greater Orthodox unity became a threat to the ethnocentric view of the jurisdiction.

Second, there was little concern for mission. Most of the jurisdictions were inward-looking. They were concerned with survival and preservation. Orthodox leaders often made bold claims about the catholicity of the Orthodox Church and the flawless character of its faith. Yet, throughout the late nineteenth century and during much of the twentieth century, many of these same leaders had little regard for reaching out to others who were not part of their jurisdiction. The ethnic emphasis of most of the Orthodox jurisdictions appeared to be incompatible with a commitment to mission.

Finally, there was very little concern for the well-being of the wider society. During the 1950s many Orthodox worked diligently to have Orthodoxy recognized as a major faith in this country. Yet, the responsibility of the church to this society usually was ignored. Each jurisdiction tended to see itself as composed of people who were not really part of American society.

The controversies of the 1970s especially were a very public expression of a process to reaffirm the fundamental nature of the Orthodox Church in this country. This process has its roots in the developments of the Orthodox Church in the United States that occurred in the period following World War II. During this period, there were major changes in the demographics of membership. There were important developments in the area of religious education and liturgical life. There were grassroots movements encouraging greater unity for the sake of mission and witness. The discussions over the autocephaly of the Metropolia/Orthodox Church in the United States and the discussions over the greater use of the vernacular languages in worship in the Greek Orthodox Archdiocese were serious and difficult. At a deeper level, however, these discussions witnessed the fact that concerns about the nature of the Orthodox Church in the United States had entered into a new stage of reflection and action.

For many Orthodox theologians, the use of the term *diaspora* began to appear inappropriate when used in reference to the church in this country. While the term may have had some sociological meaning, it distorted the fundamental conception of the church. Father Leonidas Contos, a theologian of the Greek Orthodox Archdiocese, addressed this point with boldness:

I wonder if the term "diaspora" is any longer descriptive of our situation. . . . Our numbers, relative to the strength of the Mother Church, are so great, our life so ordered, our organizations so articulated, our identity so well-defined, our aims so coherent, above all our roots so deeply thrust in this congenial soil, that to regard ourselves as a "dispersion" in any literal sense of the term, at least, tends in very subtle ways to distort our sense of self. . . . For so long as we are conditioned in our polity and our cultural life, by the diaspora complex, however subconsciously, we will be inhibited in the fullest realization of our "church-hood."[40]

This fundamental change in perspective also was going to affect other aspects of Orthodox Church life. There would be need for greater reflection on the relationship of the various jurisdictions to their mother church. There would be need for greater reflection on the role of the Ecumenical Patriarchate as a unifying force in the church in America. There would be need for greater reflection on the missionary dimension of the church's life. There would be need for greater reflection with regard to the relationship of the church to the wider society. In the wake of the emotional and bitter debates of the 1970s, Orthodox theologians began to investigate these topics with greater urgency.[41]

A PAN-ORTHODOX RESPONSE

Despite the tension among the various autocephalous Orthodox churches that were created by the grant of autocephaly to the Orthodox Church in America/Metropolia, the developments in America appear to have had a positive influence on the worldwide conciliar movement among the Orthodox. Some two years after the Fourth Pan-Orthodox Conference in 1968, the Inter-Orthodox Preparatory Commission for the Great and Holy Council met in Geneva on 15–28 July 1971. This group approved the publication of studies on aspects of the six topics approved by the Fourth Pan-Orthodox Conference. But, even more important, the commission recommended that the proposed First Pre-Conciliar Conference revise the list of study topics originally established in 1961.[42]

Between 1971 and 1976, the Ecumenical Patriarchate organized a number of theological meetings and sent delegations to all the autocephalous churches. The intent of the Patriarchate was to identify particular topics for common study that were directly related to the critical needs facing the Orthodox Church.

During this same period, Metropolitan Maximos of Sardis published his seminal book titled *The Ecumenical Patriarchate in the Orthodox Church*. Coming from one of the most respected scholars of the Ecumenical Patriarchate, the book dealt with a number of topics that had a direct bearing upon the development of the church in the so-called diaspora. The author cogently discussed the ancient canons that designated the Ecumenical Patriarchate of Constantinople as the church responsible for overseeing the development of new local churches outside the territory of established autocephalous churches. The author also discussed the formal condemnation of ethnophylitism in 1872. This term refers to the organization of regional churches along ethnic lines rather than geographical lines. The author's elucidation of this practice clearly demonstrated that the present structure of the Orthodox jurisdictions in America was contrary to the best organizational principles of Orthodox ecclesiology.[43]

When the First Preconciliar Conference was held in Chambesy (Geneva) in 21–28 November 1976, the representatives of the regional Orthodox churches formally approved a new list of topics that would be studied prior to the convocation of the Great and Holy Council. While this list included themes proposed earlier, it also reflected concern for the recent developments in America. The themes proposed were:

1. The Orthodox diaspora

2. Autocephaly and how it is proclaimed

3. Autonomy and how it is proclaimed

4. Diptychs (the official ranking of churches)

5. The question of a common calendar

6. Impediments to marriage

7. Adjustments of the rules of fasting to the conditions of the present day

8. Relation of the Orthodox churches to the rest of the Christian world

9. Orthodoxy and the ecumenical movement

10. Contribution of the local Orthodox churches to the promotion of the ideals of peace, freedom, and brotherhood among peoples, and to the eradication of racial discrimination[44]

After studies undertaken by the Preconciliar Commission, the Second Pre-Conciliar Conference was held in 1982. It approved statements on the fifth and the sixth topics. The Third Pre-Conciliar Conference met in 1986 and approved statements on the seventh, eighth, ninth, and tenth topics. This process of deliberation set the stage for the Pre-Conciliar Commission to deal with the remaining three topics.[45]

The Pre-Conciliar Commission began its discussion of the Orthodox diaspora at its meeting on 10–17 November 1990 and continued its discussion at the meeting of 7–13 November 1993. At these meetings the commission produced an important statement that contains recommendations that have been submitted to the churches. The statement indicates that the autocephalous churches recognize the critical need to address the situation of the developing Orthodox Church in places such as North and South America and Western Europe. In this text, the commission states that "every Orthodox Church is unanimous that the problem of the Orthodox diaspora be resolved as quickly as possible and that it be organized in a way that is in accordance with Orthodox ecclesiological tradition and the canonical praxis of the Orthodox Church."[46]

The report of the Pre-Conciliar Preparatory Commission was warmly greeted by both theologians and knowledgeable laypersons in this country. While many would have liked the Pre-Conciliar Commission to be even more direct with regard to the American situation, there was a sense that the representatives of the autocephalous and autonomous churches recognized the need formally to encourage greater administrative unity. The direction of the Pre-Conciliar Commission was in harmony with perspectives that had been advanced by many American Orthodox theologians from a wide variety of jurisdictions. The difficulties engendered by the controversies originating in the 1970s had not completely subsided. Yet, it appeared that many Orthodox leaders both in the United States and in other parts of the world had come to recognize that the organizational development of the Orthodox Church in this country demanded greater attention and that a resolution had to be found.[47]

10
HERITAGE AND VISION

The visit of Ecumenical Patriarch Dimitrios of Constantinople to the United States in 1990 served as an important affirmation of the significance of Orthodox Christianity in this country. While the Orthodox jurisdictions continued to look toward greater administrative unity, many signs of a mature presence and a fruitful mission were clearly visible. The Orthodox in America numbered over 3 million, gathered into over 1,500 parishes. Through their concern for liturgical and spiritual renewal, theological studies, ecumenical dialogue, and evangelization, the American Orthodox in recent decades had strengthened their own mission and witness in this country. They had also become a major influence upon Christianity throughout the world.[1]

THE VISIT OF THE ECUMENICAL PATRIARCH

Ecumenical Patriarch Dimitrios I of Constantinople, together with a delegation that included five Metropolitans made an unprecedented visit to the United States 2–29 July 1990. Among the delegation was the present patriarch, Patriarch Bartholomew, who succeeded Patriarch Dimitrios in 1991. Although other Orthodox Patriarchs had visited this country in the past, this was the first visit of the Ecumenical Patriarch. His visit had a special significance because he is viewed as the first bishop of the Orthodox Church. As such, the Ecumenical Patriarch is frequently looked upon as the spiritual leader of the 300 million Orthodox Christians throughout the world. Moreover, according to Orthodox canon law and ecclesiastical practice dating from at least the fourth century, the Patriarch of Constantinople has special responsibility for overseeing the development of the Orthodox Church in lands beyond the boundaries of other autocephalous churches.[2]

When he arrived in Washington, Patriarch Dimitrios spoke of his mission:

In particular as Ecumenical Patriarch entering this land, I reflect upon the fact that our Church took root here and flourished for whole generations, thus contributing also to the great and historic advance of the American people, to its attainments, in sharing its problems, its progress and its dreams for a better mankind. Today, Orthodoxy is not a strange and alien factor in America. It is flesh of its flesh and bone of its bones. . . . I greet warmly and without exception all the faithful children of the Orthodox in this country. . . . As the Ecumenical Patriarch, I convey to all the Orthodox of this country my love and blessing, and assure them that the full unity of the Church, by canonical order, has never ceased and will never cease to be my principal concern.[3]

The theme of greater Orthodox unity and witness in America would be repeated on many occasions as the Patriarch's limited itinerary took him from Washington to New York; Allentown and Johnstown, Pennsylvania; San Francisco; Chicago; Buffalo; and Boston. At each stop, the Patriarch not only met with members of the Orthodox Church but also met with representatives of other churches. In the former case, he stressed the need for greater Orthodox unity in America. In the latter case, he spoke strongly about the responsibility of all Christians to work for reconciliation that would lead toward visible unity rooted in the apostolic faith.

From the perspective of Orthodox unity, one of the most significant aspects of the Patriarch's visit was his meeting with Metropolitan Theodosius of the Orthodox Church in America within the context of a prayer service at St. Nicholas Cathedral in Washington, D.C., on 4 July 1990. The presence of the Ecumenical Patriarch at the cathedral of Metropolitan Theodosius was clearly a sign of a new relationship developing between the Church of Constantinople and the Orthodox Church in America, the former Metropolia. This encounter was the fruit of preliminary discussions between representatives of the Ecumenical Patriarchate and the Orthodox Church in America that had been renewed in 1989.

In his words of welcome to St. Nicholas Cathedral, Metropolitan Theodosius said:

For us in particular, your presence is a sign of renewed hope for unity, witness and mission of Orthodox Christianity in America. As the "first among equals" within the brotherhood of Orthodox bishops throughout the world, you have as your primacy a unique ministry of unity. We ask that through your prayers our ministry in America may bring ever closer the full integration of our continued efforts, that the people and the society in the midst of which we witness may see that the Orthodox Church in North America is truly united in common mission, common witness, and common purpose. At this time in our history, there has never been a greater need, nor has there been a time of greater opportunity.[4]

Patriarch Dimitrios warmly responded to the welcome. In the course of his response, the Patriarch made reference to the situation of the Orthodox Church in the United States:

It is truly a scandal for the unity of the Church to maintain more than one bishop in any given city; it clearly contravenes the sacred canons and Orthodox ecclesiology. It is a scandal that is exacerbated whenever phyletistic motives play a part, a practice soundly condemned by the Orthodox Church in the last century. The Ecumenical Patriarchate, as a supra-national Church serving the unity of the Church, is not indifferent to the condition that has evolved, and will exert every effort in cooperation with the other Holy Orthodox Churches, and in accordance with canonical order, to resolve this thorny problem.[5]

The visit of the Ecumenical Patriarch and the meetings that he and his associates had with church leaders in America were seen by many as a sign that new attention was being given to the issues related to greater unity and common witness.

DIOCESAN LIFE

The major political developments in Central and Eastern Europe, especially in the period between 1989 and 1993, enabled the Orthodox churches in those regions to reaffirm their mission and witness. As in earlier periods of this century, these European changes were reflected in developments in church life in this country. This time, however, the developments were generally very positive. In conjunction with efforts to provide assistance to the churches in the Old World as they emerged from a period of oppression, many of the dioceses in this country, which had experienced divisions in the 1950s and 1960s, were reconciled or at least brought closer together.

The Serbian Orthodox dioceses, divided since 1963, were reconciled through the personal interventions of Patriarch Paul of Serbia, who visited this country in 1992. Bishop Kyril (Yonchev), who, together with a number of clergy and laity, separated from the Orthodox Church of Bulgaria in 1963, was recognized by Patriarch Maxim and the synod of that church during a visit there in 1992. The dramatic restoration of the Orthodox Church in Albania in 1992–1993 also led to greater contact between members of the two Albanian Orthodox dioceses in this country that were divided in 1950. Finally, the two Romanian Orthodox dioceses divided since 1951 agreed to the restoration of relations in 1993.[6]

While the changes in Europe provided a catalyst for these developments, they were, at a deeper level, the fruit of the process of reconciliation that had been taking place for decades, especially at the local level. American Orthodox had become less and less troubled by the old political issues that frequently led to the diocesan divisions in the 1950s and 1960s. At the same time, most American Orthodox had matured in their appreciation of the common bonds of faith and the requirement for common mission and witness.

These developments also paralleled a renewed theological understanding of the diocese. Orthodox theologians began to reemphasize that the diocese is the expression of the "local church." It is a gathering of clergy and laity in a number of parish communities in a given place who are in communion with the diocesan bishop. They are united in common faith, witness, and service. Their unity is most visibly expressed at the celebration of the Eucharist. This understanding clearly challenged the old view of the diocese that had developed among many Orthodox in America. The old view saw the diocese or archdiocese as a jurisdiction centered upon ethnic or linguistic particularities.

Three important principles directly related to the American situation began to emerge in the renewed understanding of the diocese. First, as a manifestation of the local church, the diocese must be geographically based and unite all the Orthodox believers of a particular place or region. This challenged the notion that the diocese contains only persons of a particular ethnic background. Second, the diocesan bishop must be viewed first and foremost as a sign of the unity of the church in a particular place. This challenged the notion of the bishop as an "ethnarch" leading a particular ethnic group. Third, the diocese must reflect in its organizational life a conciliar spirit that emphasizes the interrelationship between bishop, clergy, and laity in their service to the church and to society. This challenged the notion that there is no mutual accountability among the members of the church.

How long it will take for the renewed theological understanding of the diocese to refashion the actual administrative life of each particular diocese, and indeed the larger church in the United States, is difficult to tell. As we have seen, the administrative development of the Orthodox Church in the United States has been one plagued with difficulties. But the fact that the renewed vision of the diocese is coming from many quarters is viewed by many as a hopeful sign.[7]

PARISH LIFE

Orthodox parishes have always been diverse in terms of both their size and their composition. By 1994, there were well over 1,500 Orthodox parishes in the United States, serving over 3 million parishioners. Some of these parishes include over 1,000 members. Others, considered to be missions, may include about 50 members. The vast majority of parishes average anywhere from 200 to about 500 members.

Throughout the period between 1960 and 1980 especially, many of these parishes undertook major building or remodeling campaigns in conjunction with the move of parishioners to the suburbs. Often, the new buildings were constructed in a manner that clearly reflected the principles of traditional Orthodox architecture. As the Orthodox were able to construct their church buildings in suburban locations throughout the United States, they were not reluctant to let their distinctive church architecture publicly bear witness to their presence. In many cities, the distinctive dome of the Orthodox church building has become a very visible reminder of the presence of Orthodox Christians.

While united in their profession of the same faith, the members of these parishes are quite diverse. Parishes in Alaska continue to bring together believers from the various Alaskan native peoples. Some parishes on the East Coast especially comprise newly arrived immigrants from wartorn Palestine and Lebanon. The vast majority of Orthodox parishes, however, comprise Americans of various ethnic and racial backgrounds. Some of these persons are the descendants of the Orthodox immigrants. An ever-growing number of others were raised in different religious traditions and subsequently chose to enter the Orthodox Church.

Membership in most Orthodox parishes today reflects the fact that persons have freely and consciously decided to accept the Orthodox Christian faith and to be part of an Orthodox parish community. These persons appreciate the faith and devotion of the pious immigrants who established many of the original Orthodox parishes in the late nineteenth and early twentieth centuries. They also recognize the obligation of the church to serve the spiritual needs of new immigrants. Yet, at the same time, they see their Orthodox parish less and less as an ethnic community and more as a manifestation of the church established by Christ and nurtured primarily by His gospel.

Each parish is headed by an ordained priest. The pastor is engaged in a multi-dimensional ministry that centers upon leading the liturgical services, preaching, teaching spiritual direction, and pastoral care. Increasingly, the Orthodox are placing very high expectation on their clergy. While the parishioners are usually involved in a selection process, the parish priest is ultimately appointed by the diocesan bishop. Generally, an elected parish council, with the parish priest as its president, oversees the life of the parish. The majority of Orthodox parishes have religious education programs for children and young adults. Many have special religious education programs and Bible studies for adults. Lay women and men are very active in the liturgical, educational, and charitable ministries of the parish.

Orthodox theologians recognize that these important developments in parish life have accompanied a gradual movement that has emphasized the role of the parish as a center for Christian worship and life that is rooted in the teachings of Christ as reflected in the life of the Orthodox Church throughout the ages. Those who look closely at the Orthodox parish recognize also that further maturation is required. Central to this maturation is the vision of the parish as a Christian community of faith that both shares fully in the life of the surrounding society and is able to provide, when necessary, a Christian critique of the values of the society. Father John Meyendorff addresses this point:

In America today, we Orthodox face two major temptations. The one is to lose love for Divine Truth; to capitulate before the secular and relativistic environment; to consider the Church as a social club among many, using only more elaborate "Eastern" ritual than other clubs. The other temptation is to forget that the truth of Orthodoxy—Divine Truth indeed—has not been given to us alone, as our own private possession: it is a truth which saves the entire world, and of which we have been made witnesses at our own peril. If we hide it under a bushel of our human limitations, our ethnic cultures, our prejudices, we will be judged accordingly.[8]

LITURGICAL AND SPIRITUAL RENEWAL

During the past twenty-five years, there has been a steady movement for liturgical renewal throughout the Orthodox Church in the United States. This renewal has been nurtured by the writings and lectures of Father Alexander Schmemann, as well as by Father Alkiviadis Calivas, Father Laurence of New Skete, and Dr. Paul Meyendorff. Both clergy and laity have sought to reemphasize the centrality of the Eucharist in the life of both the believer and the parish community. Orthodox Christians expect their parish to be a center for worship and prayer that aids them in their spiritual growth and Christian identity.[9]

English translations of the Eucharistic Liturgy, the Sacraments, and other prayer services have been readily available for generations. These, however, often were literal translations in an archaic form of English and not intended to be used in the liturgical services. Fortunately, some of the more recent translations have been done with an eye toward their actual use in parishes. Thus, only in recent years have clergy and congregations truly become comfortable with the actual use of prayers and hymns in English.

Alexander Schmemann wisely recognized that the Orthodox in America were required not simply to translate old liturgical texts but to capture in the English language the power of the liturgical affirmations:

As long as American Orthodoxy is only translated it is neither fully American nor fully Orthodox. It is not fully American because the literal translations of Byzantine or Russian texts remain odd and alien to the genius and result in—to say the truth—Greek or Russian services in English, but not English services. And it is not fully Orthodox because what gives these texts their power and fulfills their liturgical function—their beauty, is simply lost in these literal renderings . . . true continuity with the living Tradition requires from us more than translation: a real recreation of the same and eternal message, its true incarnation in English. The problem is not just to translate but to give again the hymns and texts of the Byzantine liturgy the power they have in the original, and which is rooted in the organic unity of meaning and "beauty."[10]

The greater use of English in worship in Orthodox congregations, in the past three decades especially, has had two important consequences. First, the liturgical services now are able to contribute to the formation of the believers. The Orthodox have always emphasized the power of the liturgical services to form and inform the believer. The Orthodox faith is experienced, affirmed, and celebrated through the worship of the church. While the services offer, first of all, the opportunity for the community to praise and thank God, they also teach the basic affirmations of the faith. There is, therefore, a very close connection between participation in the liturgical services and growth in Christian life.

Second, the increased use of English has provided the basis for greater participation by the laity in the liturgical services. While practices vary from parish to parish, the liturgical services are increasingly seen as the common worship offered and celebrated by the entire church. No longer are the services of worship seen as the activity of the clergy and their assistants, at which most of the laity are passive bystanders. There is a growing movement to involve the entire parish community in the services of worship.

Central to this renewal has been the restoration of the importance of the regular reception of Holy Communion. Not long ago, Orthodox were accustomed to receive Holy Communion only a few times during the course of the year. While the Liturgy has always been the principal service of common worship, the reception of Holy Communion by the laity on a regular basis was not always encouraged. Now, with greater emphasis upon the importance of full participation in the Eucharist, more and more clergy and laity are welcoming the restoration of the practice of frequent reception of Holy Communion. This has also been accompanied by a greater appreciation of the value of personal prayer, fasting, confession, and charity. These serve as appropriate spiritual disciplines that can also contribute one's preparation to receive Holy Communion.[11]

Orthodox theologians in America recognize that they must continue to stress the centrality of worship and the importance of spiritual growth, especially in a society that frequently places great emphasis upon secular values accentuating individualism and materialism.

At the same time, many Orthodox theologians in America recognize that a slavish preservation of minor liturgical customs and practices can, in fact, prevent the liturgical services from accomplishing their most fundamental purposes, which are to glorify God and nurture human life. The Orthodox in America have inherited a wide variety of liturgical customs from the various traditions that are part of the church in this country. While maintaining a fundamental unity in faith and sacramental life with the Orthodox throughout the world, the Orthodox in this country are now involved in a process of developing liturgical traditions that serve the needs of the church in America. This is not a novel task for Orthodox. It is, in fact, a process that has occurred in every place that the church has grown as a result of mission.

The liturgical tradition, says Father Laurence of New Skete, "is always and everywhere characterized by an ongoing process of change and adaptation giving birth to new and varied forms of expression, and, thus, keeping the fountain of life, as it were, from drying up completely." Referring to the need for a parish "order of worship," he says that "a properly parochial 'typikon' is therefore of crucial urgency. Protestations to the contrary reflect the rigid, museum frame of mind and/or the cast of mind that is frantically in need of security. The faith was never intended to be a security blanket, but the means, as St. Paul says, "whereby we find justification before the Lord."[12]

WOMEN IN CHURCH SERVICE

Women have always been involved in the development of the Orthodox Church in this country. In the early years, they were active especially in the teaching of religion, in fund-raising, and in charitable work. Some were also part of monastic communities. During the 1930s and 1940s, most parishes established associations that brought greater direction to these activities. At the same time, most jurisdictions also established national organizations especially for women. Viewed in historical perspective, these organizations were established at a time when women were expected to have their own specific group within the parish or diocese. Established in 1932, the Philoptochos Society of the Greek Orthodox Archdiocese, for example, has a well-deserved reputation for its philanthropic activity and has ably adapted itself to changing circumstances.

Orthodox women in recent decades have also begun to be involved in many more aspects of the church's pastoral, liturgical, charitable, educational, and administrative life. They have taken up responsibilities in the church that would have been nearly impossible only a few decades ago. Some women have been blessed and tonsured to undertake specific ministries within parishes. A number of theologically educated women represent their church at symposiums, conferences, and ecumenical meetings. It is now quite common for women to serve as members of parish and diocesan councils.[13]

The ancient order of the ordained deaconess has not as yet been fully restored in the contemporary Orthodox Church. At a Pan-Orthodox conference held in Rhodes in 1988, the delegates from all the regional churches formally called for the full restoration of this ancient order so that the pastoral needs of the contemporary church may be better served. Many Orthodox in America believe that the restoration of this order in this country will contribute greatly to the pastoral and charitable ministries of the local parish.[14]

Issues associated with the role and dignity of women in the Orthodox Church frequently reflect the interplay between the Old World cultures and the Orthodox faith. The questions associated with the ordained ministry and women still need to be explored more deeply by Orthodox theologians. Moreover, the Orthodox have inherited prayers, ritual prohibitions, and canons that reflect the cultural, philosophical, and medical views of women in earlier historical periods. Many Orthodox theologians in America today recognize that these critical issues deserve greater theological investigation and pastoral sensitivity so that the influences of earlier cultures can be distinguished from the fundamental convictions of the Orthodox faith. The Orthodox in America will continue to be challenged to hear the concerns of Orthodox women.[15]

THEOLOGICAL EDUCATION

The education and formation of clergy and lay leaders for specialized ministry have been concerns that have been consistently present in the American Orthodox experience since the time of the Alaskan mission. A number of early pastoral schools provided the basis for the establishment of more stable seminaries during the 1930s. These seminaries generally served the needs of specific jurisdictions by providing rudimentary education for future clergy and lay leaders in the church's teachings and liturgical practices.

Two of these seminaries rose to higher levels of competence and mission during the 1960s and 1970s. St. Vladimir's Orthodox Theological Seminary, founded in 1938 by the Russian Orthodox Metropolia, now the Orthodox Church in America, received full accreditation from the American Association of Theological Schools in 1973. Founded in 1937 by the Greek Orthodox Archdiocese, Holy Cross Greek Orthodox School of Theology was fully accredited as a graduate-level school of theology by the same agency in 1976. Its undergraduate college was given full accreditation by the New England Association of Secondary Schools and Colleges in the same year. These grants of accreditation marked important milestones for both institutions. In addition, Holy Cross has been a member since 1976 of the Boston Theological Institute, a consortium of nine theological schools. This unique association is the only association in the world to bring together fully accredited theological schools representing Orthodox, Roman Catholic, and Protestant traditions.

While these two institutions continued to prepare future clergy and lay leaders for parish service, they also have recognized their responsibility to be centers of advanced study in the various disciplines of Orthodox theology. Increasingly, their programs have attracted not only those who seek to serve in the pastoral ministry but also those who wish to pursue studies toward advanced degrees in theology and related disciplines. Likewise, both institutions have begun to attract students not only from their own jurisdictions but also from other Orthodox jurisdictions both in this country and abroad. A number of American-born theologians began to join the faculties in the late 1960s and 1970s. At about the same time, both institutions became coeducational. These developments clearly contributed to the maturation of both schools.[16]

Founded in 1965, the Orthodox Theological Society has become a significant association of theologians that sponsors a yearly meeting devoted to a particular theme. In recent years, the meetings of the society have examined such important topics as ecumenical relations, women in the church, and the role of the laity. The society has fostered greater contact among theologians from the various jurisdictions and has addressed theological issues that affect all the Orthodox in this country.

During the last twenty-five years especially, Orthodox theologians from the United States also began to become more prominent in meetings of Orthodox theologians from throughout the world. A sizable number were present at the Second International Conference of Orthodox Theological Schools held in Athens in 1970. Since that time, both Holy Cross and St. Vladimir's have hosted a number of conferences and symposia that brought together Orthodox theologians from throughout the world. Most recently, in 1987, Holy Cross hosted the Third International Conference of Orthodox Theological Schools.[17]

The important contribution that American Orthodox theologians have to make to the worldwide church has also gained greater recognition. Orthodox theologians from America have been involved in some of the meetings preparing for the Great and Holy Council. A sizable number participated in the Inter-Orthodox Conference on the Role of Women held in Rhodes in 1988. A number have been appointed to Orthodox delegations to bilateral consultations with other churches and to the various committees of the World Council of Churches.

All of these developments have been sustained by the growth of a great body of literature devoted to various aspects of Orthodox faith, history, and spirituality. Up until about 1960, there was only a handful of books available in English dealing with the Orthodox Church. With few exceptions, most of these were written primarily for students of theology and history. In the past thirty years, however, hundreds of books have appeared that deal with all facets of Orthodox Christianity. Some are written especially for scholars, while others are written for a popular audience. Four Orthodox publishing houses—Holy Cross Press, St. Vladimir's Seminary Press, Light and Life Publications, and Oakwood Publications—have been in the forefront in publishing works especially by Orthodox authors and in providing substantial studies on various aspects of the Orthodox Church.

One cannot overlook the fact that in the past twenty to thirty years there has been a renewed interest in early Christianity, in the writings of the fathers and mothers of the church, and in the history of the Liturgy and Sacraments. Many of these specialized studies and translations, by scholars, both Orthodox and Western Christians, have contributed to an understanding of early Christianity free from the partisan debates and denominational polemics that characterized previous investigations. At the same time, these studies have sparked among many Western Christians a new appreciation of the development of Eastern Christianity in general and a renewed interest in the contemporary Orthodox Church. Indeed, through these books many Western Christians have first come to know about the Orthodox Church.

ECUMENICAL WITNESS

The degree of Orthodox involvement in local expressions of ecumenical witness continued to vary from place to place, especially during the period 1970–1994. In some cities, the Orthodox parishes have been active in the local Council of Churches. In other cities, the Orthodox have consistently avoided formal involvement in ecumenical associations. As a general rule, Orthodox clergy and laity participated in local inter-Christian associations that were devoted either to theological dialogue or to local philanthropic activities. All Orthodox continue to avoid any formal type of eucharistic "intercommunion." The Orthodox believe that the restoration of eucharistic communion among Christians is primarily the fruit of reconciliation and not a means toward achieving the unity of Christians.

Orthodox involvement in the National Council of Churches of Christ (NCCC) has remained problematical. The fact that it has been traditionally dominated by Protestants has meant that its agenda and concerns have not always been of interest to the Orthodox. As a result, Orthodox involvement in its various commissions generally has been weak.

On behalf of its member jurisdictions, the Standing Conference of Orthodox Bishops suspended Orthodox involvement in the NCCC on 24 October 1991. The reasons for this dramatic decision were many. Chief among them was the concern of many Orthodox that the NCCC was advocating positions that ran contrary to historic Christian teachings and the concern that Orthodox positions were not taken seriously within the various departments of the council. The decision of the Orthodox bishops led to a series of discussions between their representatives and the representatives of the NCCC. These meetings led to a decision by the bishops of SCOBA on 23 March 1992 to "provisionally resume" ties with the NCCC.[18]

Despite these difficulties, the active presence of Orthodox theologians from this country has been especially felt in recent years in worldwide ecumenical meetings. For example, Orthodox theologians from America have been especially active in recent years in work of the Faith and Order Commission and other committees of the World Council of Churches. Among those who have been deeply involved in the activity of these committees are Father John Meyendorff, Father Stanley Harakas, Father Thomas Hopko, Father Leonid Kishkovsky, Dr. Kyriaki FitzGerald, Father Nicholas Apostola, and Dr. Constance Tarasar. Many of the Orthodox from America have been particularly adept in overcoming historic animosities and in bridging the gap between the theological differences of Eastern and Western Christianity. Certainly, many of the American Orthodox have benefited not only from their formal study of Roman Catholicism and Protestantism but also from the fact that they have had firsthand, personal relationships with Western Christian theologians.

MONASTICISM

Monasteries have always played an important role in the development of Orthodox Christianity. Orthodox monasticism did not develop particular orders as in the Christian West. Traditionally, each monastery has had the right to develop its own mission, provided that it does not run counter to the norms of community life and worship. Thus, throughout history, Orthodox monasteries, both those for men and those for women, have been involved in such diverse ministries as education, care for the needy, the preservation of manuscripts, liturgical renewal, and missions.

As we have seen, the first Orthodox missionaries who came to America in 1794 were monks. Their humble quarters on Kodiak Island were the first Orthodox monastery in North America. Dating from 1905, St. Tikhon Monastery in South Canaan, Pennsylvania, was the first one established in the continental United States. Twenty-five years later, in 1930, the Holy Trinity Monastery was founded in Jordanville, New York. Since that time numerous other monastic communities have come into existence throughout the country. Regardless of the number of members, the monasteries are communities centered upon worship and spiritual life. The traditional cycle of common prayer is the pattern about which all other activities of the monastery are structured.

One group of Orthodox monastics has described their life:

In the community life of our respective monasteries, we not only profess the Gospel but manifest our intention of seeking sanctification with God's help through growth in wisdom and spiritual understanding. In so doing, we witness to the Kingdom of God which is to come and to the fullness of the promise made at baptism to every Christian. Thus, we hope to be responsive to the prophetic character of our vocation, which, from the very inception of monasticism in the desert of Skete [in Egypt], has made monks and nuns responsible not only for their own salvation, but for that of all God's people.[19]

Increasingly, many Orthodox clergy and laypersons have come to recognize the importance of monasteries for the growth of the church in America. These monasteries have become places of pilgrimages where pilgrims can go to worship, for retreats, and to seek spiritual direction from the abbot or abbess.

Because of its distinctive witness, one monastery in America deserves special attention: the Community of New Skete in Cambridge, New York. First established in 1966, the monastery formally joined the jurisdiction of the Orthodox Church in America in 1978. New Skete actually comprises a community of monks whose house is dedicated to the Transfiguration, a separate monastic community of nuns whose house is dedicated to Our Lady of the Sign, and a separate community of married couples whose house is dedicated to the disciples of Emmaus. While each community maintains its own particular identity and mission, the members of the three houses meet daily for worship.

Thoroughly immersed in the tradition of monasticism, the members of these communities actively seek to bring the ancient spiritual insights of Orthodox spirituality into contact with the realities of twentieth-century America. Under the leadership of Father Laurence, the abbot and spiritual father, New Skete has become not only a vital monastic center but also a place of reflection and nurture that emphasizes the importance of Christian community and worship. Because of this, New Skete has also become a center that has encouraged contact, dialogue, and common endeavors for members of many of the Orthodox jurisdictions in America.

Among the ministries undertaken at New Skete, special attention has been given to the translation of liturgical texts, the composition of hymns, and the publication of liturgical books. Nurtured by their own liturgical life and enriched by their knowledge of the liturgical traditions, the members of New Skete have made their community renowned throughout the Orthodox world not only for their translations into American English but also for their efforts to restore and renew Orthodox worship in a manner both faithful to Orthodox tradition and responsive to the reality of American society.

SOCIAL CONCERN AND MISSION

The witness of American Orthodox clergy and laity can also be seen in ever-growing attention given to the social concerns of this society and the moral questions that face believers today. In sharp contrast to the lack of interest in societal issues during the early periods of Orthodox Church development in America, the Orthodox in recent decades have demonstrated far greater interest in the challenges facing America today. Archbishop Iakovos of the Greek Orthodox Archdiocese joined Dr. Martin Luther King in 1965 for the historic Selma march. This event is frequently viewed as the beginning of greater involvement in social issues by the Orthodox in this country. It is an involvement that has been nurtured by the theological insights of Father Stanley Harakas, the preeminent Orthodox ethicist in this country.[20]

Orthodox theologians have sought to articulate perspectives on social issues and moral questions that are both rooted in the distinctive faith affirmations of Orthodox Christianity and, at the same time, truly responsive to the needs of today's Christian community. These perspectives have often found forceful expression in the statements issued by national meetings of clergy and laity of the various jurisdictions. They have also found concrete expression in the growing efforts by dioceses and local parishes to work for greater justice and to serve the needy.

The dramatic political changes and social upheavals in Eastern Europe, especially between 1988 and 1992, provided the Orthodox in America with a valuable opportunity to respond by providing both humanitarian aid and catechetical materials.

The needs of Orthodox Christians in Central and Eastern Europe and in the Commonwealth of Independent States were especially highlighted during the visit of Patriarch Aleksy II of Moscow to the United States in 1991 and 1993. Traveling through this country in the wake of the historic political changes in the former Soviet Union, the patriarch called upon all the Orthodox to respond to the tremendous needs of all the people of Central and Eastern Europe and to assist the church in reestablishing its charitable and educational activities.[21]

The Standing Conference of Canonical Orthodox Bishops in America (SCOBA) formally sanctioned in 1992 the establishment of International Orthodox Christian Charities (IOCC). Initially organized by laypersons from a number of Orthodox jurisdictions, IOCC in its first year of operation organized the shipment of more than $5 million of food and medical supplies to Eastern Europe and the Commonwealth of Independent States. As IOCC began to enlarge the scope of its charitable activities, it became clear that it had become a valuable organization that provided both the vehicle for international Orthodox humanitarian aid and a new means through which Orthodox in America could cooperate in charitable endeavors.[22]

The Mission Center of the Greek Orthodox Archdiocese also entered into a new phase of its development, especially during the period after 1980. For many years the center had been active in supporting missionary work in Africa. This had involved funding the education of African Orthodox students at Hellenic College and Holy Cross Greek Orthodox School of Theology. More recently, under the leadership of Father Demetrios Couchell, the center broadened its scope to provide scholarships for students from Indonesia, Korea, and Japan. In addition, the center has supported a number of missionary teams comprising American Orthodox young adults who traveled to such countries as Uganda, Ghana, Kenya, Ukraine, Poland, Greece, and Russia. Depending upon the location, these missionaries were responsible for building or repairing churches, establishing medical clinics, and leading retreats for clergy and laypersons. The Mission Center formally became in 1993 the center for all the missionary activity supported by all the jurisdictions of SCOBA.[23]

IDENTIFICATION AND SHARING

The Orthodox in America are the inheritors of a rich tradition of faith, worship, and service that is as old as Christianity itself. This tradition was brought to North America by Russian monks in 1794. It was also brought by the pious immigrants from Greece, Asia Minor, Carpatho-Russia, and other parts of Eastern Europe and the Middle East who came to this country especially in the late nineteenth and early twentieth centuries. Often escaping religious persecution in the Old World, these immigrants carried few material possessions with them. Among them were icons and crosses. Like the monks in Alaska, one of their first tasks in this land was to construct church buildings where they could pray together and teach their faith to others. Their crosses, their icons, and their church buildings were the external signs that Orthodox Christianity was taking root in a new place, that it was to affect a new people in a new world.

Now, 200 years after the founding of the mission in Alaska, American Orthodox are traveling to other parts of the world as missionaries. Over a hundred years after the first immigrants arrived from lands rich in Christian history, American Orthodox are traveling as missionaries to Russia, the Balkans, other parts of Eastern Europe, the Middle East, Africa, and the Far East. With the prayers and financial support of their local parishes, these American Orthodox go to join Orthodox Christians in these lands to teach the faith, to build churches and clinics, and to care for the needy.

Yet, this is only a portion of a remarkable story of sharing that continues today. Both in word and in deed, the American Orthodox are contributing to the life of the church and to the life of the world. While difficulties continue to confront Orthodox Christians in America, they are part of a developing regional church that is making a profound impact upon the life of the Orthodox Church throughout the world and, indeed, upon all of contemporary Christianity. The writings of American Orthodox theologians are affecting their colleagues in Athens, Thessaloniki, Moscow, and Balamand. Religious education methods and materials from America enrich the programs in such diverse places as Syria, Indonesia, and Kenya. The participation of American Orthodox in both Orthodox conferences and in ecumenical meetings throughout the world provides an opportunity for personal contact and enrichment. Finally, all of this is nurtured by the daily liturgical prayers of the Orthodox "for peace throughout the world, the well-being of the holy churches of God, and the union of all."[24]

NOTES

CHAPTER 1

1. Maximos Aghiorgoussis, "The Dogmatic Tradition of the Orthodox Church," in *A Companion to the Greek Orthodox Church*, ed. Photios Litsas (New York: Greek Orthodox Archdiocese, 1984), pp. 160–168.

2. John Meyendorff, *The Orthodox Church* (Crestwood, N.Y.: St. Vladimir's Seminary Press, 1981), pp. 19–28.

3. Georges Florovsky, *Bible, Church, Tradition: An Eastern Orthodox View* (Belmont, Mass.: Nordland, 1972), pp. 9–16; Timothy Ware, *The Orthodox Church* (New York: Penguin Books, 1976), pp. 207–210.

4. *Ibid.*, p. 210.

5. Hans-Georg Link, ed., *Apostolic Faith Today* (Geneva: World Council of Churches, 1985), pp. 1–14; Faith and Order Commission, *Confessing the One Faith* (Geneva: World Council of Churches, 1991).

6. Thomas FitzGerald, "Toward the Reestablishment of Full Communion: The Orthodox-Oriental Orthodox Dialogue," *Greek Orthodox Theological Review* 36:2 (1991): 170–171.

7. *Ibid.*, pp. 171–182.

8. John Meyendorff, *Byzantine Theology* (New York: Fordham University Press, 1976), p. 91.

9. *Ibid.*, p. 92.

10. *Ibid.*, pp. 98–99.

11. *Ibid.*, pp. 103–115.

12. Ware, *The Orthodox Church*, p. 102.

13. *Ibid.*, p. 103.

14. *Ibid.*, pp. 104–106.

15. See Stanley Harakas, *Something Is Stirring in World Orthodoxy* (Minneapolis: Light and Life Publications, 1980).

16. Thomas FitzGerald, *The Ecumenical Patriarchate and Christian Unity* (Brookline, MA: Holy Cross Orthodox Press, 1990), pp. 10–15.

17. The order followed here is that of the ecumenical patriarchate and the one followed in inter-Orthodox meeting. The Church of Russia regards the Orthodox Church in America as an autocephalous church and the Church of Japan as autonomous.

18. Meyendorff, *The Orthodox Church,* pp. 145–149.

19. *Ibid.*, pp. v–vi.

20. Thomas FitzGerald, "Commission Discusses 'Diaspora,'" *Orthodox Theological Society Bulletin,* Series II:3 (Summer 1991): 2.

21. Maximos Aghiorgoussis, "Orthodox Soteriology," in *Salvation in Christ,* ed. John Meyendorff and Robert Tobias (Minneapolis: Augsburg, 1992), pp. 35–40.

22. *Ibid.*, pp. 41–47.

23. St. Irenaeus, *Against Heresies,* 4:20:6.

24. *Ibid.*, p. 5: preface.

25. John Meyendorff, "New Life in Christ: Salvation in Orthodox Theology," *Theological Studies* 50 (1989): 481–499.

26. Florovsky, *Bible, Church, Tradition,* p. 59.

27. *Ibid.,* p. 69.

28. Kyriaki FitzGerald, "Reflections on Spirituality and Prayer," in *Faith and Order: 1985–1989* (Geneva: World Council of Churches, 1990), pp. 180–183.

29. This phrase is taken from the Liturgy of St. John Chrysostom.

CHAPTER 2

1. On Russian Orthodox missions in this period, see S. Bolshakoff, *The Foreign Missions of the Russian Orthodox Church* (London: SPCK, 1943); Georges Florovsky, "Russian Missions: An Historical Sketch," *The Christian East* 14:1 (1933): 30–41; Nikita Struve, "Orthodox Missions: Past and Present," *St. Vladimir's Theological Quarterly* 7:1 (1964): 31–42.

2. See John Harrison, *The Founding of the Russian Empire in Asia and America* (Coral Gables, Fla.: University of Miami Press, 1971); R. J. Kerner, *The Urge to the Sea* (Berkeley: University of California Press, 1946).

3. See M. B. Ricks, *The Earliest Years of Alaska* (Anchorage: University of Alaska, 1963); Frank Golder, *Russian Expansion on the Pacific, 1641–1850* (Cleveland: Arthur Clark Company, 1914).

4. See Frank Golder, *Bering's Voyages: An Account of the Russians to Determine the Relation of America to Asia* (New York: American Geographical Society, 1932).

5. For an early description, see H. H. Bancroft, *History of Alaska 1870–1885* (New York: Antiquarian Press, 1959), pp. 64–75. Historians now generally believe that the coast of North America was sighted by an earlier expedition of I. Federov and M. Gvozdev in 1732. The report, however, was not widely circulated. See Harrison, *The Founding of the Russian Empire in Asia and America,* p. 113.

6. Raisa Makarova, *Russians on the Pacific 1743–1799,* trans. and ed. Richard Pierce and Alton Donnelly (Kingston, Ont.: Limestone Press, 1975), pp. 37–50.

7. *Ibid.,* pp. 140–144.

8. See S. M. Okun, *The Russian-American Company,* trans. Carl Ginsberg (Cambridge: Harvard University Press, 1951); P. A. Tikhmenev, *A History of the Russian-American Company,* trans. Richard Pierce and Alton Donnelly (Seattle: University of Washington Press, 1978).

9. On the mission, see Michael Oleska, *Orthodox Alaska* (Crestwood, N.Y.: St. Vladimir's Seminary Press, 1992); Bishop Gregory Afonsky, *A History of the Orthodox Church in Alaska* (Kodiak: St. Herman's Theological Seminary, 1977); Michael Kovach, *The Russian Orthodox Church in Russian America* (Ann Arbor, Mich.: University Microfilms, 1957).

10. Kovach, *The Russian Orthodox Church in Russian America,* p. 54; Tikhmenev, *A History of the Russian-American Company,* pp. 35–36.

11. Afonsky, *A History of the Orthodox Church in Alaska,* p. 20.

12. *Ibid.*, pp. 22–23.

13. Constance Tarasar and John Erickson, eds., *Orthodox America: 1794–1976* (Syosset, N.Y.: Orthodox Church in America, 1975), p. 15.

14. Tikhmenev, *A History of the Russian-American Company,* pp. 81–107.

15. Kovach, *The Russian Orthodox Church in Russian America,* pp. 52–55.

16. Colin Bearne and Richard Pierce, eds., *The Russian Orthodox Religious Mission in America, 1794–1837* (Kingston, Ont.: Limestone Press, 1978), pp. 1–8.

17. A translation of "The Life of the Valamo Monk Herman, American Missionary" can be found in Boris Borichevsky, ed. and trans., *St. Herman of Alaska* (Wilkes Barre, Pa.: Orthodox Church in America, 1970), pp. 19–39.

18. See Vsevolod Rochcau, "St. Herman of Alaska and the Defense of Alaskan Native Peoples," *St. Vladimir's Theological Quarterly* 16:1 (1972): 17–39.

19. Kovach, *The Russian Orthodox Church in Russian America,* pp. 118–121.

20. Tarasar and Erickson, *Orthodox America,* p. 25.

21. Bolshakoff, *The Foreign Missions,* p. 86.

22. Paul D. Garrett, *St. Innocent Apostle to America* (Crestwood, N.Y.: St. Vladimir's Seminary Press, 1979), p. 37.

23. The full text is found in Michael Oleska, ed., *Alaskan Missionary Spirituality* (New York: Paulist Press, 1987), pp. 80–119.

24. Kovach, *The Russian Orthodox Church in Russian America,* pp. 161–162.

25. Robert Croskey, "The Russian Orthodox Church in Alaska: Innokentii Veniamonov's Account (1858)," *Pacific Northwest Quarterly* 1 (1975): 36–49.

26. Garrett, *St. Innocent,* pp. 114–116.

27. Tikhmenev, *A History of the Russian-America Company,* pp. 196–197.

28. Garrett, *St. Innocent,* p. 141.

29. See Vsevolod Rochcau, "Innocent Veniaminov and the Russian Mission to Alaska, 1820–1840," *St. Vladimir's Theological Quarterly* 15:3 (1971): 105–120.

30. Garrett, *St. Innocent,* pp. 227–234.

31. The full text can be found in Afonsky, *A History of the Orthodox Church in Alaska,* p. 75.

32. Garrett, *St. Innocent,* pp. 310–321.

33. Barbara Smith, *Orthodoxy and the Native Americans: The Alaskan Mission* (New York: Orthodox Church in America, 1980), pp. 16–19; Kovach, *The Russian Orthodox Church in Russian America,* pp. 260–272.

34. Afonsky, *A History of the Orthodox Church in Alaska,* pp. 78–81. See also Robert Berkhofer, *Salvation and the Savage: An Analysis of Protestant Missions and the American Indian Response, 1787–1862* (Louisville: University of Kentucky Press, 1965).

35. Oleska, *Orthodox Alaska,* p. 221.

CHAPTER 3

1. Alexander Doumouris, "Greek Orthodox Communities in America Before World War I," *St. Vladimir's Theological Quarterly* 11:4 (1967): 177–178.

2. Constance Tarasar and John Erickson, eds., *Orthodox America: 1794–1976* (Syosset, N.Y.: Orthodox Church in America, 1975), pp. 38–39.

3. *Ibid.*, pp. 40–41.

4. *Ibid.*, p. 39.

5. Dimitry Grigorieff, "The Historical Background of Orthodoxy in America," *St. Vladimir's Theological Quarterly* 5:1–2 (1961): 7.

6. See E. P. Panagopoulos, *New Smyrna: An Eighteenth Century Greek Odyssey* (Gainesville: University Presses of Florida, 1966).

7. Charles C. Moscos, Jr., *Greek Americans: Struggle and Success* (Englewood Cliffs, N.J.: Prentice-Hall, 1980), pp. 8–9.

8. United States Immigration and Naturalization Service, *Annual Report, 1975* (Washington, D.C.: Government Printing Office, 1976), pp. 86–88.

9. For turn-of-the-century accounts, see Thomas Burgess, *Greeks in America* (Boston: Shermon, Trench, 1913) and Henry Pratt Fairchild, *Greek Migration to the United States* (New Haven, Conn.: Yale University Press, 1911).

10. Theodore Saloutos, *The Greeks in the United States* (Cambridge: Harvard University Press, 1964), pp. 71–78.

11. Moscos, *Greek Americans,* pp. 33–34; Saloutos, *The Greeks in the United States,* pp. 123–126.

12. Saloutos, *The Greeks in the United States,* p. 121.

13. "O Patriarchikos kai Synodikos Tomos," *Ekklesiastike Alletheia* 3 (1908): 183. See Metropolitan Silas of New Jersey, "Greek-Americans in Crisis," in *History of the Greek Orthodox Church in America,* ed. Miltiades Efthimiou and George Christopoulos (New York: Greek Orthodox Archdiocese, 1984), pp. 37–66.

14. Saloutos, *The Greeks in the United States,* p. 138.

15. Paul Robert Magocsi, "Carpatho-Rusyns," in *Harvard Encyclopedia of American Ethnic Groups,* ed. Stephen Therstrom (Cambridge: Harvard University Press, 1980), p. 200.

16. Tarasar and Erickson, *Orthodox America 1794–1976,* p. 12.

17. Paul Robert Magocsi, *Our People: Carpatho-Rusyns and Their Descendents in North America* (Toronto: Multicultural History Society of Ontario, 1984), pp. 5–15.

18. *Ibid.*, pp. 17–21.

19. Lawrence Barriger, *Good Victory: Metropolitan Orestes Chornock and the American Carpatho-Russian Orthodox Greek Catholic Diocese* (Brookline, Mass.: Holy Cross Orthodox Press, 1985), pp. 18–23.

20. *Ibid.*, p. 24.

21. Keith S. Russin, "Fr. Alexis G. Toth and the Wilkes-Barre Litigations," *St. Vladimir's Theological Quarterly* 16:3 (1972): 140–149. See also George Soldatow, ed., *Archpriest Alexis Toth, Volume One, Letters, Articles, Papers, and Sermons* (Toronto: Synaxis Press, 1978).

22. Barriger, *Good Victory,* pp. 25–26; Russin, "Father Alexis G. Toth," pp. 129–134.

23. Barriger, *Good Victory,* p. 27.

24. Tarasar and Erickson, *Orthodox America 1794–1976,* p. 51.

25. Russin, "Father Alexis G. Toth," p. 148; Barriger, *Good Victory,* pp. 26–30.

26. Barriger, *Good Victory,* pp. 30–36.

27. Department of the Interior, *Report on Statistics of Churches at the Eleventh Census: 1890* (Washington, D.C.: Government Printing Office, 1894), p. 265.

28. Department of Commerce, *Religious Bodies: 1906, Part III* (Washington, D.C.: Government Printing Office, 1910), p. 259.

29. Department of Commerce, *Religious Bodies: 1916, Part III* (Washington, D.C.: Government Printing Office, 1919), p. 225.

30. Leonid Kishkovsky, "Archbishop Tikhon in America," *St. Vladimir's Theological Quarterly* 19:1 (1975): 9–31; Serafim Surrency, *The Quest for Orthodox Church Unity in America* (New York: Saints Boris and Gleb Press, 1973), pp. 24–25.

31. Basil Benson, *Russian Orthodox Greek-Catholic Church of North America* (New York: Colonial, 1941), pp. 13–15.

32. "Documents," *St. Vladimir's Theological Quarterly* 19:1 (1975): 49–56.

33. Alexander Schmemann, "Patriarch Tikhon, 1925–1975," *St. Vladimir's Theological Quarterly* 19:1 (1975): 9–31.

34. A portion of the text is found in Tarasar and Erickson, *Orthodox America, 1794–1976*, pp. 100–101.

35. John Meyendorff, "The Russian Church After Patriarch Tikhon," *St. Vladimir's Theological Quarterly* 19:1 (1975), pp. 32–48.

36. Surrency, *The Quest for Orthodox Church Unity in America,* pp. 107–110.

37. *Ibid.*, pp. 110–112.

38. *Ibid.*, pp. 94–95.

39. See Fan Noli, *Fiftieth Anniversary Book of the Albanian Orthodox Church in America* (Boston: Albanian Orthodox Church, 1960).

40. See Vasile Hategan, *Fifty Years of the Romanian Orthodox Church in America* (Jackson, Mich.: Romanian Orthodox Episcopate in America, 1959).

41. William Essey, "Raphael: Bishop of Brooklyn," *The Word* 5 (1976): 14.

42. Surrency, *The Quest for Orthodox Church Unity in America,* pp. 29–32.

43. This claim appears early in Boris Burden, "The Holy Eastern Orthodox Catholic and Apostolic Church in North America," *The Orthodox Catholic Review* 1:1 (1927): 9.

44. Saloutos, *The Greeks in the United States,* pp. 123–124.

45. Based upon very limited evidence, it appears that the Greek Orthodox priests commemorated in liturgical services either the patriarch of Constantinople or the bishop of their home diocese. See M. Gedeon, "Ekklesiai en te Diaspora," in *E Synchronos Ellenike Ekklesia,* ed. Evgenios Kostaridou (Athens, 1921).

46. Doumouras, *"Greek Orthodox Communities in America Before World War I,"* pp. 178–182.

47. *Ibid.*, p. 47.

48. Department of Commerce, *Religious Bodies: 1906,* p. 61.

49. Tarasar and Erickson, *Orthodox America 1794–1976,* pp. 340–350.

CHAPTER 4

1. Theodore Saloutos, *The Greeks in the United States* (Cambridge: Harvard University Press, 1964), p. 281.

2. Theokletos Strangas, *Ekklesiastike Historia ek Pegon Apseudon, 1817–1967* (Athens: Papadoyanne, 1969), Vol. 2, pp. 845–850; George Papaioannou, *From Mars Hill to Manhattan* (Minneapolis: Light and Life, 1976), pp. 30–32.

3. Basil Zoustis, *O en Ameriki Ellenismos kai e Drasis aftou* (New York: D. C. Dirvy, 1953), pp. 117–125.

4. *Ibid.*, pp. 126–129.

5. *Ibid.*, pp. 132–133.

6. "Certificate of Incorporation of the Greek Orthodox Archdiocese of North and South America," Archives, Greek Orthodox Archdiocese, New York.

7. See Basil Istravidis, "O Oikoumenikos Patriarches Meletios (1921–1923)," *Theologia* 47 (1976): 159–176.

8. *Ekklesiastike Aletheia* 42 (1922): 30. A portion of the text is translated in *St. Vladimir's Theological Quarterly* 5 1–2 (1961): 114.

9. "Patriarchkos kai Synodos Tomos," *Ekklesiastike Aletheia* 42 (1922): 190; Papaioannou, *From Mars Hill to Manhattan*, pp. 33–34.

10. Stragas, *Ekklesiastike Historia*, vol. 2, pp. 988–991.

11. Saloutos, *The Greeks in the United States*, p. 285.

12. *Ibid.*, 290–291.

13. Strangas, *Ekklesiastike Historia*, vol. 2, pp. 168–172; Zoustis, *O en Ameriki Ellinismos*, p. 187.

14. In various forms, a number of Greek old calendar parishes and dioceses have continued to exist.

15. *Orthodoxia* 5 (1930): 131; Zoustis, *0 en Ameriki Ellenismos*, pp. 188–189: Saloutos, *The Greeks in America*, pp. 298–304.

16. Papaioannou, *From Mars Hill to Manhattan*, pp. 37–40.

17. Basil Benson, *The Russian Orthodox Greek Catholic Church of North America* (New York: Colonial, 1941), pp. 15–17.

18. Dimitry Grigorieff, "The Historical Background of Orthodoxy in America," *St. Vladimir's Theological Quarterly* 5:1–2 (1961): 13.

19. Ibid., pp. 14–18.

20. Benson, *The Russian Orthodox Greek Catholic Church of North America*, pp. 17–18.

21. Constance Tarasar and John Erickson, eds., *Orthodox America: 1794–1976* (Syosset, N.Y.: Orthodox Church in America, 1975), pp. 128–129.

22. *Ibid.*, p. 128.

23. Grigorieff, "The Historical Background of Orthodoxy in America," p. 20.

24. "The Archdiocese of North America and the Aleutian Islands," in *Inventory of Church Archives in New York City, Eastern Orthodox Churches*, ed. Charles Baker (New York: Historical Records Survey, 1940): 62–67.

25. For an analysis of the Living Church movement, see Sergius Troitsky, "The Living Church," in *Religion in Soviet Russia*, ed. William Emhardt (Milwaukee: Morehouse, 1929), pp. 298–379.

26. "Decision of His Holiness Patriarch Tikhon and the Sacred Synod, January 16, 1924," in Serafim Surrency, *The Quest for Orthodox Church Unity in America* (New York: Saints Boris and Gleb Press, 1973), p. A125.

27. *Ibid.*, p. A126.

28. Alexander Bogolepov, *Toward an American Orthodox Church* (New York: Morehouse Barlow, 1963), pp. 78–83.

29. David Abramtsov, "The November 1920 Decree and Russian Orthodoxy Abroad," *One Church* 25:5 (1971): 202–204.

30. Michael Rodzianko, *The Truth About the Russian Church Abroad* (Jordanville, N.Y.: Holy Trinity Monastery, 1975), p. 8. For the limitations placed upon the Russian bishops, see *Echoes d'Orient* 23 (1924): 365; *Tserkovnya Viedomosti* 15–16 (1924): 7–8.

31. Nicholas Zernov, "The Schism Within the Russian Church in the Diaspora: Its Causes and the Hopes of a Reconciliation," *Eastern Churches Review* 7:1 (1975): 63. For the official account of the conference, see *Dieianiia Russkago Vsegranichnago Tserkovnago Sobra* (Sremski-Karlovtsy, 1922). The views of the Russian émigrés are discussed in Robert Williams, *Culture in Exile: Russian Emigres in Germany, 1881–1941* (Ithaca, N.Y.: Cornell University Press, 1972).

32. "Letter from Archbishop Thaddeus to Metropolitan Evlogius, April 22, 1922," *St. Vladimir's Theological Quarterly* 19:1 (1975): 53–55.

33. The full text can be found in Matthew Spinka, *The Church and the Russian Revolution* (New York: Macmillan, 1927), pp. 285–290.

34. See I. M. Andrreev, *Kratkii Obzor Istorii Russkoi Tserkvi ot Revoliutsii do Nashikh Dnei* (Jordanville, N.Y.: Holy Trinity Monastery, 1961).

35. Grigorieff, "The Historical Background of Orthodoxy in America," pp. 31–33.

36. William Essey, 'The Antacky-Russy Dilemma," *The Word* 9 (1976): 7–9.

37. Surrency, *The Quest for Orthodox Church Unity in America*, pp. 110–111.

38. *Ibid.*, p. 108.

39. *Ibid.*, p. 105.

40. *Ibid.*, pp. 92–93.

41. *Ibid.*, pp. 94–95.

42. *Ibid.*, p. 112.

43. *Ibid.*, pp. 112–113.

44. See Lawrence Barringer, *Good Victory* (Brookline, Mass.: Holy Cross Orthodox Press, 1985).

45. Archbishop Aftimios, "Present and Future of Orthodoxy in America in Relation to Other Bodies and to Orthodox Abroad," *Orthodox Catholic Review* 1:4–5 (1927): 145.

46. Surrency, *The Quest for Orthodox Church Unity in America*, pp. 38–40. A valuable review of various groups is offered in John Bacon, "Orthodoxy and Canonicity" (Th.M. thesis, Holy Cross Greek Orthodox School of Theology, Brookline, Mass., 1992).

47. Metropolitan Maximos of Sardis, *The Oecumenical Patriarchate in the Orthodox Church* (Thessaloniki: Patriarchal Institute, 1976), pp. 303–309.

48. John Meyendorff, "One Bishop in One City," *St. Vladimir's Theological Quarterly* 5:1–2 (1961): 54–61.

49. John Meyendorff, "Orthodoxy in the U.S.A.," in *Orthodoxy: A Sign from God* (Athens: Zoe, 1964), p. 355.

CHAPTER 5

1. George Papaioannou, *From Mars Hill to Manhattan* (Minneapolis: Light and Life, 1976), pp. 57–60.

2. "Archbishop Apollinary, Confessor of Orthodoxy in America," *Orthodox Word* 6:1 (1970): 37–41.

3. "The Historical Road of the Orthodox Church in America," *Diakonia* 6:1 (1970): 172–173.

4. Papaioannou, *From Mars Hill to Manhattan*, pp. 103–113.

5. Basil Bensin, *The Russian Orthodox Greek Catholic Church of North America* (New York: Colonial, 1941), pp. 19–21.

6. Alexander Doumouras, "St. Athanasius Greek Orthodox Seminary: 1921–1923," *Upbeat* 9:6 (1976): 10–15.

7. Basil Bensin, "Twenty Years Ago," *St. Vladimir's Theological Quarterly* 2:3 (1958): 14.

8. *Ibid.*, p. 15.

9. See George Tsoumas, "The Founding Years of Holy Cross Greek Orthodox Theological School," *Greek Orthodox Theological Review* 12:3 (1967): 241–282.

10. *Ibid.*

11. Constance Tarasar and John Erickson, eds., *Orthodox America 1794–1976* (Syosset, N.Y.: Orthodox Church in America, 1975), pp. 205–210.

12. "Letter from Metropolitan Anthony to Metropolitan Theophilos," October 7, 1937, Archives, Greek Orthodox Archdiocese.

13. "Letter from Archbishop Athenagoras to Metropolitan Theophilus," 2 October 1937, cited in Papaioannou, *From Mars Hill to Manhattan*, p. 173.

14. *Ibid.*

15. Serafim Surrency, *The Quest for Orthodox Church Unity in America* (New York: Saints Boris and Gleb Press, 1973), pp. 47–49.

16. *Ibid.*

17. Quoted in Papaioannou, *From Mars Hill to Manhattan*, p. 176.

18. *Ibid.*, pp. 176–177.

19. Surrency, *The Quest for Orthodox Church Unity in America*, pp. 49–50.

20. *Ibid.*, p. 51.

21. *Ibid.*, p. 52.

22. Papaioannou, *From Mars Hill to Manhattan*, pp. 196–201.

CHAPTER 6

1. Dimitry Pospielovsky, *The Russian Church Under the Soviet Regime 1917–1982, Vol. 1* (Crestwood, N.Y.: St. Vladimir's Seminary Press, 1984), pp. 199–203.

2. *Ibid.*, Vol. 2, pp. 301–325. See also William Fletcher, *A Study in Survival: The Church in Russia, 1927–1943* (London: S.P.C.K., 1965); William Fletcher, *The Russian Orthodox Church Underground, 1917–1970* (New York: Oxford University Press, 1971).

3. The English translation is found in Wassilij Alexeev and Theofanis Stavrou, *The Great Revival: The Russian Church Under German Occupation* (Minneapolis: Burgess, 1976), p. 91. For an elaboration on the position of the Synod Abroad, see George Grabbe, *The Canonical and Legal Position of the Moscow Patriarchate* (Jerusalem: Russian Mission, 1971).

4. "Letter from Metropolitan Anastasy to Adolph Hitler," *Diakonia* 5:3 (1970): 277–278.

5. "Addresse du Patriarche de Moscou et de toutes les Russies Alexis aux eveques et membres du clerge de l'orientation dite karlovtzienne, 10 aout 1945," *Russie et Chretiente* 1 (1945): 120–122.

6. "Letter of Metropolitan Anastasy, January, 1946," *Orthodox Life* 27:6 (1977): 29–36.

7. Seraphim Surrency, *The Quest for Orthodox Church Unity in America* (New York: Saints Boris and Gleb Press, 1973), pp. 52–53.

8. *Ibid.*, p. 54.

9. "Memorandum on the Status of the Russian Orthodox Church in America," in Surrency, *The Quest for Orthodox Church Unity in America,* p. A137.

10. *Ibid.*

11. *Ibid.,* p. 139.

12. Surrency, *The Quest for Orthodox Church Unity in America,* p. 56.

13. *Ibid.,* p. 54.

14. *Ibid.,* p. 59.

15. Constance Tarasar and John Erickson, eds., *Orthodox America 1784–1976* (Syosset, N.Y.: Orthodox Church in America, 1975), p. 214.

16. Anthony Ugolnik, *The Illuminating Icon* (Grand Rapids, Mich.: William B. Eerdmans, 1989), pp. 241–249.

17. See *The Romanian Orthodox Missionary Episcopate in America: A Short History* (Detroit: Romanian Orthodox Missionary Episcopate, 1967); Vasile Hategan, *Fifty Years of the Romanian Orthodox Church in America* (Jackson, Mich.: Romanian Orthodox Episcopate, 1959).

18. Arthur Piepkorn, *Profiles in Belief, Vol. 1* (New York: Harper and Row, 1977), p. 79.

19. *Ibid.*

20. *Ibid.,* p. 80.

21. Some of the documents are published in Dionisije Milivojevech, *Patriarch German's Violation of the Holy Canons, Rules and Regulations of the Serbian Orthodox Church in Tito's Yugoslavia* (Libertyville, Ill: Serbian Orthodox Diocese, 1965).

22. *The New York Times,* 22 June 1976, p. 22.

23. Surrency, *The Quest for Orthodox Church Unity in America,* pp. 94–95; Piepkorn, *Profiles in Belief,* p. 81.

24. Metropolitan Fan Noli, *Fiftieth Anniversary Book of the Albanian Orthodox Church in America 1908–1958* (Boston: Albanian Orthodox Church, 1960), pp. 105–113.

25. Surrency, *The Quest for Orthodox Church Unity in America,* pp. 92–94.

26. For a review of the situation in the Ukraine both prior to World War II and after it, see Pospielovsky, *The Russian Church Under the Soviet Regime 1917–1982,* pp. 73–77, 236–241; Bohdan Bociurkiw, "The Renovationist Church in the Soviet Ukraine, 1922–1939," *Annals of the Ukrainian Academy of Arts and Sciences in the U.S.* 9:1–2 (1961): pp. 41–42. Central to many of these difficulties was the decision of some nationalistically minded Ukrainian Church leaders to convene a council in Kiev in 1921. At this council, Vasil Lypkivsky was said to be made a bishop through a ceremony in which only priests and laymen participated. Such an act was contrary to Orthodox understanding of the episcopacy and episcopal ordinations. Lypkivsky then claimed to have ordained others as bishops and priests. Because of this, the Orthodox Church forbade sacramental contact with this group, which was generally known as the Autocephalists.

27. Surrency, *The Quest for Orthodox Church Unity in America,* pp. 113–114.

CHAPTER 7

1. George Papaioannou, *The Odyssey of Hellenism in America* (Thessaloniki: Patriarchal Institute, 1985), pp. 379–392; Constance Tarasar and John Erickson, eds., *Orthodox America 1794–1976* (Syosset, N.Y.: Orthodox Church in America, 1975), pp. 141–142.

2. Arthur Peipkorn, *Profiles in Belief,* Vol. 1 (New York: Harper and Row, 1977), pp. 69–84.

3. Robert Donus, "Greek-Americans in a Pan-Orthodox Parish," *St. Vladimir's Theological Quarterly* 18:1 (1974): 44–52.

4. John Meyendorff, *Vision of Unity* (Crestwood, N.Y.: St. Vladimir's Seminary Press, 1987), pp. 66–67.

5. *Ibid.*, pp. 70–71.

6. Georges Florovsky, "The Responsibility of Orthodox Believers in America," *The Russian Orthodox Journal* 2:6 (1949): 15–18.

7. George Nicozisin, *The Road to Orthodox Phronema* (Brookline, Mass.: Department of Religious Education, 1977), pp. 33–38; Tarasar and Erickson, *Orthodox America*, p. 202.

8. Nicozisin, *The Road to Orthodox Phronema*, pp. 42–47.

9. Tarasar and Erickson, *Orthodox America*, p. 234.

10. *Ibid.*

11. *Ibid.*, p. 235.

12. Andrew Blane, ed., *Georges Florovsky: Russian Intellectual-Orthodox Churchman* (Crestwood, N.Y.: St. Vladimir's Seminary Press, 1993), p. 100.

13. Ernest Villas, "Toward Unity of Orthodox Youth in America," *St. Vladimir's Theological Quarterly* 2:4 (1954): 31–32.

14. A valuable list of significant books of this period is in Dean Timothy Andrews, *The Eastern Orthodox Church: A Bibliography* (New York: Greek Orthodox Archdiocese, 1957).

15. *Ibid.*, pp. 25–36.

16. Metropolitan Antony, "The Antiochian Church and Christian Unity," *The Word* 1:6 (1957): p. 145.

17. Paul Schneirla, "A New Tendency in Anglican-Orthodox Relations," *St. Vladimir's Theological Quarterly* 4:1 (1960): 23–31.

18. Paul Schneirla, "American Orthodoxy and Ecumenism, " *Orthodoxy* 10:9 (1966): 266–267; Georges Florovsky, "The Challenge of Disunity," *St. Vladimir's Theological Quarterly* 3:1/2 (1954–1955): 31–36.

19. "Survey of the Second Assembly," *St. Vladimir's Theological Quarterly* 3:1/2 (1954–1955): 5–15; Blane, *Georges Florovsky*, pp. 106–109.

20. Archbishop Michael, "Reflections on Evanston," *Istina* 2 (1955): 202.

21. See Paul Minear, ed., *The Nature of the Unity We Seek* (St. Louis: Bethany Press, 1958).

22. Alexander Schmemann, "Report on Oberlan," *St. Vladimir's Theological Quarterly* 2:1 (1958): 36–41.

23. "Statement of the Representatives of the Eastern Orthodox Church," in Minear, *The Nature of the Unity We Seek,* pp. 159–163.

24. Alexander Schmemann, "Notes on Evanston," *St. Vladimir's Theological Quarterly* 3:1/2 (1954): 16–22.

25. Miltiades Efthimiou and George Christopoulos, eds., *History of the Greek Orthodox Church in America* (New York: Greek Orthodox Archdiocese, 1984), pp. 371–376.

CHAPTER 8

1. Appreciation for insights into themes discussed in this chapter is extended to Fathers Timothy Andrews, John Zenetos, and James Christon.

2. Antony Bashir, "The Bishops Meet," *The Word* 4:5 (1960): 3–5.

3. Joseph Hayden, *Slavic Orthodox Christianity in the United States: From Culture Religion to Sectarian Church,* (Ann Arbor, Mich.: University Microfilms, 1973), pp. 125–143.

4. William Paul Schneirla, "The Bishop's Conference," *St. Vladimir's Theological Quarterly* 4:1 (1960): 47–48.

5. Serafim Surrency, *The Quest for Orthodox Church Unity in America* (New York: Saints Boris and Gleb Press, 1973), p. 62.

6. Alexander Schmemann, "The Standing Conference of Orthodox Bishops in America," *St. Vladimir's Theological Quarterly* 6:1 (1962): 42–43.

7. Archbishop Iakovos, "The State of the Church Address, July 20, 1968," *Congress Album* (New York: Greek Orthodox Archdiocese, 1968), p. 40.

8. Vasilios Stavridis, *Istoria tou Oikoumenikou Patriarcheiou* (Athens, 1967), pp. 206–207.

9. *Towards the Great and Holy Council: Introductory Reports of the InterOrthodox Commission in Preparation for the Next Great and Holy Council of the Orthodox Church* (London: S.P.C.K., 1972).

10. Thomas FitzGerald, *The Ecumenical Patriarchate and the Quest for Christian Unity* (Brookline, Mass.: Holy Cross Orthodox Press, 1990), pp. 8–9.

11. John Meyendorff, "The Standing Conference of Canonical Orthodox Bishops," in Constance Tarasar and John Erickson, eds., *Orthodox America 1794–1976* (Syosset, N.Y.: Orthodox Church in America, 1975), p. 243.

12. FitzGerald, *The Ecumenical Patriarchate of Constantinople and the Quest for Christian Unity,* p. 7.

13. *Ibid.,* p. 10.

14. *Ibid.,* p. 14.

15. "The Discipline of Holy Communion," *St. Vladimir's Theological Quarterly* 9:1 (1965): 8.

16. *Ibid.*

17. *Guidelines for the Orthodox in Ecumenical Relations* (New York: Standing Conference of Orthodox Bishops, 1966).

18. Nils Ehrenstrom, ed., *Confessions in Dialogue* (Geneva: World Council of Churches, 1975), pp. 57, 117, 89, 113.

19. John Meyendorff, *Witness to the World* (Crestwood, N.Y.: St. Vladimir's Seminary Press, 1987), p. 17.

20. "Epistle of Bishops at the Church Council of the Russian Orthodox Church Outside of Russia to the God-Loving Flock Now in Dispersion, October 18, 1958," *Orthodox Life* 6 (1959): 10.

21. "Pastoral Address of Metropolitan Anastasy, October 18, 1958," *Orthodox Life* 6 (1959): 8.

22. "Letter from Metropolitan Anastasy to Archbishop Iakovos, June 19, 1960," Archives, Greek Orthodox Archdiocese.

23. Archimandrite Constantine, "The Spiritual State of the World and the Task of the Russian Orthodox Church Outside of Russia," *Orthodox Life* 4 (1962): 11.

24. Arthur Piepkorn, *Profiles in Belief, Vol. 1* (New York: Harper and Row, 1977), pp. 83, 79.

25. Archbishop Nikon of Washington, "Archpastoral Epistle, " *Orthodox Life* 3 (1962): 6.

26. Eugene Rose, "Witness of Orthodoxy," *Orthodox Word* 4:6 (1968): 268.

27. Eugene Rose, "Orthodoxy in the Contemporary World," *Orthodox Word* 5:6 (1969): 232.

28. "On the Heresy of Ecumenism," *Orthodox Word* 7:6 (1991): 297.

29. John Meyendorff, *Witness to the World* (Crestwood, N.Y.: St. Vladimir's Seminary Press, 1987), p. 212.

30. Metropolitan Antony Bashir, "Memorandum to the Prelates Invited to the Inter-Jurisdictional Meeting," *The Word* 4:5 (1960): 8.

31. Surrency, *The Quest for Orthodox Church Unity in America*, p. 66.

32. "Report of the Ad Hoc Commission on Unity," in Surrency, *The Quest for Orthodox Church Unity in America*, pp. A149–A150.

33. *Ibid.*, p. 67.

34. *Ibid.*, p. 70.

35. "Appeal of the Standing Conference of Canonical Orthodox Bishops in America to the Forthcoming Pan-Orthodox Conference," in Surrency, *The Quest for Orthodox Church Unity in America*, p. A151.

CHAPTER 9

1. Constance Tarasar and John Erickson, eds., *Orthodox America: 1794–1976* (Syosset, N.Y.: Orthodox Church in America, 1975), pp. 183–185.

2. Serafim Surrency, *The Quest for Orthodox Church Unity in America* (New York: Saints Boris and Gleb Press, 1973), pp. 42–45.

3. *Ibid.*, pp. 55–59.

4. "Letter from Archbishop Alexander to Metropolitan Platon, April 10, 1930." Archives, Greek Orthodox Archdiocese.

5. Tarasar and Erickson, *Orthodox America*, p. 285.

6. *Ibid.*, p. 263.

7. Letter from Patriarch Alexis of Moscow to Patriarch Athenagoras of Constantinople, August 25, 1965, *One Church* 20:1–3 (1966): 38; "Declaration of Metropolitan Nikodim at the Pan-Orthodox Conference in Geneva," 9–15 June 1968, *One Church* 22:5 (1968): 22–23.

8. Tarasar and Erickson, *Orthodox America*, p. 269.

9. *Ibid.*, p. 263.

10. Surrency, *The Quest for Orthodox Church Unity in America*, p. 82.

11. *Ibid.*, pp. 84–86.

12. *Ibid.*, p. 87.

13. Tarasar and Erickson, *Orthodox America*, p. 264.

14. *Ibid.*, p. 277.

15. *Ibid.*, pp. 294–300.

16. *Ibid.*, p. 313.

17. Surrency, *The Quest for Orthodox Church Unity in America*, p. 95.

18. Tarasar and Erickson, *Orthodox America*, pp. 305–306.

19. John Erickson, "Autocephaly in Orthodox Canonical Literature to the Thirteenth Century," *St. Vladimir's Theological Quarterly* 15:1/2 (1971): 28–41.

20. Alexander Schmemann, "A Meaningful Storm," *St. Vladimir's Theological Quarterly* 15:1/2 (1971): 3.

21. See *Autocephaly: The Orthodox Church in America* (Crestwood, N.Y.: St. Vladimir's Seminary Press, 1971); Panagiotes Trembellis, *The Autocephaly of the Metropolia in America* (Brookline, Mass.: Holy Cross Press, 1973); *Russian Autocephaly and Orthodoxy in America* (New York: Orthodox Observer Press, 1972).

22. *Autocephaly: The Orthodox Church in America,* pp. 42–43.

23. *Ibid.,* p. 43.

24. *Ibid.*

25. *Russian Autocephaly,* p. 68.

26. George Papaioannou, *From Mars Hill to Manhattan* (Minneapolis: Light and Life, 1976), pp. 230–238.

27. Archbishop Iakovos, "Address to the Archdiocesan Council, January 23, 1979," Archives, Greek Orthodox Archdiocese.

28. Archbishop Iakovos, *Toward the Decade 1970–1980* (New York: Greek Orthodox Archdiocese, 1970), p. 22.

29. *Decisions of the 20th Biennial Clergy-Laity Congress* (New York: Greek Orthodox Archdiocese, 1970), p. 55.

30. Papaioannou, *From Mars Hill to Manhattan,* pp. 248–252.

31. "Encyclical of Patriarch Athenagoras, September 12, 1970," Archives, Greek Orthodox Archdiocese; Papaioannou, *From Mars Hill to Manhattan,* p. 253.

32. Basil Vasiliades, "Ecumenical Patriarchate," *Orthodox Observer* 41 (1975): 1.

33. Spiro Vryonis, *A Brief History of the Greek Orthodox Community of St. George in Memphis* (Malibou, Tenn.: Undena, 1982), p. 119.

34. *Charter of the Greek Orthodox Archdiocese, November 29, 1977* (Brookline, Mass.: Holy Cross Orthodox Press, 1977), p. 2.

35. "Letter from Patriarch Athenagoras to Archbishop Iakovos, December, 1970," Archives, Greek Orthodox Archdiocese; Surrency, *The Quest for Orthodox Church Unity in America,* pp. A174–A175.

36. John Meyendorff, *Vision of Unity* (Crestwood, N.Y.: St. Vladimir's Seminary Press, 1987), p. 78.

37. Peter Gillquist, *Metropolitan Philip* (Nashville: Thomas Nelson, 1991), pp. 181–190.

38. "Encyclical of Metropolitan Theodosius and Metropolitan Philip, Great Lent, 1989," *The Word* 18:3 (1989): 3.

39. See Peter Gillquist, *Coming Home* (Brentwood, Tenn.: Wolgemuth and Hyatt, 1989); see also Sarah Loft, *Converts Respond* (Syosset, N.Y.: Orthodox Church in America, 1984); Theodore Bobosh, ed., *Come and See: Encountering the Orthodox Church* (Syosset, N.Y.: Orthodox Church in America, 1983).

40. Leonidas Contos, *2001: The Church in Crisis* (Brookline, Mass.: Holy Cross Orthodox Press, 1982), p. 24.

41. *Ibid.,* p. 26.

42. Stanley Harakas, *Something Is Stirring in World Orthodoxy* (Minneapolis: Light and Life, 1978), pp. 7–11.

43. Metropolitan Maximos of Sardis, *The Oecumenical Patriarchate in the Orthodox Church* (Thessaloniki: Patriarchal Institute, 1976).

44. Harakas, *Something Is Stirring in World Orthodoxy,* pp. 15–17.

45. "Second Pre-Conciliar Conference," *Journal of the Moscow Patriarchate* 1 (1983): 62; "Third Pre-Conciliar Pan Orthodox Conference," *Journal of the Moscow Patriarchate* 2 (1987): 48.

46. Thomas FitzGerald, "Commission Discusses 'Diaspora,'" *Orthodox Theological Society in America Bulletin,* Series II, 3 (Summer 1991): 2.

47. Inter-Orthodox Preparatory Commission, "Orthodox Diaspora," *Orthodox Theological Society in America Bulletin,* Series II, 3 (Summer 1991): 3.

CHAPTER 10

1. For insights into themes discussed in this chapter, appreciation is expressed to Father Nicholas Apostola, Father Anthony Nicklas and Father Joseph Mirowski.

2. See Nikki Stephanopoulos and Robert Stephanopoulos, eds., *Dimitrios in the U.S.A.* (New York: Greek Orthodox Archdiocese, 1991); Thomas FitzGerald, "The Visit of the Ecumenical Patriarch to the United States," *Ecumenical Trends* 19:7 (1990): 103–105.

3. "Remarks of Patriarch Dimitrios," *The Orthodox Church,* 26:9/10 (1990): 9.

4. "Greeting by Metropolitan Theodosius," *The Orthodox Church* 26:9/10 (1990): 8.

5. "Remarks of Patriarch Dimitrios," *The Orthodox Church* 26:9/10 (1990): 9.

6. See *The Orthodox Church* 29:7/8 (1993): 1; 29:9/10(1993): 14.

7. Thomas Hopko, "On Ecclesial Conciliarity," in *The Legacy of St. Vladimir,* ed. J. Meyendorff et al. (Crestwood, N.Y.: St. Vladimir's Seminary Press, 1990), pp. 217–220.

8. John Meyendorff, *Witness to the World* (Crestwood, N.Y.: St. Vladimir's Seminary Press, 1987), p. 150.

9. See Thomas Fish, "Schmemann's Theological Contribution to the Renewal of the Churches," in *Liturgy and Tradition,* ed. Thomas Fisch (Crestwood, N.Y.: St. Vladimir's Seminary Press, 1990), pp. 1–20.

10. Alexander Schmemann, "Problems of Orthodoxy in America III: The Spiritual Problem," *St. Vladimir's Theological Quarterly* 9:4 (1965): 181.

11. John Meyendorff, *Vision of Unity* (Crestwood, N.Y.: St. Vladimir's Seminary Press, 1987), pp. 115–116.

12. Abbot Laurence, *A Book of Prayers* (Cambridge, N.Y.: New Skete, 1988), pp. xx–xxi.

13. Kyriaki FitzGerald, "Orthodox Women and Pastoral Praxis: Observations and Concerns for the Church in America," in *Orthodox Perspectives on Pastoral Praxis*, ed. Theodore Stylianopoulos (Brookline, Mass.: Holy Cross Orthodox Press, 1988), pp. 101–104; Deborah Belonick, "Women in the Church," in *Orthodox Perspectives on Pastoral Praxis*, ed. Theodore Stylianopoulos (Brookline, Mass.: Holy Cross Orthodox Press, 1988), pp. 81–83.

14. FitzGerald, "Orthodox Women and Pastoral Praxis," pp. 104–114.

15. See A Sub-Committee of the Ecumenical Task Force, *Women and Men in the Church* (Syosset, N.Y.: Orthodox Church in America, 1980).

16. See Alkiviadis Calivas, "The Fiftieth Anniversary of Holy Cross," in *Orthodox Perspectives on Pastoral Praxis,* ed. Theodore Stylianopoulos (Brookline, Mass.: Holy Cross Orthodox Press, 1988), pp. xi–xiv; John Meyendorff, et al., *A Legacy of Excellence: St. Vladimir's Orthodox Theological Seminary* (Crestwood, N.Y.: St. Vladimir's Seminary Press, 1988).

17. The papers of this conference will soon be published by Holy Cross Press. The editor is Lewis J. Patasaros.

18. "SCOBA Hierarchs Unite in Decision to Suspend NCCC Membership," *The Orthodox Church* 27:10/11 (1991): 1; "Orthodox Provisionally Resume NCCC Membership," *The Orthodox Church* 28:5 (1992): 8; Anthony Ugolnik, "An Ecumenical Estrangement: Orthodoxy in America," *Christian Century* (June 17–24, 1992): 610–616.

19. *Monastic Typicon* (Cambridge, N.Y.; New Skete, 1980), p. 2.

20. Stanley Harakas, *Let Mercy Abound* (Brookline, Mass.: Holy Cross Orthodox Press, 1983), p. 33.

21. "Ten Memorable Days," *The Orthodox Church* 28:1/2 (1992): 8–9.

22. "IOCC Established," *The Orthodox Church* 28:5 (1992): 6.

23. Alexander Veronis, "Eastern Europe: An Historic Challenge for Orthodoxy," *Mission* 8:1 (1992): 12.

24. These words are from prayer petitions offered at the Eucharist and at most other services of common prayer in the Orthodox Church.

Part Two
A BIOGRAPHICAL DICTIONARY OF ORTHODOX LEADERS

ABBREVIATIONS USED IN THIS VOLUME

DAS   *Dictionary of American Scholars,* 8th edition, 4 vols. (New York, 1982).

DCA   *Dictionary of Christianity in America* (Downers Grove, IL, 1990).

GOTR   *The Greek Orthodox Theological Review.*

OA   *Orthodox America: 1794–1976* (Syosset, NY, 1975).

OC   *The Orthodox Church.*

OO   *The Orthodox Observer.*

RLA   *Religious Leaders of America* (Detroit, 1991).

SVTQ   *St. Vladimir's Theological Quarterly.*

WWR   *Who's Who in Religion* (Chicago, 1977, 1985, 1992). Edition specified by year in the bibliography.

A

AGHIORGOUSSIS, MAXIMOS DEMETRIOS (5 March 1935, Chios, Greece–). *Education:* diploma, Patriarchal Theological School of Halki, Turkey, 1957; B.Phil., University of Louvain, 1964; Dr. Theol., 1964. *Career:* ordained a priest, 1957; pastorates in Brussels, Belgium, 1961–62; Louvain, Belgium, 1959–64; Rome, Italy, 1965–66; professor of systemic theology, Holy Cross School of Theology, 1967–78; consecrated titular bishop of Diokleia, 1978; visiting professor, Christ the Savior Seminary, 1979–present; visiting professor, St. Vladimir's Seminary, 1991–92; bishop of Pittsburgh, 1979–present.

Bishop Maximos is regarded as the preeminent Orthodox systematic theologian in the United States. He is a specialist on the writings of St. Basil the Great and on the relationships between Orthodoxy and Roman Catholicism. Prior to his teaching and pastoral responsibilities in this country, he represented the Ecumenical Patriarchate at the Second Vatican Council. Since coming to the United States in 1966, Bishop Maximos has served the Ecumenical Patriarchate and Greek Orthodox Archdiocese at a number of theological gatherings, especially those dealing with ecumenical witness. Since 1967 he has been a member of the Orthodox-Roman Catholic Bilateral Consultation and is presently its Orthodox chairman. He has also served (1979–81) as a vice president of the National Council of Churches.

Bibliography

A. *La dialectique de l'image de Dieu d'après Saint Basile le Grand* (Louvain, 1964); *San Francisco d'Assisi e la Spiritualita Ortodossa* (Rome, 1966); "East Meets West: Gifts of the Eastern Tradition to the Whole Church," *SVTQ* 37:1 (1993), 3–22.
B. *WWR* (1992), 332.

AJALAT, CHARLES   (4 March 1947, Los Angeles, CA–   ). *Education:* B.A., Harvard College, 1968; J.D., University of California at Berkeley Law School, 1971. *Career:* private law practice, 1971–present; chancellor, Antiochian Orthodox Christian Archdiocese, 1991–present.

A member of the Antiochian Orthodox Christian archdiocese, Charles Ajalat serves this jurisdiction as its chancellor and is a member of a number of its committees. He has been active in Pan-Orthodox activities, especially as chief executive officer for Orthodox Christian Charities (1991–92) and as a member of the Task Force on Mission and Evangelization of the Standing Conference of Orthodox Bishops. He also serves as coordinator for the Committee on Common English Translations. He is a member of the Central Committee of the World Council of Churches.

ALLEN, JOSEPH   (31 January 1943, Wilkes-Barre, PA–   ). *Education:* B.S., Kutztown State University, 1964; M. Div., St. Vladimir's Seminary, 1969; S.T.M., Union Theological Seminary, 1971; Th.D., General Theological Seminary, 1978. *Career:* ordained a priest, 1967; pastor in Bergenfield, NJ, 1967–92; assistant professor, Holy Cross Seminary, 1977–92; professor of pastoral theology, St. Vladimir's Seminary, 1978–92; vicar general, Antiochian Orthodox archdiocese, 1983–92; director of theological education and assistant to the metropolitan, Antiochian Orthodox archdiocese, 1992–present.

A priest of the Antiochian Orthodox archdiocese, Joseph Allen has been a pioneer in the development of an approach to pastoral theology that is both rooted in the spiritual traditions of the Orthodox faith and sensitive to the insights of the social sciences. His extensive writings have also demonstrated a concern for issues related to pastoral preparation and renewal.

Bibliography

A. *Out of the Depth* (Brookline, MA, 1979); *Orthodox Synthesis* (Crestwood, NY, 1981); *The Mystery of Fidelity* (Brookline, MA, 1984); *The Ministry of the Church* (Crestwood, NY, 1986); *Inner Way: Eastern Christian Spiritual Direction* (Grand Rapids, MI, 1994).

ANDREWS, TIMOTHY   (2 January 1914, Salem, MA–   ). *Education:* B.A., Gorden College, 1937; B. Div., Holy Cross School of Theology, 1942; B.L.S., Pratt Institute, 1944; M.A., Columbia University, 1950. *Career:* librarian, Pratt Institute, New York, 1943–53; ordained a priest, 1953; pastorates in San Antonio, TX; Lawrence, MA; Ipswich, MA; Brookline, MA, 1953–79; librarian, Hellenic College–Holy Cross Greek Orthodox School of Theology, 1954–79; active retirement, 1979–present.

As librarian at Holy Cross Greek Orthodox School of Theology, Timothy Andrews worked diligently to establish one of the most comprehensive collections of books dealing with Orthodox Christianity in this part of the world. In addition, he generously provided generations of students and scholars with bibliographical information and guidance on sources.

Bibliography

A. *The Eastern Orthodox Church: A Biography* (New York, 1953, rev. ed., 1957).
B. *Pomfret the Golden Decade*, ed. George Poulis (Brookline, MA, 1988), 79.

APOSTOLA, NICHOLAS (30 April 1951, Sturbridge, MA–). *Education:* B.A., University of Massachusetts, Amherst, 1973; M. Div., Holy Cross School of Theology, 1980; Ph.D., Boston University, 1995. *Career:* coordinator, Eastern Orthodox Council of Churches of Central Massachusetts, 1978–present; ordained a priest, 1980; pastor, Worcester, MA, 1980–present; secretary, Romanian Orthodox Missionary archdiocese, 1980–present; faculty member, Hellenic College–Holy Cross School of Theology, 1985–91.

Nicholas Apostola is a priest of the Romanian Orthodox Missionary Archdiocese. In his lecturing and scholarly work, he has explored the relationship between the Orthodox faith and values of modern society. He has also been active in the movement toward greater administrative unity among the Orthodox. He is a member of the Study and Planning Committee of the Standing Conference of Orthodox Bishops. He also serves on the Orthodox-Roman Catholic Consultation and upon the Unit I Commission of the World Council of Churches.

Bibliography

A. Editor, *A Guide to the Music of the Eastern Orthodox Church* (Brookline, MA, 1984); *A Report on Baptism, Eucharist, and Ministry of the Orthodox Theological Society* (Brookline, MA, 1984); "The Reestablishment of the Greek Catholic Church in Romania Following the December, 1989 Revolution," *GOTR* 35:4 (1990), 299–316.

ARSENIEV, NICHOLAS (1888, Stockholm, Sweden–18 December 1977, New York). *Education:* graduate studies at the Universities of Moscow, Freiburg, and Berlin. *Career:* lecturer in the history of religions, University of Moscow, 1914–18; professor of religions, University of Saratov, 1918–20; professor of Russian culture, University of Köningsberg, 1920–26; professor of New Testament and comparative religions, University of Warsaw, 1926–48; professor of New Testament and apologetics, St. Vladimir's Theological Seminary, 1948–72.

After an early career teaching at Moscow and Saratov, Arseniev left Russia during the civil war and then taught at Köningsberg and Warsaw. Coming to the United States in 1948, he became a professor at St. Vladimir's Theological Seminary. He was known for a breadth of knowledge that included the ancient Greek philosophers, the New Testament, and the church fathers, as well as Pushkin and Tolstoy.

Bibliography

A: *We Beheld His Glory* (New York, 1936); *Holy Moscow* (New York, 1940); *Mysticism and the Eastern Church* (Crestwood, NY, 1979); *Russian Piety* (Crestwood, NY, 1975); *Revelation of Eternal Life* (Crestwood, NY, 1982).
B: *SVTQ* 34:1 (1988), 74–75.

ASHANIN, CHARLES B. (15 November 1920, Montenegro, Yugoslavia–   ). *Education:* B.D., University of Glasgow, Scotland, 1952; Ph.D., 1955. *Career:* assistant professor of religion, University College of Ghana, 1955–60; associate professor of philosophy of religion, Allen University, Columbia, SC, 1960–65; associate professor of religion, Claflan University, Orangeburg, SC, 1965–67; professor of early church history, Christian Theological Seminary, Indianapolis, 1967–90; active retirement, 1990–present.

Charles Ashanin left his native Yugoslavia in 1945 for Italy and later for England and Scotland. Coming to the United States in 1960, he served at a number of academic institutions, teaching in the area of religion. His most recent appointment at Christian Theological Seminary helped to expose many Protestant students to the traditions of early Christianity and to the Orthodox Church. Active in programs in spiritual renewal, Ashanin is a popular speaker on Orthodox spirituality and religious developments in Eastern Europe.

Bibliography

A. *Essays on Orthodox Christianity and Church History* (Indianapolis, 1990).
B. *DAS* (1974), 14.

B

BARROIS, GEORGES A. (17 February 1898, Les Hautes-Rivières, France–27 August 1987, Princeton, NJ). *Education:* doctorate in theology, Tournai (Belgium), 1924; *Prolyta in Sacra Scriptura,* Vatican, 1932. *Career:* Dominican monk and Roman Catholic priest, ordained in 1923; taught Old Testament in Rome, France, Belgium, and Jerusalem, 1924–40; left the Roman Catholic Church in 1940 and subsequently married in 1942; professor of history and theology, Princeton University, 1945–68; entered the Orthodox Church in 1968; visiting professor of Old Testament, St. Vladimir's Theological Seminary, 1968–86.

When the theological and spiritual journey finally led Georges Barrois to join the Orthodox Church in 1968, he already had a reputation as a foremost scholar of the Old Testament. As a Dominican monk, he had received his early training in theology in Tournai, Belgium. After military service for France in Syria as part of a League of Nations mandate, he returned to Tournai, received his doctorate in theology in 1942, and joined the French Biblical School in Jerusalem. Having received the special degree of *Prolyta in Sacra Scriptura* at the Vatican, Barrois returned to Etiolles, France, as professor of Old Testament studies.

In the years prior to World War II, an antimodernist movement supported by Pope Pius XII was directed against the French Dominican biblical scholars in Jerusalem. Because of this, Barrois traveled to the United States and taught briefly at Catholic University. Deeply troubled by the circumstances of his order and the actions of Rome, he subsequently left the Roman Catholic Church. Between 1945 and 1968, Barrois taught at Princeton Theological Seminary as professor of history and theology of the medieval church. While there, he also developed a friendship with Father John Turkevich and Father Georges Florovsky. This association provided the formal basis for Barrois's entrance into the Orthodox Church in 1968. After retiring from Princeton in the same year, Barrois became a visiting professor at St. Vladimir's Theological Seminary and was very active in the work of Orthodox biblical scholarship until his death in 1987.

Bibliography

A. *Precis d'Archeologie Biblique* (Paris, 1935); *Manuel d'Archeologie Biblique* (Paris, 1939–53); *The Face of Christ in the Old Testament* (Crestwood, NY, 1974); *Scripture Readings in Orthodox Worship* (Crestwood, NY, 1977); *Jesus Christ in the Temple* (Crestwood, NY, 1980); *The Fathers Speak* (Crestwood, NY, 1986).
B. *SVTQ* 31:4 (1987), 283–84.

BASHIR, ANTONY   (15 March 1898, Douma Lebanon–15 February 1966, Boston, MA). *Education:* diploma, Balamand Theological Seminary, Tripoli, Lebanon, 1916; diploma, American University of Beirut. *Career:* ordained a priest, 1916; professor at the American University of Beirut; began pastoral work in the United States, 1922; archbishop of Syrian Antiochian Orthodox archdiocese, 1935–66.

Before coming to this country, Bashir was known for his work as a translator of Arabic literature in Lebanon. Following his arrival in the United States, he spent about thirteen years traveling throughout the country strengthening and organizing parishes that served the needs of Arab Orthodox immigrants. Highly regarded for his pastoral and organizational skills, he was elected to succeed Archbishop Victor AbuAssaly in 1936 as head of the jurisdiction directly related to the Patriarchate of Antioch. This diocese had been established in 1924 and included many of the parishes, composed of Arab Orthodox immigrants, that had been previously associated with the Russian Orthodox Metropolia.

Metropolitan Antony's authority was immediately challenged by Metropolitan Samuel David. Consecrated a bishop on the same day, Samuel David organized a diocese composed of parishes that opposed Antony's leadership. This rival jurisdiction was eventually recognized by the Patriarch of Antioch. But the full integration of the two jurisdictions did not take place until 1975, under Antony's successor, Metropolitan Philip Saliba, and David's successor, Archbishop Michael Shaheen.

Metropolitan Antony had a strong commitment to the establishment of an indigenous Orthodox Church in America. Within his own jurisdiction, he encouraged the use of English in liturgical services, advocated a strong program in religious education, and welcomed persons from other religious traditions who wished to become Orthodox. He was one of the organizers of the Federation of Primary Jurisdictions in 1938 and the Standing Conference of Orthodox Bishops in 1960.

Bibliography

A. *Studies in the Greek Orthodox Church* (New York, 1960).
B. *DCA,* 120; *OA,* 195.

BELLAVIN, TIKHON BASIL (19 January 1865, Klin, Russia–7 April 1925, Moscow). *Education:* diploma, St. Petersburg Theological Academy, 1888. *Career:* ordained a priest, 1891; bishop of Lubin, 1897; bishop of Aleutian Islands and North America, 1898; archbishop, 1905–07; archbishop of Iaraslav and Rostov, 1907–13; archbishop of Lithuania and Vilna, 1914–17; Metropolitan of Moscow, 19 June 1917; Patriarch of Moscow and all Rus, 5 November 1917–25; proclaimed a saint, 1989.

When Tikhon was elected bishop of the Aleutian Islands and Alaska in 1898, he became responsible for the Russian Orthodox mission in North America begun in 1794. With the permission of the synod of the Church of Russia, he guided the transfer of the diocesan center from San Francisco to New York in 1905 in order to be closer to the parishes in the East recently established by immigrants from Carpatho-Russia, the Ukraine, the Balkans, and the Middle East. The title of the Archdiocese had been changed in 1900 to include all of North America. After 1904, he was assisted by two auxiliary bishops, Innocent Pustynsky and Raphal Hawaweeny.

Given the title archbishop in 1905, Tikhon traveled through his vast Archdiocese. He was an early proponent of Orthodox unity in America. He made a bold proposal in 1905 to the synod of the Church of Russia for the organization of the church in America. He recognized the missionary character of the church in America and the need to unite the various Orthodox immigrant groups into a single church. He was also a forceful advocate of the use of English in liturgical services.

Tikhon was called back to Russia to serve in Iaraslav in 1907 and in Vilna in 1914. He was elected Metropolitan of Moscow in 1917 following the abdication of Tzar Nicholas II. The historic Church Council of 1917–18 in Moscow restored the office of patriarch, suppressed by Peter the Great in 1700, and elected Tikhon by lot from three candidates on 5 November 1917.

In the face of the Bolshevik revolution and the Russian civil war, Tikhon excommunicated those whom he termed the "enemies of Christ, open or disguised," on 1 November 1918, although he maintained political neutrality and advised the Russian clergy to do the same. He opposed the Living Church movement within Russia and did not sanction the Russian émigrés who advocated the restoration of the monarchy. He was imprisoned from May 1922 to June 1923. Under mysterious circumstances, he died on 7 April 1925. Long venerated as a confessor of the faith by Orthodox both in Russia and in the United States, Tikhon was formally canonized as a saint in 1989.

Bibliography

B. Leonid Kishkovsky, "Archbishop Tikhon in America," *SVTQ* 19:1 (1975), 9–31.

BELONICK, DEBORAH MALACKY (13 July 1951–). *Education:* B.S., Kent State University; M.Div., St. Vladimir's Orthodox Theological School. *Career:* researcher, author, and lecturer, 1975–present.

Deborah Belonick is among those Orthodox theologians who has successfully used the rich insights of the patristic tradition to illuminate contemporary concerns regarding the identity of the human person. With a firm understanding of Orthodox theology, she has done pioneering work in her writings and lectures to address many of the issues raised by feminist theologians. She served on the Faith and Order Commission of the National Council of Churches from 1978 to 1984. She was also involved in consultations of the World Council of Churches at Epiney in 1979 and Sheffield in 1981 dealing with the theme of "The Community of Women and Men in the Church." As a theologian of the Orthodox Church in America, she serves as a member of its Department of External Affairs and as the editor of the journal *Jacob's Well.* A popular lecturer at conferences and retreats, she is a member of the Orthodox Theological Society in America.

Bibliography

A. *Feminism and Christianity: An Orthodox Christian Response* (Syosset, NY, 1983); "The Spirit of the Female Priesthood," in *Women and the Priesthood,* ed. Thomas Hopko (Crestwood, NY, 1983), pp. 135–168; "Feminist Theology: An Orthodox Christian Perspective," in *Rome and Constantinople,* ed. Robert Barriger (Brookline, MA, 1984), pp. 73–85; "Women in Orthodoxy," *Ecumenism* 77:3 (1985), 14–17; "Revelation and Metaphors: The Significance of the Trinitarian Names, Father, Son and Holy Spirit," *Union Seminary Quarterly Review* 40:3 (1985), 31–42.

BJERRING, NICHOLAS   (1831 Denmark–c. 1884, New York). *Education:* University of Breslau, Denmark. *Career:* professor, St. Mary's Seminary, Baltimore, 1868–70; ordained an Orthodox priest, 1870; founder of first Orthodox parish in New York, 1870; editor of *Oriental Church Magazine,* 1879–81.

Born and educated in Denmark, Nicholas Bjerring became a naturalized citizen following his appointment as professor of philosophy and history at St. Mary's Roman Catholic Seminary in Baltimore in 1868. After the promulgation of the dogma of papal infallibility in 1870, he published a major statement opposing the new doctrine. It was widely circulated and translated into a number of languages. Following contacts with Europeans who had recently entered the Orthodox Church, Bjerring petitioned the Church of Russia to receive him. During a visit to St. Petersburg, he was received into the Orthodox Church in 1870 and was subsequently ordained a priest in St. Petersburg. He arrived in New York in the same year with a mandate from the Holy Synod of the Church of Russia to establish an Orthodox parish there. Created in 1870, his parish in New York City was the first Orthodox church on the East Coast.

During the next decade, Bjerring was also engaged in translating Orthodox liturgical texts and doctrinal essays into English. He was responsible for establishing and editing the quarterly *Oriental Church Magazine* (1879–81). This was the first journal devoted to the Orthodox Church to be published in the United States. His ministry, lectures, translations, and publications enabled many Americans of the late nineteenth century to gain a deeper appreciation of the Orthodox church.

Bibliography

A. *Office for Admission and Reception of Converts into the Orthodox Church* (New York, 1872); trans., *The Divine Liturgies of Our Holy Fathers John Chrysostom and Basil the Great* (New York, 1873); *The Offices of the Oriental Church* (New York, 1884).
B. *OA*, 40–41.

BOLOTOV, JOSEPH IVAN ILYICH   (22 January 1761, Kashin Ujezd, Russia–? May 1799, Alaskan coast). *Education:* Tver Seminary and Valaam Monastery, c. 1786. *Career:* appointed head of mission to Alaska, 1793; arrived in Alaska, 1794; elected first Orthodox bishop for North America, 1799; consecrated bishop of Kodiak in Irkutsk, 10 April 1799.

Father Joseph (Ioasaf) was selected to head the first group of Russian Orthodox missionaries sent to Alaska in 1794. The original group included seven other monks and two novices. Joseph had studied at the Tver Seminary. Yet, little else is known about his background or that of the others. After journeying 293 days and covering over 7,327 miles, the missionaries arrived in Kodiak on 24 September 1794. With a few months, they established the Holy Resurrection Church in Kodiak, which served as the center of their missionary work among the native population. In 1799, Joseph was recalled to Russia and was elected the first bishop of Kodiak. He was consecrated on 10 April 1789 in Irkutsk. Archbishop Benjamin of Irkutsk was the sole ordaining bishop. On the return trip to Alaska, the ship with Bishop Joseph aboard capsized, and all perished. Not until 1840 was another bishop elected to oversee the Alaskan mission: Bishop Innocent Veniaminov, who had served as a missionary there since 1824.

Bibliography

B. Michael Oleska, ed., *Alaskan Missionary Spirituality* (Mahwah, NJ, 1987) and *Orthodox Alaska* (Crestwood, NY, 1992).

BOOJAMRA, JOHN LAWRENCE   (8 June 1942, Brooklyn, NY–   ). *Education:* B.S., Brooklyn College, 1964; M.Div., St. Vladimir's Orthodox Theological Seminary, 1967; M.A., Fordham University, 1970; Ph.D., 1976. *Career:* teacher, Brooklyn Technical High School, 1968–present; adjunct professor in Christian education and church history, St. Vladimir's Seminary, 1977–present; lecturer in history, Fordham University, 1985–present.

A member of the Antiochian Orthodox Christian archdiocese, John Boojamra has been actively involved both in the study and teaching of Orthodox Church history and in the study and teaching of religious education. For over ten years, he has served as the director of Christian education for his archdiocese and as the executive secretary of the Orthodox Christian Education Commission.

Bibliography

A. "Emperor Theodosius and the Establishment of Christianity," *Byzantina* 9 (1977),
384–407; "Problems Concerning Autocephaly," *GOTR* 24 (1979), 129–200; "Anas-
tasios of Constantinople," *Church History* 48 (1979), 27–48; "Socialization Theory
as the Basis for an Historical Model of Christian Education," *SVTQ* 25 (1979),
219–37; *Church Reform in the Late Byzantine Empire* (Thessalonika, Greece,
1982); *Foundations of Christian Education* (Crestwood, NY, 1987).

BRECK, JOHN R.   (8 January 1939, New York City–   ). *Education:* A.B.,
Brown University, 1960; M.Div., Yale Divinity School, 1965; Dr. Theol.,
Ruprecht-Karl Universitat, Heidelberg, 1972; postdoctoral studies, St. Sergius
Theological Institute, Paris, 1973–75. *Career:* director of continuing education for
pastors, Neuchâtel, Switzerland, 1972–75; professor of New Testament and patristics, St. Herman Seminary, Kodiak, AK, 1975–78; ordained a priest, 1977; professor of New Testament, St. Sergius Theological Institute, Paris, 1978–84;
professor of New Testament and ethics, St. Vladimir's Orthodox Theological Seminary, 1984–present.

John Breck is well known among the Orthodox here and abroad both for his
scholarly work in New Testament studies and for his investigations in the area of
medical ethics. He is among the very few Orthodox theologians to have written
and spoken on topics related to genetic engineering and biomedical technology. A
priest of the Orthodox Church in America, he has served it through membership
on a number of committees dealing with issues related to ministry and theological
education. He has served as the editor of *St. Vladimir's Theological Quarterly*
since 1985.

Bibliography

A. *The Power of the Word* (Crestwood, NY, 1986); "Bio-Medical Technology: Of the Kingdom or of the Cosmos?" *SVTQ* 32:1 (1988), 5–26; "Selective Treatment of the Ter-
minally Ill," *SVTQ* 33:3 (1989), 261–72; *The Spirit of Truth: The Origins of
Johannine Pneumatology* (Crestwood, NY, 1991); "John 21: Appendix, Epilogue or
Conclusion?" *SVTQ* 36:1–2 (1992); "Divine Initiative: Salvation in Orthodox Theology," in *Salvation in Christ,* ed. J. Meyendorff and R. Tobias (Minneapolis, 1992).

BURDEN, BORIS   (15 July 1898, North East, PA–26 March 1973, Amsterdam,
NY). *Education:* A.A., William and Mary College, 1921; graduate studies, Yale
Divinity School, c. 1925. *Career:* ordained a priest, 1922; administrative duties,
St. Nicholas Cathedral, New York, 1922–c. 1940; pastoral responsibilities, Buf-
falo, NY, 1940–73.

Boris Burden was deeply devoted to greater unity among the Orthodox jurisdictions at times when such a conviction was not held by many. He established the
Orthodox Catholic Review in 1927 as a vehicle for exposing Orthodox teachings
to the wider society. For some years after this, he was associated with attempts to

establish an American Orthodox Church. When this attempt was not successful, Burden returned to the jurisdiction of the exarchate of the Patriarchate of Moscow. He was one of the organizers of the Federation of Orthodox Greek Catholic Primary Jurisdictions in 1940. It was the first successful attempt to bring together for common efforts the representatives of a number of diocesan jurisdictions. He established the Orthodox Catholic Alliance in 1944 as an association devoted primarily to Orthodox unity. This association developed a sizable collection of books on the Orthodox Church, which were donated to the State University of New York in Buffalo in 1973.

Bibliography

A. "The Holy Eastern Orthodox Catholic and Apostolic Church, *Orthodox Catholic Review* 1:1 (1927), 7–16.

B. *One Church* 27:5 (1973), 224; *Diakonia* 9:2 (1974), 186–87.

C

CALIVAS, ALKIVIADIS (2 December 1932, Buliarate, Albania, Northern Epiros–). *Education:* B.A., Holy Cross School of Theology, 1956; S.T.B., General Theological Seminary, 1960; Th.M., St. Vladimir's Seminary, 1970; Th.D., University of Thessaloniki, 1982. *Career:* ordained a priest, 1956; pastorates in Brooklyn, NY, and Washington Heights, NY; faculty member, Holy Cross School of Theology, now professor of liturgics, 1978–present, and dean, 1980–93.

A priest of the Greek Orthodox Archdiocese, Alkiviadis Calivas is one of the foremost authorities on the Byzantine liturgical tradition. Through his teaching and administrative service at Holy Cross School of Theology, he has also been a preeminent spokesman for the significance of theological education in the church today.

Bibliography

A. *The Divine Liturgy: The Time of Its Celebration* (Thessaloniki, 1978); *Come Before God* (Brookline, MA, 1986); *Great Week and Pascha in the Greek Orthodox Church* (Brookline, MA, 1992); "The Date of Pascha, the Need to Continue the Debate," *GOTR* 35:3 (1990), 333–43.

CHORNOCK, ORESTES (11 July 1883, Ortutova, Austro-Hungarian Empire–17 February 1977, Stamford, CT). *Education:* diploma, Presov Theological Academy, 1906. *Career:* married and ordained a priest, 1906; pastor, St. Michael Greek Catholic Church, Osturna, 1906–8; arrived in the United States and served parishes in Chicago, Cleveland, Duquesne, and Bridgeport, 1908–38; entered the jurisdiction of the ecumenical patriarchate of Constantinople and ordained bishop of Agathonikeia, 1938; head of the Carpatho-Russian Greek Catholic diocese, 1938–77.

Orestes Chornock and his wife came to the United States in 1908 to serve within the Eastern-Rite Catholic diocese, chiefly serving Carpatho-Russian (Ruthenian) immigrants from the old Austro-Hungarian Empire. Division among the Carpatho-Russians who remained Greek Catholics and related to Rome and those who entered into the Russian Orthodox diocese dated from the late nineteenth century.

Shortly after coming to this country, Chronock became associated with Greek Catholic clergymen who challenged the intention of the Vatican to prevent married men from being ordained for the Eastern Catholic parishes in this country. This was expressed in the decrees *Ea Semper* of 1908 and in *Cum Data Fuerit* of 1929. The opponents of these decrees claimed that the Vatican's desire to require a celibate priesthood among the Eastern Catholics in the United States not only was a violation of the principles of the Unions of the sixteenth and seventeenth centuries but also was an infringement upon the legitimate traditions of the Carpatho-Russian people.

While serving at the parish in Bridgeport, Connecticut, Chornock became a vocal critic of the Vatican's policy and of his bishop, Basil Takach, who refused to ordain married men to the priesthood. Chornock, together with four other priests, was suspended from pastoral duties in 1931. Despite their appeals to Rome, the Vatican refused to reconsider its policy on celibacy and reaffirmed the suspensions of the priests. Unwilling to accept the Vatican's position and be reconciled with Bishop Takach, Chornock and the others continued to serve their parishes and to challenge the actions of the bishop.

The opponents to Bishop Takach established a new diocese in 1935, and Chornock was selected as its administrator. Following the death of his wife in 1936, many began to propose him as a potential bishop. Following the formal excommunication of Chornock and five other priests in 1937, the leaders of the new diocese recognized that association with the Roman Catholic Church was no longer possible, and they began to investigate the establishment of a canonical relationship with the Orthodox Church. Fearing Russification in the Russian Orthodox archdiocese, the Carpatho-Russians turned to Archbishop Athenagoras of the Greek Orthodox archdiocese. He proposed to the ecumenical patriarchate the acceptance of the Carpatho-Russian diocese and the consecration of Chornock as its first bishop. This formally took place in Constantinople in 1938.

Although plagued by court battles over parish property, Chornock set out immediately to provide his diocese with a firm administrative and educational basis. After losing control of his Bridgeport cathedral, Chornock established a new cathedral and diocesan center in Johnstown, Pennsylvania in 1950. A year later, in 1951, he started Christ the Saviour Seminary in Johnstown. This school continued the modest seminary he had established in New York in 1940. Prior to his death in 1977, Chornock headed a diocese that contained about seventy parishes.

Bibliography

B. Lawrence Barriger, *Good Victory* (Brookline, MA, 1985).

CONIARIS, ANTHONY MICHAEL   (4 April 1936, Boston–   ). *Education:* B.A.TH., Holy Cross Greek Orthodox School of Theology, 1948; M.Div., Northwestern Theological Seminary, 1949. *Career:* ordained a priest, 1950; pastor, St. Mary Church, Minneapolis, 1953–93; president, Light and Life Publications, 1953–present; pastor emeritus, 1993–present.

Anthony Coniaris is priest of the Greek Orthodox Archdiocese who is widely regarded for his pastoral ministry in Minneapolis. He has made a major contribution to religious formation and education through the publication of well over twenty books and booklets dealing with Orthodox spirituality and worship. The founder of Light and Life Publications, Coniaris has also been instrumental in publishing books and pamphlets by a number of other Orthodox authors dealing with a wide variety of topics. A popular preacher and lecturer, he is a frequent speaker at retreats and conferences.

Bibliography

A. *Eastern Orthodoxy: A Way of Life* (Minneapolis, 1966); *No Man Ever Spoke as This Man* (Minneapolis, 1969); *Orthodoxy: A Creed for Today* (Minneapolis, 1971); *Getting Ready for Marriage in the Orthodox Church* (Minneapolis, 1972); *Gems from the Sunday Gospels* (Minneapolis, 1975); *Making God Real in the Orthodox Christian Home* (Minneapolis, 1977).
B. *WWR* (1977), 128.

CONSTANTELOS, DEMETRIOS   (27 July 1927, Spelia, Greece–   ). *Education:* B.A., Holy Cross School of Theology, 1958; Th.M., Princeton Theological Seminary, 1959; M.A., Rutgers University, 1963; Ph.D., 1965. *Career:* ordained a priest, 1955; pastorates in Perth Amboy, NJ, 1955–64, and Lexington, MA, 1965–67; associate professor of history, Hellenic College, 1965–71; professor of history and religious studies, Richard Stockton College of New Jersey, 1971–86; Charles Cooper Townsend Distinguished Professor of history and religious studies, 1971–present.

A priest of the Greek Orthodox archdiocese, Demetrios Constantelos is widely regarded as a foremost expert on issues of social welfare in the Byzantine Empire. His major writings have investigated the theme of philanthropy as it was expressed in the ancient world, within the early Christian tradition, and finally within the life of Byzantine society. Both in this country and abroad, he has been active in scholarly associations as well as ecumenical and interfaith dialogues.

Bibliography

A. *An Old Faith for Modern Man* (New York, 1964); *Byzantine Philanthropy and Social Welfare* (New Brunswick, NJ, 1968; rev. ed., New Rochelle, NY, 1991); *Marriage, Sexuality, Celibacy: A Greek Orthodox Perspective* (Minneapolis, 1974); *Understanding the Greek Orthodox Church* (New York, 1982); *Poverty, Society and Philanthropy* (New Rochelle, NY, 1992); *Christian Hellenism* (New Rochelle, NY, 1993).
B. *WWR* (1977), 68.

CONSTANTINIDES, MICHAEL   (27 May 1892, Marinia, Greece–13 July 1958, New York). *Education:* diploma, Patriarchal Theological School of Halki, 1915; student, theological academies of Kiev and St. Petersburg, Russia, 1915–19. *Career:* ordained a priest and served in parishes in Turkey and Russia, 1919–27; dean, St. Sophia Cathedral, London, 1927–39; elected a bishop and Metropolitan of Corinth, 1939; elected archbishop of America, 1949.

Archbishop Michael succeeded Archbishop Athenagoras, who had served the Greek Orthodox Church from 1930 to 1948, when he was elected Ecumenical Patriarch of Constantinople. Prior to coming to the United States, Michael had distinguished himself as a parish priest in London and later as Metropolitan of Corinth. Having studied both in Constantinople and in Russia, Michael had the much-deserved reputation as a theologian prior to becoming archbishop of America. He participated in early ecumenical meetings in Lausanne in 1927 and Edinburgh in 1937.

During his service in America, Michael guided a vast archdiocese comprising over 400 parishes throughout North and South America. While his predecessor had done much to unite the previously divided parishes, composed chiefly of recent immigrants, Michael was confronted with an archdiocese composed chiefly of persons born and raised in this country. In order to respond to this reality, Michael encouraged the publication of Orthodox literature in English, including the archdiocese's journal, the *Orthodox Observer,* improved the religious education program, established the association known as the Greek Orthodox Youth of America, and strengthened the financial basis of the archdiocese. He led his archdiocese into membership in the National Council of Churches and served as one of the copresidents of the World Council of Churches.

Bibliography

A. *The Orthodox Church* (London, 1930; Brookline, MA, 1952)
B. *RLA*, 316.

CONTOS, LEONIDAS C.   (1929, Newburyport, MA–   ). *Education:* diploma, Holy Cross Greek Orthodox School of Theology, 1943; B.A., University of Bridgeport, 1950; Dr. Theol., Oxford University, 1963. *Career:* pastorates, Stamford, CT, 1944–51, and Los Angeles, CA, 1951–65; director of communications and ecumenical relations, Greek Orthodox archdiocese, 1965–66; president,

Hellenic College–Holy Cross School of Theology, 1966–72; senior editor, *Saturday Review,* 1972–73; pastorate, Belmont, CA, 1979–78; professor of Orthodox studies, Graduate Theological Union, Berkeley, CA, 1987–present.

Leonidas Contos is well known both for his contributions to Orthodox theological education and for his involvement in religious broadcasting. He is the founder and director of the Patriarch Athenagoras Orthodox Institute at the Graduate Theological Union at Berkeley, California. He has recently become involved in liturgical translations.

Bibliography

A. *Critical Text of St. Gregory Palamas' "Contra Akindynum"* (Thessaloniki, Greece, 1970); *In Season and Out of Season* (New York, 1972); *2001: The Church in Crisis* (Brookline, MA, 1982).

COUCHELL, DIMITRIOS (JAMES)   (17 February 1938, Greenville, SC–   ). *Education:* B.A., Holy Cross Greek Orthodox School of Theology, 1957–63; graduate studies, Yale University, 1963–64. *Career:* director, campus ministry, 1964–71; editor, *Concern Magazine,* 1966–71; editor, *Orthodox Observer,* 1971–81; director of ecumenical relations, Greek Orthodox archdiocese, 1979–81; director, St. Photios Foundation, 1981–present; ordained a priest, 1983; director, Archdiocesan Mission Center, 1985–present.

From being very active in the Orthodox youth movement in this country, Dimitrios Couchell has continued to serve the church in a number of positions related to publications, ecumenical witness, and missions. He has been on the forefront in reviving the spirit of missions within the Orthodox Church in this country. Under his direction, Orthodox mission teams have gone to serve in Africa, Eastern Europe, and Russia.

COUCOUSIS, IAKOVOS (JAMES) DEMETRIOS   (29 July 1911, St. Theodore, Imbros, Turkey–   ). *Education:* diploma, Patriarchal Seminary of Halki, 1934; S.T.M., Harvard Divinity School, 1946. *Career:* instructor, Holy Cross Greek Orthodox School of Theology, 1939; archdeacon, 1939; ordained a priest, 1940; pastorates in Hartford, New York, St. Louis, and Boston, 1940–54; consecrated titular bishop of Melita, 1955; representative of the Patriarchate of Constantinople to the World Council of Churches, 1955–59; archbishop of North and South America, 1959–present.

Archbishop Iakovos is the best-known Orthodox clergyman in America today. A native of Turkey, Iakovos received his early education in the schools associated with the Patriarchate of Constantinople at a time when wars and the transfer of populations ravaged much of the Balkans and Asia Minor. At the invitation of Archbishop Athenagoras of the United States, Coucousis came to this country in

1935 to teach at the newly established theological school then in Pomfret, Connecticut, and to pursue further studies. He was soon ordained a priest, in 1940. He was dean of the Annunciation Cathedral in Boston from 1942 to 1954. There, as well as in his previous parishes, he came to be known for his preaching, his pastoral sensitivities, and his concern for the younger generation.

After becoming a bishop in 1954, Iakovos was appointed by Patriarch Athenagoras to the newly created position as representative of the ecumenical patriarchate at the World Council of Churches (WCC). In this position, Iakovos quickly became recognized as a preeminent spokesmen for Orthodox theology. He helped many Orthodox to recognize that their obligation to be involved in the quest for Christian reconciliation did not mean a denial of Orthodox teachings. He also called upon Roman Catholics and Protestants to look beyond their divisions and to appreciate the insights of Orthodox Christianity. His involvement in the WCC helped to pave the way for greater and deeper Orthodox participation in its activities and the ecumenical movement generally. Between 1959 and 1968, he served as one of the copresidents of the WCC.

Elected Archbishop of the Greek Orthodox Archdiocese of North and South America in 1959, Iakovos returned to a local church that he knew well. Within his own vast archdiocese, Iakovos has acted to strengthen the mission and witness of the national church. He has encouraged the development of religious education programs both for the young and for adults. He has guided the development of Hellenic College and Holy Cross Greek Orthodox School of Theology. He has supported scholarly and popular publications dealing with Orthodox theology. He has overseen the restructuring of the vast archdiocese that created a number of dioceses headed by a diocesan bishop. He has called upon the members of his own flock to recognize the challenges that face the Orthodox and to affirm their distinctive mission in this society.

The influence of Archbishop Iakovos has reached far beyond the confines of his own archdiocese. Among the Orthodox in America, he is seen as their principal spokesman and leader. He was the initiator of the Standing Conference of Orthodox Bishops in 1960, and he has served as its chairman since then. Recognizing the obligation that the Orthodox have to this society, he became a forceful advocate of civil rights and marched with Dr. Martin Luther King in Selma in 1965.

Bibliography

A. *Faith for a Lifetime: A Spiritual Journey* (New York, 1988).
B. George Poulos, *Breath of God; A Biography of Archbishop Iakovos* (Brookline, MA, 1984).

D

DABOVICH, SABASTIAN JOHN   (21 June 1863, San Francisco–30 November 1940, Zitcha, Yugoslavia). *Education:* diploma, St. Petersburg Theological Academy, 1887. *Career:* ordained a priest, 1892; missionary in California, Washington, Minnesota, 1892–1905; administrator of Serbian Orthodox parishes, 1905–10; instructor at Orthodox Seminary, Tenafly, NJ, 1913–16; service in the Orthodox Church in Serbia, 1916–40.

Sabastian Dabovich was the first native-born Orthodox to be ordained a priest in San Francisco in 1892 following studies in Russia. During the last decade of the nineteenth century, he served a number of Orthodox immigrant communities both on the West Coast and in Minneapolis, where he followed Father Alexis Toth. In 1894 he established the first parish to serve Serbian Orthodox immigrants in Jackson, California. With the establishment of other parishes serving Serbian Orthodox immigrants, he was appointed their administrator by Archbishop Tikhon in 1896. Prior to going to Serbia in 1916, he taught briefly at the Orthodox Seminary in Tenafly, New Jersey.

Bibliography

A. *The Ritual Services and Sacraments of the Holy Orthodox Church* (San Francisco, 1896).
B. *OA*, 96; DCA, 566.

DONAHUE, PHOTIOS F. M.   (18 December 1913, Pittsburgh–1 November 1983, Lansing, MI). *Education:* M.A., Michigan State University, 1948; Ph.D., 1954. *Career:* ordained a priest, 1940; pastorates in New York, Chicago, East Lansing, MI, 1940–83; professor of religious studies, Michigan State University, c. 1954–78.

Photios Donahue was a leading cleric in the exarchate of the Moscow Patriarchate. He was active in promoting contact between the Church of Russia and the United States. He also was involved in the meetings of the National Council of Churches and World Council of Churches as a delegate of the Patriarchal Exarchate. Donahue was instrumental in organizing in 1954 the Eastern Orthodox Catechetical Association, one of the first Pan-Orthodox associations in this country. From its inauguration, it gathered together clergy and laity involved in religious education for a weeklong conference held in East Lansing, Michigan. He was editor of the journal *One Church* from 1962 to 1976.

Bibliography

B. *One Church* 37:5–6 (1983), 224.

E

EFTHIMIOU, MILTON   (20 January 1935, Boston–). *Education:* B.D., Holy Cross School of Theology; S.T.M., Boston University; Ph.D., Miami of Ohio University, 1974. *Career:* ordained a priest, 1958; pastoral and administrative position, Greek Orthodox archdiocese, 1958–present, now director of the office of church and society.

Milton Efthimiou is a priest of the Greek Orthodox Archdiocese. He has served that jurisdiction in a number of capacities in the areas of ecumenical witness and social concern. He has also represented the archdiocese and Ecumenical Patriarchate at national and international conferences.

Bibliography

A. *Greeks and Latins on Cyprus* (Brookline, MA, 1976); *A History of the Greek Orthodox Church in America* (New York, 1984).

ERICKSON, JOHN H.   (4 October 1943, Frostbite Falls, MN–). *Education:* A.B., Harvard College, 1966; M.Phil., Yale University, 1970; M.Th., St. Vladimir's Seminary, 1984. *Career:* instructor in canon law and church history, St. Vladimir's Seminary, 1973–85; director of studies, 1976–present; associate professor, 1985–91; assistant professor, 1991–present.

A theologian of the Orthodox Church in America, John Erickson is recognized as one of the foremost experts in Orthodox canon law. In addition to his graduate studies, he has also been a Robbins Fellow at the University of California School of Law and a Fellow at Dumbarton Oaks Center for Byzantine Studies. Erickson has served on a number of its commissions dealing with topics related to canon law, inter-Orthodox relations, and ministries. Widely respected for his contribution to ecumenical dialogues, he presently serves as a member of the Orthodox-Roman Catholic Consultation and the Anglican-Orthodox Consultation. He is a past president of the Orthodox Theological Society.

Bibliography

A. Coeditor, *Orthodox America, 1794–1976* (Syosset, NY, 1975); "*Oikonomia* in Byzantine Canon Law," in *Law, Church and Society,* ed. K. Pennington and R. Somerville (Philadelphia, 1977), 225–36; *The Challenge of Our Past* (Crestwood, NY, 1990).

F

FITZGERALD, KYRIAKI ANTONIA KARIDOYANES (17 January 1956, Boston–). *Education:* B.A., Hellenic College, 1977; M.Div., Holy Cross School of Theology, 1980; Certificate of Advanced Studies, School of Theology, University of Thessaloniki, 1978–79; Ph.D., Boston University, 1985. *Career:* assistant professor and pastoral counselor, Holy Cross School of Theology, 1984–90; adjunct clinical faculty, Andover Newton Theological School, 1986–91; director of Orthodox pastoral counseling, the Worcester Pastoral Counseling Center, Worcester, MA, and the Eastern Orthodox Council of Churches for Central Massachusetts, 1986–92; director of education and associate director of training, Institute of Pastoral Training, the Worcester Pastoral Counseling Center, 1987–91; licensed psychologist in private practice, 1990–present; visiting professor, the Ecumenical Institute, World Council of Churches, Geneva, Switzerland, 1992 and 1994; staff psychologist, Gosnold Counseling Center, Falmouth, MA, 1992–present; visiting professor in pastoral theology, St. Vladimir's Orthodox Theological Seminary, 1994–present.

With formal training in both Orthodox theology and psychology, Kyriaki FitzGerald has examined in her writings themes related to spirituality, pastoral care, and women in the church. As a member of the Faith and Order Commission of the World Council of Churches, she is a frequent participant in ecumenical conferences. A fellow in the American Association of the Pastoral Counselors, she is noted also for her lectures on the relationship between psychology and spiritual development.

Bibliography

A. *Religious Formation and Liturgical Life* (Ann Arbor, MI, 1985); "The Ministry of Women," *Journal of Ecumenical Studies* 20:4 (1983), 558–75; "The Characteristics and Nature of the Order of the Deaconess," in *Women and the Priesthood,* ed. Thomas Hopko (Crestwood, NY, 1983), 75–95; "Orthodox Women and Pastoral Praxis," in *Orthodox Perspectives on Pastoral Praxis,* ed. T. Stylianopoulos (Brookline, MA, 1988), 101–26; "The Spirit as Fire and Light," in *Come Holy Spirit,* ed. G. Limouris (Brookline, MA, 1990), 255–61; "Reflections on Spirituality and Prayer," in *Faith and Order 1985–89,* ed. T. Best (Geneva, 1990), 180–84; "Walls of the Heart," *Ecumenical Trends* 22:4 (1993), 13–16.

FLOROVSKY, GEORGES VASILYEVICH (28 August 1893, Odessa, Russia–11 August 1979, Princeton, NJ). *Education:* diploma, 1911; Magister Philosophiae, University of Novorosisk, 1919; Magister Philosophiae, Russian Academic Group, Prague, 1923. *Career:* instructor of the philosophy of law, University of Prague, 1922–26; professor of patristics, St. Sergius Theological Academy, Paris, 1926–48; professor of theology, St. Vladimir's Theological Seminary, 1948–55; dean, 1950–55; visiting professor of church history, Boston University, 1954–55; professor of patristics, Holy Cross Greek Orthodox School of Theology, 1955–59, 1963–65; professor of eastern church history, Harvard Divinity School, 1956–64; emeritus professor, 1964; professor of Slavic studies, Princeton University, 1964–79; visiting professor of Patristics, Princeton Theological Seminary, 1973–79.

Georges Florovsky is widely recognized as the most influential Orthodox theologian of the twentieth century. Born and raised in Odessa, Florovsky was deeply immersed in the religious and cultural renaissance of the late nineteenth century in Russia. His father was the rector of the Odessa Theological Academy and dean of the city's Cathedral of the Transfiguration. His mother, Klaudia Popruzhenko, was the daughter of a professor of Greek and Russian.

Florovsky's early education was in law and the social sciences. His first published article was written under the direction of a student of Pavlov and was entitled "On Reflex Salivary Secretions." Not until after his marriage on 27 April 1922 to Xenia Ivanova Simonova did he begin to deepen his long-standing interest in church history and theology. The Florovskys' move to Paris in 1926 brought them into contact with the vibrant Russian émigré community, where religious, political, and cultural issues were constantly discussed. Florovsky became one of the leaders of the Paris School of Orthodox theology centered at St. Sergius Institute. He was ordained a priest under the jurisdiction of the Patriarchate of Constantinople in 1932.

While serving as professor of patristics at St. Sergius Institute, Florovsky authored three monumental works in Russian dealing chiefly with the writings of the early fathers of the church. In *Eastern Fathers of the Fourth Century* (1931), *The Byzantine Fathers of the Fifth-Sixth Centuries* (1933), and *The Ways of Russian Theology* (1937), Florovsky not only provided a fresh perspective on the early Christian teachers but also called for a "neo-patristic synthesis." Florovsky believed that a renewed interest in the patristic themes and spirit could reinvigorate

Orthodox theology, which had become influenced by Western Christian perspectives and polemics, especially in Russia during the eighteenth and nineteenth centuries.

Florovsky also became one of the Orthodox Church's most respected representatives in the fledgling ecumenical contacts and dialogues in Europe during the 1930s and 1940s. He participated in the first Conference on Faith and Order in Edinburgh in 1937. His concern for Christian reconciliation was a topic of many of his scholarly articles in this period. He is regarded as having a major influence upon the formation of the World Council of Churches, finally established in 1948. His involvement in the activities of the World Council of Churches and the National Council of Churches continued following his move to America. He is regarded as one of the Orthodox theologians who forged a theological basis for Orthodox participation in ecumenical dialogues and associations.

The Florovskys made a monumental decision to move to the United States and to become associated with St. Vladimir's Seminary in 1948. The move was dictated by two major factors. First, Florovsky's relationships with some of his colleagues at St. Sergius were not always easy. This was due, in part, to his criticism of the theological teachings on Sophiology by Father Sergius Bulgakov. Second, Florovsky was frustrated with the lack of a Pan-Orthodox spirit and missionary concern in many of the older members of the St. Sergius faculty and supporters. Florovsky saw America as a place in which a unified Orthodox Church could make a major contribution to the religious and spiritual life of this country. He became a naturalized American citizen in 1954.

Florovsky became dean of St. Vladimir's in 1950 and immediately set out to strengthen its identity. He oriented the seminary toward the realities of America. Under his direction, English became the principal language of instruction and worship. While associated with the Russian Orthodox Metropolia, St. Vladimir's Seminary became more of a Pan-Orthodox institution. These developments were greatly aided by other professors who followed Florovsky from Paris. Among them were Alexander Schmemann (1951), Serge Verhovskoy (1952), and John Meyendorff (1959).

In 1955, Florovsky resigned and eventually accepted teaching positions at Holy Cross Greek Orthodox School of Theology and at the Harvard Divinity School. While at Holy Cross, Florovsky continued to advocate a return to the fathers and a concern for a united Orthodox Church in America that would transcend ethnic differences and Old World antagonisms. Through his teaching at Harvard, Florovsky had a profound effect upon a number of young scholars of various religious traditions who appreciated deeply his own command of the history and theology of the Orthodox Church as well as the hospitality of his home. Following his retirement from Harvard, he continued his teaching at Princeton until his death in 1979. He was a member of the Academy of Athens, the American Academy of Arts and Sciences, and the British Academy. He was one of the founding members of the Fellowship of St. Alban and Sergius and the Orthodox Theological Society in America.

Florovsky was both a scholar and an Orthodox theologian who was equally at home in the so-called secular institutions and in the so-called religious ones. His life and career bridged many worlds. Paris, St. Vladimir's, Holy Cross, Harvard, and Princeton have been enriched by his presence. He was convinced that one could detect the mind of the church in the writings of the fathers. His writings sought to bring patristic insights to bear upon contemporary challenges. His devotion to the Orthodox Church did not prevent him from forging bonds of love and interests with Roman Catholics and with Protestants. His books and articles continue to nurture and inspire both scholars and laypersons.

Bibliography

A. *Collected Works; Volumes 1–14* (Belmont, MA, 1972–89).
B. Alexander Schmemann, "In Memoriam, Georges Florovsky," *SVTQ* 23 (1979), 132–33; Thomas Bird, "In Memoriam, Georges Florovsky," *GOTR* 24 (1979), 342–50; W. A. Visser T'Hooft, "Fr. Georges Florovsky's Role in the Formation of the WCC," *SVTQ* 23 (1979), 135–38; Andrew Blane, ed. *Georges Florovsky: Russian Intellectual and Orthodox Churchman* (Crestwood, NY, 1993).

G

GEANAKOPLOS, DENO JOHN (11 August 1916, Minneapolis–). *Education:* B.A., University of Minnesota, 1941; M.A., 1946; D.Litt., University of Pisa, Italy, 1946; Ph.D., Harvard University, 1953. *Career:* instructor, Brandeis University, 1953–54; professor, University of Illinois, 1954–59; professor of medieval and Renaissance history, Yale University, 1967–present.

Deno Geanakoplos has introduced many to the Byzantine period of the Orthodox Church through his scholarly writings and lectures. His writings frequently examine the intricate relationships between the Christians of the East and West during the Middle Ages. He has been a visiting lecturer at universities in Athens, Paris, Rome, Thessaloniki, and Oxford. A member of the Greek Orthodox Archdiocese, he has served it in a number of capacities related to ecumenism, education, and church history.

Bibliography

A. *Emperor Michael Paleologis and the West* (Cambridge, 1959); *Greek Scholars in Venice* (Cambridge, 1962); *Byzantine East and Latin West in the Middle Ages and Renaissance* (New York, 1966); *Interaction of Sibling Byzantine and Western Cultures in the Middle Ages and Renaissance* (New York, 1975).
B. *DAS*, 1, 217–18.

GILLQUIST, PETER (13 July 1938, Minneapolis–). *Education:* B.A., University of Minnesota, 1960; graduate study, Dallas Theological Seminary, 1960–61; Wheaton College Graduate School, 1961–62. *Career:* regional director, Campus Crusade for Christ, 1960–68; director of development, Memphis State

University, 1969–72; freelance writing, 1972–76; senior editor, Thomas Nelson Publishing, 1976–86; president, Evangelical Orthodox Church, 1977–87; ordained a priest, 1987; chairman, Department of Missions, Antiochian Orthodox Christian archdiocese, 1987–present.

Peter Gillquist was one of the leaders who guided more than 2,000 evangelical Christians into the Orthodox Church in 1987. Beginning his ministry as an evangelical youth minister, Gillquist became increasingly interested in the teachings of the fathers of early Christianity. He and a number of other evangelical ministers established the Evangelical Orthodox Church in 1977. Ten years later, most of its members entered into full communion with the Orthodox Church through the Antiochian Orthodox Christian Archdiocese. Since then, Gillquist has devoted himself to writing and lecturing on the Orthodox faith and the church's mission in America.

Bibliography

A. *Making America Orthodox* (Brookline, MA, 1984); *Becoming Orthodox: A Journey to the Ancient Christian Faith* (Brentwood, TN, 1989); *Metropolitan Philip: His Life and Dreams* (Nashville, TN, 1991).

H

HADDAD, ROBERT MITCHELL (10 October 1930, New York–). *Education*: B.S., University of Pittsburgh, 1952; M.A., University of Michigan, 1954; Ph.D., Harvard University, 1965. *Career:* lecturer, Smith College, 1963–65; assistant professor, 1965–68; associate professor, 1968–73; professor of history and religion, 1973–82; Sophia Smith Professor of History and Professor of Religion, 1982–93; president, American University of Beirut, 1993–present.

Robert Haddad is a scholar specializing in the area of Islamic history and the relationship of Christians and Muslims in the Middle East. He is widely respected for his scholarly writings in these areas. Active in the affairs of the Antiochian Orthodox Christian Archdiocese, he has served it in areas related to interfaith relations, ecumenism, and education. He is presently a member of the Orthodox-Roman Catholic Consultation. He is the first Orthodox Christian of Arab background to serve as the president of the American University of Beirut.

Bibliography

A. *Syrian Christians in Muslim Society: An Interpretation* (Princeton, NJ, 1970); "Constantinople over Antioch, 1516–1724: Patriarchal Politics in the Ottoman Era," *Journal of Ecclesiastical History* 41:2 (1990); "The Conversion of Eastern Christians to the Unia," in *Conversion and Continuity: Indigenous Christian Communities in Islamic Lands,* ed. Michael Graves and Ramzi Jibran Bikhazi (Toronto, 1990).
B. *DAS*, 1, 250.

HAPSBURG, MOTHER ALEXANDRA (PRINCESS ILEANA) (5 January 1909, Bucharest, Romania–21 January 1991, Youngstown, OH). *Education:* private education for the Romanian royal family. *Career:* princess; married Anton Hapsburg, archduke of Austria, 1931; settled in Newton, MA, 1945; nun, Monastery of Bussy-en-Othe, France, 1961; established Monastery of Holy Transfiguration, Ellwood City, PA, 1964; abbess, 25 March 1969; active retirement, 1987–91.

The daughter of King Ferdinand and Queen Marie of Romania, Princess Ileana was related to many of the members of the royal families of Europe. Married to Anton Hapsburg, they had six children while living in Sonnberg, Austria. She returned with her family to Romania in 1944 and provided funds for the erection of a hospital in memory of her mother at the foot of the family castle at Braun. Throughout the war years, she personally cared for the.wounded. With the Communist takeover of Romania, she and her family fled their country in 1944, first to Switzerland and then to Argentina. With little means of support, she finally settled in Newton, Massachusetts, with her children in 1950. She supported her family through lecturing and writing. Her book *I Live Again* chronicles her early life.

As her children reached adulthood, Ileana decided to go to France to become a nun in 1961. She was given the name Alexandra. In 1964, she returned to the United States to establish a monastery for women. With the assistance of Archbishop Valerian, she located and purchased land in Ellwood City, Pennsylvania. The first stage of the monastery was blessed in 1968. Appointed abbess in 1969, she directed a community that included about twelves nuns. Mother Alexandra wrote popular books and booklets on Orthodox doctrine and spirituality. A much sought-after lecturer, she was frequently invited to speak about monasticism and spirituality.

Bibliography

A. *I Live Again* (New York, 1952); *Meditations on the Nicene Creed* (New York, 1958); *The Holy Angels* (Still River, MA, 1981).
B. "Mother Alexandra," *OC* 27:4 (1991), 1; Basil Pennington, *In Search of True Wisdom* (Garden City, NY, 1979), 159–72.

HARAKAS, STANLEY SAMUEL (13 January 1932, Pittsburgh–), *Education:* B.A., Holy Cross Greek Orthodox School of Theology, 1954; B.D., Holy Cross Greek Orthodox School of Theology, 1958; Th.D., Boston University, 1964. *Career:* ordained a priest, 1956; pastorates in Lancaster, PA, Peabody, MA, Lexington, MA, and Sharon, MA, 1956–present; instructor, Holy Cross School of Theology, 1966; assistant professor, 1967; associate professor, 1971; dean, 1971–79; professor of Christian ethics, 1972.

Stanley Harakas is the Archbishop Iakovos Professor of Orthodox Theology at Holy Cross School of Theology. A prolific author, Harakas has written especially in the areas of Christian ethics. He is recognized internationally as one of the foremost Orthodox theologians writing in this field. His work stands behind many of the position papers on social and moral issues produced by the Greek Orthodox Archdiocese. Often called upon to be a participant in ecumenical dialogues, he served as a member of the Orthodox-Reformed/Lutheran Dialogue, 1968–71. He is presently a member of the Orthodox-Roman Catholic Consultation and a member of the World Council of Churches Unit III Commission. A popular speaker, he has lectured at scholarly symposia, church assemblies, youth retreats, and college campuses.

Bibliography

A. *Living the Liturgy* (Minneapolis, 1976); *Contemporary Issues: Orthodox Christian Perspectives* (New York, 1976); *Something Is Stirring in World Orthodoxy* (Minneapolis, 1978); *The Melody of Prayer* (Minneapolis, 1979); *Contemporary Moral Issues* (Minneapolis, 1982); *Let Mercy Abound* (Brookline, MA, 1983); *Toward Transfigured Life* (Minneapolis, 1983); *Health and Medicine in the Eastern Orthodox Tradition* (New York, 1990); *Living the Faith: The Praxis of Eastern Orthodox Ethics* (Minneapolis, 1992).
B. *WWR* (1992), 271.

HARVEY, SUSAN   (7 June 1953, Rochester, NY–   ). *Education:* B.A., Grinnell College, 1975; M. Litt., University of Birmingham, England, 1977; Ph.D., 1982. *Career:* instructor in Syriac, University of Birmingham, 1978–82; lecturer in theology, 1980–82; lecturer in New Testament studies and Christian origins, University of North Carolina, 1982–83; assistant professor of religious studies, University of Rochester, 1983–87; associate professor of religious studies, Brown University, 1987–91; associate professor, 1991– present.

Susan Harvey is widely recognized for her studies, especially in the Syriac Christian tradition. As a member of the Antiochian Orthodox Archdiocese, she has been active in ecumenical dialogues. She is presently a member of the Orthodox–Roman Catholic Consultation and the Faith and Order Unit of the Rhode Island Council of Churches.

Bibliography

A. *Holy Women of the Syrian Orient* (Berkeley, 1987); *Asceticism and Society in Crisis: John of Ephesus and the "Lives of the Eastern Saints"* (Berkeley, 1990).

HAWAWEENY, RAPHAEL   (8 November 1860, Damascus, Syria–27 February 1915, New York). *Education:* diploma, Patriarchal Theological School of Halki, 1887. *Career:* ordained a priest and studied at the Theological School of Kiev, 1888; professor of Arabic, Theological School of Kiev, 1894; arrived in the United States to serve the mission to Arab Orthodox, 1895; bishop of Brooklyn, 1904–15.

A native of Damascus, Raphael Hawaweeny had studied both at Constantinople and in Russia prior to coming to the United States as a missionary priest in 1895 to serve the growing numbers of Arab Orthodox in New York and in other cities along the East Coast. He published a *Book of Services* in Arabic in 1898. On 12 March 1904, he was ordained as the bishop of Brooklyn by Archbishop Tikhon at St. Nicholas Church in that city. He was the first Orthodox bishop consecrated in America. Having special responsibility for the Arab Orthodox immigrants, Bishop Raphael served as a vicar to Tikhon in the North American mission directed by the Holy Synod of the Church of Russia. He founded in 1905 the magazine *Al-Kalemat,* later known as *The Word.* Known for his piety, pastoral care, linguistic ability, and theological insights, Raphael oversaw about thirty Orthodox parishes serving about 25,000 Arab immigrants at the time of his death. They were usually referred to as Syrian Orthodox.

Bibliography

B. *DCA,* 513; *OA*, 95.

HERMAN (1760, Serpoukhov, Russia–13 December 1837, Spruce Island, Alaska). *Education:* Holy Trinity-St. Sergius Monastery, St. Petersburg; Valaam Monastery, 1778–94. *Career:* tonsured a monk, c. 1776; missionary in Alaska, 1794–1836; proclaimed a saint, 1970.

Little is known of the early years of Herman. As a monk at the Valaam Monastery, he came under the influence of the charismatic abbot, Father Nazary, and developed a reputation for simplicity and piety. After about sixteen years at Valaam, Herman was selected to be part of the mission team being organized to go to Alaska. Herman was among the original eight monks who left St. Petersburg on 25 December 1793 and arrived on Kodiak on 24 September 1794. Their task was not simply to serve the Russian merchants and traders but to do missionary work among the native population.

Although he was never ordained, Herman is remembered as the most devoted and pious of the first missionaries. When the leader of the mission, Joseph Bolotov, left for Russia to be made a bishop, Herman was given preference over the clergy to provide temporary leadership. Following Bolotov's death at sea on his return voyage, Herman became the formal leader of the mission. During his forty years in Alaska, Herman instructed the natives in the basics of Christianity and taught them agricultural techniques. He staunchly defended the rights of the natives in the face of the exploitation by the Russian merchants and was twice exiled to Spruce Island, which became his home. He referred to it as New Valaam.

During his life, the natives recognized his genuine piety and unselfish love. Within thirty years after his death, in 1837, they began to collect stories about him and the miracles attributed to his intercession. By 1900, the Church of Russia was considering his canonization. However, the Bolshevik revolution intervened. Frequently, the Russian Orthodox in America proposed his formal recognition as a saint, especially in 1936, 1953, and 1957. Finally, the formal canonization took place on Kodiak Island on 9 August 1970. He is honored as the first canonized Orthodox saint in America. His relics are in the Holy Resurrection Cathedral in Kodiak.

Bibliography

B. Michael Oleska, *Alaskan Missionary Spirituality* (Mahwah, NJ, 1987); Vsevolod
    Rochcau, "St. Herman of Alaska and the Defence of Alaskan Native Peoples,"
    SVTQ 16:1 (1972), 17–39; *DCA*, 522–23.

HOPKO, THOMAS JOHN   (28 March 1939, Endicott, NY–   ). *Education:*
B.A., Fordham University, 1960; M. Div., St. Vladimir's Seminary, 1963; M.A.,
Duquesne University, 1968; Ph.D., Fordham University, 1982. *Career:* ordained a
priest, 1963; pastorates in Warren, OH; Wappingers Falls, NY; Jamaica Estates,
NY, 1963–83; faculty member, now professor of dogmatic theology, St. Vladimir's
Seminary, 1968–present; dean, 1992–present.

Thomas Hopko is an internationally recognized Orthodox theologian who is
presently dean and professor of dogmatic theology at St. Vladimir's Seminary. He
is a member of the Orthodox Church in America and a former president of the Orthodox Theological Society in America. A gifted and thoughtful lecturer on university campuses and at retreats, Hopko has authored a number of books dealing
with various themes in Orthodox theology and spirituality. His popular four-volume study, *The Orthodox Faith,* has been translated into ten languages.

In addition to being active in the Orthodox Church in America, Hopko is highly
regarded in ecumenical circles. From 1975 to 1991, he was an active participant in
the Faith and Order Commission of the World Council of Churches (WCC). He
was one of the theologians directly involved in the preparation of the historic WCC
document, *Baptism, Eucharist and Ministry* (1982).

Bibliography

A. *Christian Spirituality East and West* (Chicago, 1968); *The Orthodox Faith: An Elementary Handbook,* 4 vols. (New York, 1972–76); *The Spirit of God* (Danbury, CT,
    1976); *All the Fullness of God* (Crestwood, NY, 1982); *The Lenten Spring* (Crestwood, NY, 1983); *Women and the Priesthood* (Crestwood, NY, 1983); *The Winter
    Pascha* (Crestwood, NY, 1984).

J

JORGENSON, JAMES WAYNE (1 September 1943, Evanston, IL–). *Education:* B.A., St. Meinrad College, 1966; M. Div., St. Vladimir's Seminary, 1969; Ph.D., Boston University, 1979. *Career:* ordained a priest, 1969; pastorates in Lublin, WI, 1969–71; Minneapolis, 1971–74; Chelsea, MA, 1974–79; Dallas, 1979–81; Detroit, 1981–91; associate professor of church history, Sacred Heart Major Seminary, Detroit, MI, 1988–present; Dearborn Heights, MI, 1991–present.

A priest of the Orthodox Church in America, James Jorgenson has specialized in the relationship between Orthodoxy and Protestantism. He serves as a member of the Orthodox-Lutheran Bilateral Dialogue as well as the Faith and Order Commission of the National Council of Churches.

Bibliography

A. "Reflections on the Lima Statement," *SVTQ* 27:4 (1983), 239–50; "Fr. Alexis Toth and the Transition of the Greek Catholic Community in Minneapolis to the Russian Orthodox Church," *SVTQ* 32:2 (1988), 119–38.

K

KESICH, VESELIN (1921, Bosansko Grahhovo, Yugoslavia–). *Education:* diploma, Dorchester College, Oxford, 1949; B. Div., St. Vladimir's Seminary, 1957; Ph.D., Columbia University, 1959. *Career:* faculty member, St. Vladimir's Seminary, most recently professor of New Testament, 1955–91; professor emeritus, 1991–present.

Veselin Kesich is a Serbian Orthodox theologian who has made a rich and valuable contribution to Orthodox biblical studies. Besides his teaching at St. Vladimir's, he has also taught at Sarah Lawrence College, New York University, and Hofstra University. He has specialized in studies of the Scriptures and comparative religions, focusing on Buddhism, Hinduism, Judaism, and Islam.

Bibliography

A. *The Passion of Christ* (Crestwood, NY, 1965); *The First Day of the New Creation* (Crestwood, NY, 1982); *The Gospel Image of Christ* (rev. ed., Crestwood, NY, 1991).

B. *SVTQ* 35:2/3 (1991), 101–5.

KISHKOVSKY, LEONID (1943, Warsaw, Poland–). *Education:* B.A., University of Southern California, 1965; graduate studies, St. Vladimir's Seminary, 1964–67. *Career:* ordained a priest, 1969; pastorates in San Francisco, 1969–74, Sea Cliff, NY, 1974–present; administrator, Orthodox Church in America, 1974–present; editor, *The Orthodox Church,* 1984–present; president, National Council of Churches, 1990–92.

A priest of the Orthodox Church in America, Leonid Kishkovsky has been active in both inter-Orthodox and ecumenical associations. He has frequently participated in consultations and visitations related to the Orthodox Church in Russia and Eastern Europe. A past president of the National Council of Churches, he serves on the Central Committee of the World Council of Churches.

Bibliography

A. "Archbishop Tikhon in America," *SVTQ* 19:1 (1975), 9–31.

KOULOMZIN, SOPHIE SHIDLOVSKY   (1903, St. Petersburg, Russia–). *Education:* advanced studies, University of Berlin, Germany, 1922–26; M.A., Columbia University, New York, 1927. *Career:* director of education, Russian Student Christian Movement, Paris, 1927–c. 1938; executive secretary Orthodox Christian Education Commission, New York, 1956–69; instructor, St. Vladimir's Orthodox Theological Seminary, 1956–73; active retirement, 1973–present.

The daughter of the vice president of the Russian Duma, Sophie Shidlovsky was privileged to have outstanding social and educational advantages in the years prior to the October revolution of 1917. In the wake of the revolution, she traveled with her family first to Estona, then to Berlin and Paris. In Paris she became active in the Russian Student Christian Movement. In 1949, she married Nikita Koulomzin and had four children.

From the time of her arrival in America in 1949, Sophie Koulomzin has devoted her talents to religious education. She became the inspiration for a genuine renewal of Orthodox religious education in the United States in 1956, when she organized the Orthodox Christian Education Commission. Both in her teaching and in her writing, she has continued to call the church to respond to the unique needs of the young for religious direction and spiritual formation.

Bibliography

A. *Lectures in Orthodox Religious Education* (New York, c. 1956); *Our Church and Our Children* (Crestwood, NY, 1975); *Many Worlds: A Russian Life* (Crestwood, NY, 1980).
B. *OA*, 235.

L

LAZAR, THEODOSIUS THEODORE   (27 October 1933, Canonsburg, PA–   ). *Education:* B.A., Washington and Jefferson College, 1960; M. Div., St. Vladimir's Orthodox Theological Seminary, 1961. *Career:* ordained a priest, 1961; consecrated bishop of Washington, 1967; elected bishop of Alaska, 1967; bishop of Pittsburgh, 1972; metropolitan of America (Orthodox Church in America), 1978–present.

Metropolitan Theodosius has been intimately involved in many of the important developments affecting the Orthodox in America during the past quarter of a century. During his five-year tenure as bishop of Alaska, he directed a renewal of missionary activity in that vast area and oversaw preparations for the canonization of St. Herman of Alaska in 1970. In the spring of 1970, he participated in the funeral of Patriarch Alexis I of Moscow. Within a few days, he returned to Moscow, where he received on 18 May 1970 the Tomos of Autocephaly, the document granting self-governing status to the former Metropolia.

At the Fifth All American Council of the Orthodox Church of America in 1977, Bishop Theodosius was elected to succeed Metropolitan Ireney, who had announced his intention to resign due to failing health. The new Metropolitan was the first primate of the Orthodox Church in America and of its predecessor, the Metropolia, to be an American-born cleric. During his tenure, Metropolitan Theodosius has emphasized the importance of religious education, stewardship, and evangelization. He has been a proponent of Orthodox ecumenical witness. As president of St. Vladimir's Seminary, St. Tikhon Seminary, and St. Herman's Seminary, he has been a strong advocate of the importance of theological education both for clergy and for lay leaders.

Metropolitan Theodosius has expressed a special concern for the need for greater unity among the Orthodox in America. Under his direction, official conversations were begun between the Orthodox Church in America and the Patriarchate of Constantinople in 1990. In the same year, he welcomed Patriarch Dimitrios of Constantinople to St. Nicholas Cathedral in Washington. Metropolitan Theodosius made a historic visit to the Ecumenical Patriarchate of Constantinople in 1992.

Bibliography

B. *OC* 28:5 (1992), 1–5.

L'HUILLIER, PETER PAUL (3 December 1926, Paris–). *Education:* diploma, Institute of St. Denys, Paris, 1949; graduate studies, University of Paris, 1949; Lic. Theol., Moscow Theological Academy, Moscow, 1962; Dr. Theol., 1985. *Career:* tonsured a monk and ordained a priest, 1954; pastorates, Paris, 1954–68; professor, Catholic University, Paris, 1966–78; consecrated bishop, 1968; bishop of Chersone, Russian Orthodox Diocese of Western Europe, 1968–79; bishop of New York, 1971–81; bishop of Brooklyn, 1979–81; adjunct professor, St. Vladimir's Seminary, 1980–present; archbishop of New York and New Jersey, Orthodox Church in America, 1990–present.

Archbishop Peter is widely regarded as one of the foremost experts in the development of canonical legislation during the first five centuries. In addition to his pastoral responsibilities, he has frequently lectured on the topic of canon law both in his native France as well as in the United States. He has served as the chairman of the External Affairs Department, Orthodox Church in America, and as an adviser on canonical matters for the Standing Conference of Orthodox Bishops.

Bibliography

A. "Novella 89 of Leo the Wise on Marriage," *GOTR* 32:3 (1987), 153–62; "The Indissolubility of Marriage in Orthodox Canon Law and Practice," *SVTQ* 32:4 (1988), 199–221; "Episcopal Celibacy in the Orthodox Tradition," *SVTQ* 35:2/3 (1991), 271–300; "The Development of the Concept of an Ecumenical Council," *GOTR* 36:3/4 (1991), 243–62.

B. *WWR* (1977), 221.

M

MANCUSO, LAURENCE (30 June 1934, Utica, NY–   ). *Education:* S.T.B., St. Bernard Seminary, 1956; S.T.M., St. Mary Seminary, 1960; graduate studies, Georgetown University, 1959–60; Fordham University, 1961–62. *Career:* provincial counselor and master of clerics, 1956–66; tonsured a monk, Byzantine Franciscan Monastery, 1957; ordained a priest, 1960; chaplain, St. Basil Seminary, 1960–66; founder and abbot of the Monastery of New Skete, 1966–present; received into the Orthodox Church in America, 1979; received rank of archimandrite, 1985.

Abbot Laurence of New Skete is the foremost exponent of monastic spirituality and liturgical life in the Orthodox Church in this country. In 1966, he and a number of other monks established the Monastery of New Skete in Cambridge, New York, as a center that would be rooted in the spirituality of Eastern Christianity. Since then, New Skete has grown to include three flourishing monastic communities and a parish, which Abbot Laurence serves as spiritual father. The early members of these communities were received into full communion with the Orthodox Church in 1979.

For more than thirty years, Abbot Laurence and the members of New Skete have been involved in liturgical translations and in the composition of liturgical music that reflects the richness of the Eastern Christian heritage. Under his direction, new translations of the liturgies of the Orthodox Church, the daily services, and the Psalms have been made. These translations are among the best available for use in Orthodox worship in America today. The restored liturgical services are the heart of the life of the monastic communities of New Skete. These services not only have enriched the lives of the many visitors who come to the monastery chapel but also have attracted the attention of liturgical scholars throughout the world. Under the leadership of Abbot Laurence, New Skete has become a center where the rich traditions of authentic monastic life have become accessible to a wide variety of persons.

Bibliography

A. *A Prayerbook* (Cambridge, NY, 1976); *Troparia and Kontakia* (Cambridge, NY, 1984); *A Service Book* (Cambridge, NY, 1984); *The Psalter* (Cambridge, NY, 1984); *Hymns of Entreaty* (Cambridge, NY, 1987); *The Divine Liturgy* (Cambridge, NY, 1986); *A Book of Prayers* (Cambridge, NY, 1988); *Monastic Typicon* (Cambridge, NY, 1988).

MASTRANTONIS, GEORGE   (10 March 1906, Karystos, Greece–14 August 1988, St. Louis, MO). *Education:* diploma, University of Athens, 1936; graduate study, University of Leipzig, 1939; M.T.S., Concordia Theological Seminary, 1969. *Career:* ordained a priest in 1936; chancellor, metropolis of Corinth, 1937–39; pastorates in Chicago, 1940–53, St. Louis, 1953–59; pastor emeritus, 1959–88.

Although they were born and received their early education in Greece, George and his wife, Pareskevi, Mastrantonis had a strong missionary spirit that bore fruit in the United States following their arrival in 1940. In 1950 they were instrumental in organizing the Hellenic Foundation, which provided assistance both to recent immigrants and to the elderly. In the same year, George Mastrantonis led the establishment of the Federation of Eastern Orthodox Churches of Greater Chicago. His concern for greater Orthodox unity continued during his subsequent pastorate in St. Louis.

Mastrantonis is best remembered for his devotion to the educational ministry of the church. He founded a publishing house known as OLOGOS (Orthodox Love of the Gospel of Our Savior) in 1956. Its purpose was to publish inexpensive pamphlets and booklets dealing with all aspects of the life of the Orthodox Church. He was the author of these texts, which not only helped generations of Orthodox deepen their knowledge of the faith but also introduced the general public to the teachings and practices of the Orthodox Church. While his activities were reduced after 1959 because of Parkinson's disease, Mastrantonis continued his research and writings. He made a new translation of the "Liturgy of St. John Chrysostom" in 1966. He prepared a comprehensive catechism in 1969. He also made a major contribution to the field of church history with his translation of the sixteenth-century correspondence between Patriarch Jeremiah of Constantinople and Lutheran theologians at Tübingen.

Bibliography

A. *The Divine Liturgy of St. John Chrysostom* (St. Louis, 1966); *A New Style Catechism on the Eastern Orthodox Faith for Adults* (St. Louis, 1969); *Augsburg and Constantinople* (Brookline, MA, 1982).
B. *RLA*, 294.

MAXIMOVICH, JOHN MICHAEL   (4 June 1896, Kharkov, Russia–19 June 1966, Seattle, WA). *Education:* diploma, University of Belgrade, 1925. *Career:* tonsured a monk and ordained a priest, 1926; instructor, St. John Seminary, Bitol, Serbia, 1926–34; ordained bishop of Shanghai, China, 1934; came to the United States, 1950; bishop in Western Europe, 1951–60; bishop of San Francisco (Russian Orthodox Church Outside of Russia), 1960–66.

At the time of the Russian revolution of 1917, the young Maximovich and his family were among the thousands who fled their homeland for Constantinople, various parts of the Balkans, the Far East, Western Europe, and the United States. The family finally settled in Belgrade. While his family thought that he should study law, Maximovich eventually graduated from the University of Belgrade with a diploma in theology. After becoming a monk and a priest in 1926, Maximovich began teaching at a seminary in Bitol, Serbia. There he gained a reputation for study of the lives of the saints and for his own piety.

At the age of thirty-eight, Maximovich was ordained a bishop in the Russian Orthodox Church Outside of Russia and assigned to serve the Russian émigré parish in Shanghai, China. He was deeply devoted to the community and established an orphanage for homeless children. Following the Chinese revolution, he led the Russian exiles first to the Philippines and then to the United States in 1950. Assigned to serve the Russian Orthodox parishes in Western Europe in 1951, he remained there until he was elected bishop of San Francisco in 1960. While deeply rooted in the piety of prerevolutionary Russia, Archbishop John had a profound influence not only upon his own immigrant flocks but also upon Americans seeking insight into Orthodox spirituality.

Bibliography

A. *The Orthodox Veneration of the Mother of God* (Platina, CA, 1978).
B. *RLA*, 299; Bishop Savas of Edmonton, *Bishop John* (Platina, CA, 1979).

METAXAKIS, MELETIOS EMMANUEL   (21 September 1871, Lasithi, Crete–27 July 1935, Alexandria, Egypt). *Education:* graduate, Holy Cross Orthodox Seminary in Jerusalem, 1902. *Career:* secretary to the Jerusalem Patriarchate, 1903–9; Metropolitan of Kition (Crete) 1910–18; Metropolitan of Athens, 1918–20; organizer of the Greek Orthodox Church in America, 1921; Ecumenical Patriarch of Constantinople, 1921–23; Patriarch of Alexandria, 1926–35.

Meletios Metaxakis first came to the United States in 1919 in his capacity of Metropolitan of Athens. The Patriarchate of Constantinople had temporarily transferred its jurisdiction in America to the Church of Greece in 1908. Until this time, the developing Greek Orthodox parishes had little formal oversight. The immigrants in the postwar years, however, were deeply divided over the political issues of Greece. Deposed from his see due to political pressure, Metaxakis returned to the United States again in 1921. During this visit he acted to legally establish the Greek Orthodox Archdiocese of America.

During the same year, he was elected Patriarch of Constantinople and became the last to serve under Ottoman rule. He restored the jurisdiction of the Patriarchate over the Orthodox in Europe and America in 1922 and canonically established the Orthodox Archdiocese of North and South America, intending to unite all the Orthodox here. In the same year, he convened a Pan-Orthodox Conference in Constantinople. Continued political strife in Turkey forced Meletios to resign in 1923. After a brief stay in Athens, he was elected Patriarch of Alexandria in 1926. There, he continued to have special interest in relations between Orthodoxy and Anglicanism. He had affirmed the validity of Anglican orders in 1922, an opinion not shared by all Orthodox churches.

Bibliography

B. George Bebis, "Metaxakis in Profile," in *A History of the Greek Orthodox Church,* ed. M. Efthimiou (New York, 1984), 93–113.

MEYENDORFF, JOHN   (17 February 1926, Neuille-sur-Sein, France–22 July, 1992, Montreal, Quebec). *Education:* diploma, St. Sergius Orthodox Theological Seminary, Paris, 1949; doctor of letters, Sorbonne, 1958. *Career:* instructor of church history, St. Sergius, 1950–59; ordained a priest in 1959; professor of patristics and church history, St. Vladimir's Orthodox Theological Seminary, New York, 1959–92; dean, 1984–92.

Recognized as one of the most distinguished Orthodox theologians and church historians of this century, John Meyendorff was the son of Russian émigré parents living in France. Following the completion of his education there, he came to New York to assume a teaching position at St. Vladimir's Seminary in 1959 and to become associated with Dumbarton Oakes, Harvard's Byzantine research center in Washington. During his tenure at St. Vladimir's, Meyendorff also taught at Fordham University, Columbia University, and Union Theological Seminary.

As a member of the Orthodox Church in America, formerly the Metropolia, Meyendorff was deeply involved in its affairs. Throughout his thirty-three years in this country, he was a thoughtful guide for his church as it developed internal polity and missionary spirit. He was adept in bringing historical insights to bear upon contemporary challenges. He also was instrumental in the negotiations that led to the grant of autocephalous status to the Metropolia by the Patriarchate of Moscow in 1970. Always an active proponent of greater Orthodox unity and witness in America, Meyendorff was active in the establishment of the Standing Conference of Canonical Bishops in 1960 and the Orthodox Theological Society in 1964. In the years prior to his death, he was very active in discussions with the Ecumenical Patriarchate aimed at the establishment of a unified Orthodox Church in the United States.

A strong supporter of movements toward Christian reconciliation, Meyendorff was a frequent representative of the Orthodox Church in America on the Central Committee of the World Council of Churches and the Faith and Order Commission. He served as the moderator of the latter from 1967 to 1975. He was among the Orthodox theologians who were active in promoting dialogue between the Orthodox Church and the Roman Catholic Church. For a number of years, Meyendorff served as a member of the Orthodox-Roman Catholic Consultation in the United States, founded in 1965.

Widely recognized in this country as the preeminent historian of Byzantine civilization, Meyendorff was a prolific writer and the author of numerous books and scholarly articles, which have appeared in many languages. His presence at St. Vladimir's Seminary helped to project it as a major center of Orthodox thought. From 1962 to 1984, he was the editor of *St. Vladimir's Theological Review.* From 1965 to 1984, he served as editor of his church's monthly newspaper, the *Orthodox Church.* Retiring from his responsibilities at St. Vladimir's Seminary only weeks before his death from cancer in 1992, Meyendorff envisioned doing additional research and writing. Always rooted in the liturgical traditions of the church and with a deep understanding of Orthodox history, Meyendorff accomplished much to uncover the rich theological heritage of Orthodox Christianity and to make it accessible to a wider audience.

Bibliography

A. *A Study of Gregory Palamas* (New York, 1959); *Orthodoxy and Catholicity* (New York, 1966); *Living Tradition* (Crestwood, NY, 1968); *Christ in Eastern Christian Thought* (New York, 1969); *Byzantine Theology* (New York, 1973); *Marriage: An Orthodox Perspective* (Crestwood, NY, 1975); *Byzantium and the Rise of Russia* (Crestwood, NY, 1980); *The Byzantine Legacy in the Orthodox Church* (Crestwood, NY, 1981); *Catholicity and the Church* (Crestwood, NY, 1983); *Witness to the World* (Crestwood, NY, 1987); *Vision of Unity* (Crestwood, NY, 1987); *Imperial Unity and Christian Division* (Crestwood, NY, 1989).

B. *WWR* (1977), 448; *OC* 28:8–9 (1992), 1, 4.

MEYENDORFF, PAUL   (2 November 1950, Paris–   ). *Education:* B.A., Trinity College, 1972; M.Div., St. Vladimir's Seminary, 1975; Ph.D., University of Notre Dame, 1987. *Career:* assistant professor, St. Vladimir's Seminary, 1987–91; adjunct professor, Drew University, 1989; associate professor, 1991–present; visiting professor, University of Notre Dame, 1991, 1993.

Paul Meyendorff occupies the Alexander Schmemann Chair of Liturgical Theology at St. Vladimir's Seminary. Actively involved in issues related to worship and liturgical translations for the Orthodox Church in America, Meyendorff was a student of Alexander Schmemann. He has published a number of books and scholarly articles in the area of liturgical theology.

Bibliography

A. *St. Germanos of Constantinople* (Crestwood, NY, 1984); "The Liturgical Reforms of Peter Moghila, a New Look," *SVTQ* 29 (1985), 101–14; "The Orthodox Practice of Penance," *Studia Liturgica* 18 (1988), 108–11; "Reflections on the Russian Liturgy," *SVTQ* 33 (1989), 21–34; "Sacramental Theology and Pastoral Care," *Dictionary of Pastoral Care and Counseling* (Nashville, TN, 1990); *Russia, Ritual, and Reform: The Liturgical Reforms of Nikon in the 17th Century* (Crestwood, NY, 1991).

N

NICKLAS, ANTHONY (17 August 1958, Aliquippa, PA–). *Education:* B.A., Hellenic College, 1979; M.Div., Holy Cross School of Theology, 1982; D. Min., St. Vladimir's Theological Seminary, 1988. *Career:* ordained a priest, 1982; pastorates in Greenlawn, NY, 1982–83; Schenectady, NY, 1983–90; Lexington, MA, 1990–present; instructor in pastoral theology, Holy Cross School of Theology, 1990–present.

Anthony Nicklas is a priest in the Greek Orthodox archdiocese. He is regarded as an expert in the area of clergy development. He has also been involved in developing programs for aiding spiritual growth and parish renewal.

Bibliography

A. *Factors Related to Positive Clergy Development* (Crestwood, NY, 1988); *The Vespers of St. Nicholas* (Lexington, MA, 1991).

NICOZISIN, GEORGE (22 March 1927, St. Louis–). *Education:* B.A., Holy Cross School of Theology, 1956; S.T.M., Colgate-Rochester Divinity School, Rochester, NY, 1970; M.Th., Holy Cross School of Theology, 1981. *Career:* ordained a priest, 1956; pastorates in San Francisco, 1956–58; Waukegan, IL, 1958–63; San Jose, CA, 1963–67; Rochester, NY, 1967–73; Manchester, NH, 1973–77; director of religious education, Greek Orthodox Archdiocese, 1973–77; pastor, St. Nicholas Church, St. Louis, 1977–present.

A priest of the Greek Orthodox Archdiocese, George Nicozisin has combined a number of fruitful pastorates with an active commitment to Orthodox religious education. In his position as director of the office of religious education for the Greek Orthodox Archdiocese, Nicozisin oversaw the development of a new curriculum that took into account insights from both learning theory and faith development. In his own writings, he has demonstrated a particular concern for adult religious formation.

Bibliography

A. *A History of the Church* (Brookline, MA, 1971); *The Creed: Simplified Dogmatics* (Brookline, MA, 1972); *Sacraments in the Orthodox Church,* coauthored with Frieda Upson (Brookline, MA, 1973); *The Road to Orthodox Phronema* (Brookline, MA, 1977); *Your Marriage in the Orthodox Church* (St. Louis, 1985).

NOLI, THEOFAN (FAN)   (6 January 1882, Ibrik Tepe, Thrace, Turkey–13 March 1965, Boston). *Education:* A.B., Harvard College, 1912; A.B., New England Conservatory of Music, 1940; Ph.D., Boston University, 1947. *Career:* ordained a priest, 1908; organized St. George Cathedral, Boston, 1908; administrator of Albanian Orthodox parishes under the Russian Orthodox Archdiocese, 1918; nominated as bishop, 1919; consecrated Metropolitan of Durres, Gora, and Shpata and primate of Illyria, Albania, 1923; minister of foreign affairs (Albania), 1924; primate of Albanian Orthodox Archdiocese, 1930–65.

Theofan Noli arrived in America at the age of twenty-one and settled briefly in Jamestown, New York, where there was a small center of Albanian immigrants. He later moved to Boston to continue working with Albanian immigrants and became a leader of a movement advocating independence for Albania. Following his ordination in 1908, Noli became a champion of the use of the Albanian language in liturgical services in parishes serving Albanian immigrants. His own translations became central to this endeavor.

A renowned orator, Noli helped to organize the Pan-Albanian Federation in Boston in 1912, the same year that an independent Albania came into being. His interest in Albanian independence took him to Europe, where he spoke on behalf of the cause. His efforts contributed greatly to the admission of Albania into the League of Nations in 1920. He was subsequently named a delegate to the league and later became a member of Parliament and minister of foreign affairs. In the midst of these political developments, Noli was consecrated a Metropolitan-bishop in 1923. He served for six months as premier in 1924. But, in the same year, his political and ecclesiastical career ended when he was overthrown and forced to leave the country. During the next six years, spent in Germany, Noli translated many classics of literature into Albanian.

Upon his return to the United States in 1931, Noli turned his attention again to the three Albanian Orthodox parishes here. He established a diocese that was nominally related to the Church of Albania, which was granted autocephalous status by the Patriarchate of Constantinople in 1937. At the same time, Noli maintained cordial relationships with the Russian Orthodox Metropolia.

In the period following World War II especially, Noli became more interested in the movement toward greater Orthodox unity in America. In earlier years, Noli had devoted much attention to the translation of liturgical texts into Albanian. Now, he recognized the needs of a new generation. In addition to preparing a catechism in English, he was among the first to translate and publish liturgical texts in English.

Bibliography

A. *Eastern Orthodox Prayer Book* (Boston, 1949); *Eastern Orthodox Catechism* (Boston, 1954); *Three Liturgies of the Eastern Orthodox Church* (Boston, 1955); *Gospel Lectionary of the Eastern Orthodox Church* (Boston, 1956); *Epistle Lectionary of the Eastern Orthodox Church* (Boston, 1957); *Fiftieth Anniversary Book of the Albanian Orthodox Church in America, 1908–1958* (Boston, 1960).

B. *RLA*, 342.

O

OLESKA, MICHAEL   (16 March 1947, Allentown, PA–   ). *Education:* B.A., Georgetown University, 1969; M.Div., St. Vladimir's Seminary, 1973; Th.D., Orthodox Theological Faculty, Prague, 1990. *Career:* ordained a priest, 1974; pastorates in western Alaska, 1974–present; lecturer, St. Herman's Seminary, 1974–present; assistant professor of religion, University of Alaska, 1976–present.

While serving parishes in Alaska, Michael Oleska has become the foremost expert on the history and character of the Orthodox Church in that state. His recent writings have explored the Orthodox missionary tradition and have paid special attention to the relationship of faith and culture.

Bibliography

A. *Alaskan Missionary Spirituality* (New York, 1987); *Orthodox Alaska: A Theology of Mission* (Crestwood, NY, 1992).

P

PATRINACOS, NICON   (1911, Laconia, Greece–1989, New York, NY). *Education:* diploma, School of Theology, University of Athens, 1936; A.B., A.M., University of Queensland, Australia, 1947; D. Phil., Oxford, 1950. *Career:* ordained a priest, 1936; pastor, St. Louis, 1950–53; instructor, Washington University, St. Louis, 1950–53; dean and professor of psychology, Holy Cross Greek Orthodox School of Theology, 1953–54; teacher, St. Basil Academy, Garrison, NY, 1954–76; director of studies, Greek Orthodox Archdiocese, 1976–89.

After coming to the United States in 1950, Nicon Patrinacos devoted much of his time to teaching and to writing on themes related to Orthodox Church doctrine and practices. He was the founder and first editor of *The Greek Orthodox Theological Review* in 1953. A priest of the Greek Orthodox Archdiocese, he also was involved in interchurch and ecumenical relations.

Bibliography

A. *The Orthodox Church on Birth Control* (New York, 1975); *All That a Greek Orthodox Should Know* (New York, 1976); *The Orthodox Liturgy* (New York, 1976); *The Individual and His Orthodox Church* (New York, 1979); *A Dictionary of Greek Orthodoxy* (New York, 1984).
B. *GOTR* 34:4 (1989): 415–16.

PATSAVOS, LEWIS J.   (4 June 1937, Everett, MA–   ). *Education:* Lic. Theol., University of Athens, 1961; graduate studies, University of Nuremberg, 1962; University of Munich, 1962–65; Dr. Theol., University of Athens, 1973. *Career:*

faculty member, now professor of canon law and director of field education, Holy Cross School of Theology, 1973–present.

A theologian in the Greek Orthodox Archdiocese, Lewis Patsavos is widely recognized as a foremost authority on Orthodox canon law. He has served as an adviser on canonical matters both for his own Archdiocese as well as for other Orthodox jurisdictions in this country. His work in the area of field education has sought to integrate the traditional disciplines of theology with the development of the skills needed in pastoral service. He is one of the founders of the Society of Law of the Eastern Churches. He is also an active member of the Orthodox-Roman Catholic Bilateral Consultation.

Bibliography

A. *Entry into the Clergy During the First Five Centuries* (Athens, 1973); *The Canon Law of the Orthodox Catholic Church* (Brookline, MA, 1975); *The Primacy of the See of Constantinople in Theory and Practice* (Brookline, MA, 1994).

PHILIPS, ANGELOS   (25 March 1936, Sparta, Greece–   ). *Education:* B.D., Holy Cross School of Theology, 1958; Th.M., Princeton Theological Seminary, 1960; D. Phil., Oxford University, 1965. *Career:* lecturer in philosophy, Hellenic College, 1966–68; associate professor of church history and patristics, Boston University, 1968–72; independent research, 1972–present.

A specialist in the writings of St. Gregory of Nyssa, Angelos Philips acquainted many graduate students with the spirituality and teachings of the fathers, especially during his teaching career at Boston University. In recent years, he has participated in symposia devoted to patristic themes and occasionally has lectured.

Bibliography

A. *The Eschatology of Gregory of Nyssa* (Oxford, 1964); *The Orthodox Ethos* (Oxford, 1964); *Orthodoxy: Life and Freedom* (Oxford, 1973).

POLIZOIDIS, GERMANOS   (1897, Chalcedon, Turkey–13 July 1993, New York). *Education:* diploma, Patriarchal Theological School of Halki, 1919. *Career:* ordained priest, 1927; pastor, Astoria, NY, 1927–43; titular bishop of Nyssa, 1941; titular metropolitan of Hierapolis, 1959–93.

Germanos Polizoidis came to the United States as a young deacon in 1920. Ordained a priest in 1927, he began his ministry at a time when the Greek Orthodox were sharply divided by political differences. A close associate of Metropolitan Meletios Metaxakis, Polizoides was one of the organizers of the Greek Orthodox Archdiocese in 1921–22. From that time, he was a trusted adviser to the four archbishops who have led the archdiocese from 1922 to the present. In addition to having pastoral responsibilities in the New York area throughout most of his career,

Polizoidis also was, for a time, editor of the *Orthodox Observer* and a lecturer at Holy Cross Greek Orthodox School of Theology. He recognized the need for Orthodox literature in English and was the author of a number of articles, pamphlets, and books.

Bibliography

A. *A Catechism of the Eastern Orthodox Church* (New York, 1953).
B. *OO* 58 (August 1993), 8–9.

R

REXINE, JOHN EFSTRATIOS (6 June 1929, Boston–23 October 1993, Hamilton, NY). *Education:* A.B., Harvard College, 1951; M.A., Harvard University, 1953; Ph.D., 1964. *Career:* instructor, Brandeis University, 1954–57; professor of classics, Colgate University, 1957–92; active retirement, 1992–93.

John Rexine was a scholar whose teaching and writings often dealt both with the value of the classical tradition and with the significance of Orthodox Christianity. During his distinguished career at Colgate, he also served as chairman of the Department of Classics, director of the Division of the Humanities, and associate dean of the faculty. He also served as the editor of the *Classic Outlook* and as an associate editor of the *Greek Orthodox Theological Review.*

Bibliography
A. *Religion in Plato and Cicero* (New York, 1959); *The Hellenic Spirit* (Belmont, MA 1981).
B. *OO* (November 1993), 17.

ROSE, SERAPHIM EUGENE (1934–2 September 1982, Platina, CA). *Education:* B.A., Pomona College; M.A., University of California, Berkeley. *Career:* cofounder of St. Herman of Alaska Brotherhood, 1963; cofounder of the *Orthodox Word,* 1965; ordained a priest-monk, 1979.

Seraphim Rose was raised in a Protestant family and came under the influence of Zen Buddhism through his contacts with Alan Watts in Berkeley. His personal quest for knowledge and truth was deeply affected in 1961 when he heard a lecture on Orthodox Christianity delivered by Abbot Herman Podmoshensky. Rose almost immediately decided to join the Orthodox church. He was subsequently made a monk and took the name Seraphim. He was deeply influenced by the piety and writings of Archbishop John Maximovich.

With Abbot Herman, Seraphim founded St. Herman of Alaska Brotherhood in San Francisco. The purpose of this monastic fellowship was to assist Americans to come into contact with Orthodox Christianity through lectures, books, and icons. The journal *Orthodox Word* was established in 1965. The brotherhood moved its center from San Francisco to Platina, California, in 1969. At that time, it was under the jurisdiction of the Russian Orthodox Church Outside of Russia. Under the direction of Seraphim, *Orthodox Word* became an important Orthodox journal that published essays on Orthodoxy, translations of saints' lives, and liturgical services. Ordained a priest in 1979, Seraphim wrote a number of essays that appeared first in the *Orthodox Word* and were subsequently published in book form. A sizable portion of his extensive writings remains unpublished.

Bibliography

A. *Orthodoxy and the Religion of the Future* (Platina, CA, 1983); *Little Russian Philokalia* (Platina, CA, 1983).

B. *RLA*, 400; Damascene Christiensen, "The Literary Inheritance of Father Seraphim Rose," *Orthodox Word* 18:3 (1982), 108–14.

ROZHDESTVENSKY, PLATON PORPHYRY (23 February 1866, Kursk, Russia–20 April 1934, New York). *Education:* diploma, Kiev Theological Academy, 1895. *Career:* ordained a priest, 1887; rector of the Kiev Theological Academy, 1902; bishop of Chigrin, 1902–7; archbishop of Aleutians Islands and North America, 1904–14; archbishop of Kishinev and Kotin, 1914–15; archbishop of Kartalin and Kakhetin (Georgia), 1915; Metropolitan of Kherson and Odessa, 1918–20; administrator of North American Archdiocese, 1922; Metropolitan of North America, 1923–34.

Following his ordination in 1887, Platon served as a priest in the Kursk region of Russia. After the death of his wife, he became a monk in 1894 and continued his studies at the Kiev Theological Academy. He became rector of the academy and was ordained a vicar bishop of Kiev in 1902. He was transferred to America to replace Archbishop Tikhon in 1907. Returning to Russia in 1914, he occupied a number of sees before being appointed Metropolitan of Kherson and Odessa. After the Bolshevik Revolution, he fled Odessa and returned to America in 1922 and was subsequently reappointed head of the North American Archdiocese, which was deeply divided and financially weak due to the developments in Russia. Platon continued to head the archdiocese after it became a temporarily self-governing church, independent from the beleaguered Church of Russia in 1924. Composed then of about 250 parishes, it became known as the Russian Orthodox Greek Catholic Church or the Metropolia. Platon helped to bring stability and direction to the Metropolia at a very critical time.

Bibliography

B. *OA*, 128–29.

S

SALIBA, PHILIP ABDALLAH   (10 June 1931, Abou Mizan, Lebanon–   ). *Education:* diploma, Assiyeh College, Damascus, 1951; advanced studies, Kelham Theological School, Nottinghamshire, England, University of London and Holy Cross Greek Orthodox School of Theology, Brookline, MA, 1953–56; B.A., Wayne State University, Detroit, 1959; M. Div., St. Vladimir's Orthodox Theological Seminary, Crestwood, NY, 1965. *Career:* ordained a priest, 1959; elected primate of the Syrian (Antiochian) Orthodox Archdiocese and consecrated a bishop, 1966–present.

A native of Lebanon, Philip Saliba was raised close to the church and knew well the leaders of the Patriarchate of Antioch. During his elementary and secondary school education in church-related schools, he began to acquire the spirit of mission and renewal that was beginning to emerge in the Patriarchate. With a desire to further his education, Saliba came to the United States in 1956 as a young deacon.

After his ordination as a priest in 1959, he became the pastor of St. George Church in Cleveland. There, he became well known both for his preaching and for his humanitarian concerns. Upon the death of Metropolitan Antony Bashir in 1966, Saliba was the overwhelming choice of clergy and laity of the Syrian (Antiochian) Orthodox Archdiocese to become the new primate. He was formally elected by the synod of the Church of Antioch and consecrated a bishop in 1966.

Metropolitan Philip immediately set about to strengthen his archdiocese. Central to this was the fact that he prompted the change of name of the archdiocese from Syrian Orthodox to Antiochian Orthodox Christian, thereby recognizing its changing character. He also called for greater support for the education of future priests, redirected the archdiocese's national youth movement, and organized a national organization for women of his archdiocese.

In recent years, two events are especially important. Metropolitan Philip joined with Archbishop Michael Shaheen in 1975 to unify the Antiochian Orthodox parishes, which had been divided into two rival dioceses since 1936. Second, Metropolitan Philip was instrumental in receiving into the Orthodox Church through his archdiocese about 2,000 members of the former Evangelical Orthodox Church who were gathered into about seventeen communities. Their journey to the Orthodox Church took ten years and was based upon a thorough study of the beliefs and practices of the early church. Both of these events were expressions of Metropolitan Philip's commitment to the unity of Orthodoxy in America and to its witness in this country.

Bibliography

B. Peter E. Gillquist, *Metropolitan Philip: His Life and His Dreams* (Nashville, 1991).

SCHMEMANN, ALEXANDER (13 September 1921, Ravel, Estonia–13 December 1983, Crestwood, NY). *Education:* diploma, St. Sergius Orthodox Theological Institute, Paris, 1940–44; doctorate in theology, 1959. *Career:* instructor of church history, St. Sergius Institute, 1945–51; ordained a priest, 1946; faculty member, most recently professor of church history and liturgical theology, St. Vladimir's Orthodox Theological Seminary, 1951–83; dean, 1962–83.

Born of Russian émigré parents and raised in France, Alexander Schmemann matured within the context of "Russian Paris," which contained tens of thousands of migrants, many of whom hoped to return one day to their native land. Following his early education in Russian schools, Schmemann studied at St. Sergius under some of the most prominent Russian Orthodox theologians of the day. These included Anton Kartashev, Cyprian Kern, Nicholas Afanassieff, and Georges Florovsky. Rooted deeply in the liturgical and theological traditions of Orthodoxy, Schmemann was always open to the wider world. The movement for liturgical and theological renewal within French Roman Catholicism in the 1940s did not go unnoticed by the young Schmemann, who was developing a greater interest in Orthodox liturgical theology. After briefly teaching at St. Sergius, Schmemann followed Georges Florovsky to America. Schmemann had come to admire Florovsky's theological mind, his devotion to Orthodox mission, his criticism of nationalistic stereotypes, and his openness to the best theological movements in Western Christianity.

Schmemann became a member of the faculty at St. Vladimir's Seminary in New York in 1951 at the invitation of Florovsky, who was its new dean. At that time, the seminary was located in modest quarters in Manhattan. By the time Florovsky resigned as dean in 1955, the seminary had already gained a reputation as a center of Orthodox thought. After the seminary acquired its present campus in Crestwood in 1962, Schmemann became its dean. Under Schmemann's leadership until his death in 1983, St. Vladimir's Seminary became a center for Pan-Orthodox theological education, for liturgical renewal, and for publications. Schmemann succeeded at the same time in integrating the mission of the seminary into the broader life of the jurisdiction of the Russian Orthodox Metropolia.

An active participant in the affairs of the Metropolia, Schmemann was instrumental in the negotiations that led to the grant of autocephalous status by the patriarchate of Moscow in 1970. From then, the Metropolia has been known as the Orthodox Church in America. Schmemann hoped that the creation of this church would lead the way to the unification of all the Orthodox jurisdictions in America.

Schmemann was a skilled preacher, teacher, and lecturer. He was also a prolific writer who addressed many of the themes and challenges associated with the Orthodox Church today. He was one of the architects of the Standing Conference of Canonical Orthodox Bishops in 1965 and the Orthodox Theological Society in 1964. Active in commissions of both the National Council of Churches and World Council of Churches, he became a familiar and respected representative of his church.

Schmemann's enduring contribution to the church comes especially through his lectures and writing in the area of liturgical theology. He became the champion of the reaffirmation of the significance of baptism, the centrality of the Eucharist, the importance of the regular reception of Holy Communion, and the essential participation of the laity in liturgical services. In all of this, he constantly emphasized the value of the liturgical services both to form and to inform the believer.

Bibliography

A. *The Historical Road of Eastern Orthodoxy* (New York, 1954, 1963, 1977); *Sacrament and Orthodoxy* (New York, 1965); *The World as Sacrament* (London, 1966); *Introduction to Liturgical Theology* (London, 1966); *The World as Sacrament* (Crestwood, NY, 1966); *Great Lent* (1969, 1974); *For the Life of the World* (Crestwood, NY, 1973); *Of Water and the Spirit* (Crestwood, NY, 1974); *Ultimate Questions* (Crestwood, NY, 1977); *Church, World and Mission* (Crestwood, NY, 1979); *The Eucharist* (Crestwood, NY, 1987).

B. *SVTQ* 28:1 (1984), 3–48; Paul Garrett, "Fr. Alexander Schmemann: A Chronological Bibliography," *SVTQ* 28:1 (1984), 11–26; Thomas Fisch, ed., *Liturgy and Tradition: Theological Reflections of Alexander Schmemann* (Crestwood, NY, 1990).

SCHNEIRLA, PAUL W. S. (11 April 1916, Ophir, Alaska–). *Education:* B.A., University of Western Ontario, 1937; M.Div., St. Vladimir's Seminary, 1963. *Career:* ordained a priest, 1943; pastorates in Iron Mountain, MI; Allentown, PA; and Brooklyn, NY, 1951–present; adjunct professor, St. Vladimir's Seminary, 1953–present; secretary, Standing Conference of Orthodox Bishops (SCOBA), 1960–present.

A priest of the Antiochian Orthodox Christian Archdiocese, Paul Schneirla has been a trusted adviser to the primates of that jurisdiction and has also served as its ecumenical officer. He has served as a member of the Orthodox-Roman Consultation, the Orthodox-Anglican Consultation, and the Orthodox-Polish National Catholic Consultation. He has been a member of the General Board of the National Council of Churches since 1953. Active in the movement toward greater Orthodox administrative unity, Schneirla was a member of the committee that provided the constitution for SCOBA. He has remained a driving force behind its work since 1960.

Bibliography

A. "The Western Rite in the Orthodox Church," *SVTQ* 2:2 (1958), 20–46; "A New Tendency in Anglican-Orthodox Relations," *SVTQ* 4:1 (1960), 23–31; "The Future of American Orthodoxy," *SVTQ* 5:4 (1961), 24–42; "Roma locuta?" *SVTQ* 6:2 (1962), 79–92.

SCOTT, ANTHONY (21 January 1949, Wichita Falls, TX–). *Education:* B.A., University of California at Berkeley, 1971; M.Div., St. Vladimir's Seminary, 1975. *Career:* ordained a priest, 1974; pastorate in Portland, OR, 1975–77; Wichita, KS, 1977–87; director of institutional development, St. Vladimir's Seminary, 1987–present.

A priest of the Orthodox Church in America, Anthony Scott has been active in areas related to theological education, evangelization, and youth ministry. He has been especially active in encouraging lay participation in the support of theological education and in projects related to Pan-Orthodox unity.

SPYROU, ATHENAGORAS ARISTOCLIS (25 March 1886, Vasilikon, Epirus, Ottoman Empire–6 July 1972, Constantinople). *Education:* diploma, Patriarchal Theological School of Halki, Turkey, 1910. *Career:* ordained a deacon, 1910; service in the diocese of Pelagonia, 1910–16; archdeacon in Athens, 1916–22; ordained a priest, 1922; consecrated a bishop, 1922; Metropolitan of Corfu, 1922–31; Archbishop of North and South America, 1931–48; Ecumenical Patriarch of Constantinople, 1948–72.

One of the most significant Orthodox Church leaders of the twentieth century, Patriarch Athenagoras had a distinguished career as a clergyman serving the Orthodox in the old Ottoman Empire, on the island of Corfu, in the United States, and finally as Patriarch in Constantinople. In each of these places, his ministry was characterized by a profound sense of pastoral service, which found rich expression in his care for the needy, his concern for renewal, and his efforts at reconciliation.

Having already achieved a reputation as a preacher, teacher, and administrator, Athenagoras was elected Metropolitan of Corfu in 1922. He came to that troubled island in the wake of the tragic wars that placed profound strains on family life and filled Corfu with refugees escaping the disasters of Asia Minor. At once, the new bishop established employment agencies and orphanages under the aegis of the church. At the same time, he called upon the clergy to recognize the challenges of society to recommit themselves to the well-being of their flock. He placed special emphasis upon the importance of preaching and teaching. And, at a time when relationships between Orthodox and Roman Catholics were limited and strained, Athenagoras took a bold initiative. He sought to cultivate better relations with the Roman Catholic clergy on the island and called for cooperation in serving the poor and needy.

Athenagoras was elected Archbishop of the Greek Orthodox Archdiocese of North and South America in 1931. His election was clearly designed to bring to America a respected clergyman who could effectively deal with the difficulties afflicting the immigrant Greek Orthodox community. In the two decades prior to his arrival, the Greek Orthodox had become deeply divided over issues rooted in Greek politics. Party politics had infected the parishes and had created rival factions.

With the full authority of the Ecumenical Patriarchate and with the support of the Church of Greece, Athenagoras once again became a reconciler and healer throughout his vast archdiocese. At the same time, he established a new constitution for the archdiocese. While greater emphasis was placed upon a centralized church administration, the new constitution also did much to overcome the earlier abuses that had contributed to divisions. His concern for the needy found fresh expression in his establishment of a society for women known as *Philoptohos,* meaning "friend of the poor." Likewise, his concern for the formation of clergy and lay leaders led to the establishment of Holy Cross School of Theology in 1937.

Early on in his ministry in America, Athenagoras recognized the need for greater cooperation and unity among all the Orthodox. The divisions that affected his own flock were frequently compounded by Old World animosities among the various Orthodox immigrant groups. Recognizing this harsh fact, Athenagoras became a champion for greater unity among all the Orthodox in this country. He proposed a Pan-Orthodox theological school in 1934 and a Pan-Orthodox church newspaper in 1941. He was one of the organizers in 1943 of the first successful attempt to gather together the leaders of a number of Orthodox ecclesiastical jurisdictions. Known as the Federated Orthodox Greek Catholic Primary Jurisdictions, this organization was a bold effort to encourage cooperation and to coordinate Orthodox witness.

Recognized by both religious and political figures as the preeminent representative of Orthodoxy in America, Athenagoras was elected Ecumenical Patriarch of Constantinople in 1948, and he was taken to his new assignment in the private airplane of President Harry Truman. In his new ministry, Athenagoras continued to pursue many of the same goals that he had on Corfu and in America. Among his first tasks was to deepen the relationships among the various autocephalous churches, which had become severely strained throughout the first half of the century. His meetings with the other Patriarchs led to four historic Pan-Orthodox conferences held between 1961 and 1968. These conferences marked a formal renewal of conciliarity and set in motion a process designed to lead to the convocation of a Great and Holy Council.

Athenagoras also significantly increased the participation of the Orthodox in the ecumenical movement. He encouraged greater Orthodox involvement in the World Council of Churches. He also took bold steps to initiate a dialogue between the Orthodox Church and the Roman Catholic Church. A new spirit of dialogue was inaugurated in conjunction with his meeting with Pope Paul VI in Jerusalem in 1964 and in the "Lifting of the Anathemas of 1054" between the two churches in 1965. Both of these actions laid the groundwork for the establishment of a formal theological dialogue between representatives of the two churches in the United States in 1965 and worldwide in 1979.

Despite the demands of his new position, Athenagoras never neglected the development of Orthodoxy in America. Because he understood both the challenges and the unique opportunities for the church in this country, he took special interest in the elections and the ministries of his successors, Archbishop Michael (1949–58) and Archbishop Iakovos (1959–   ). While he was never able to return to the United States for a pastoral visit, Athenagoras continued to have an influence upon the development of the church in this country.

Bibliography

B. George Papaioannou, *From Mars Hill to Manhattan* (Minneapolis, MN, 1976); Demetrios Tsakonas, *A Man Sent by God: The Life of Patriarch Athenagoras of Constantinople* (Brookline, MA, 1977).

STEPHANOPOULOS, ROBERT GEORGE   (19 November 1934, Neochorion, Greece–   ). *Education:* B.A., Holy Cross School of Theology, 1958; B.Div., 1959; graduate study, University of Athens, 1958–59; Ph.D., Boston University, 1970. *Career:* ordained a priest, 1958; pastorates in Fall River, MA; Rye, NY; Cleveland, OH; and New York City, 1982–present; adjunct professor, St. John's University, Queens, NY, 1986–present.

As dean of the Holy Trinity Greek Orthodox Cathedral in New York, Robert Stephanopoulos has been active in the various ministries of the Greek Orthodox Archdiocese and in its ecumenical witness. He has also been active in the work of the National Council of Churches and the Orthodox-Roman Catholic Consultation.

Bibliography

A. *A Study of Recent Greek Orthodox Ecumenical Relations* (Ann Arbor, 1970); *Guidelines for Orthodox Christians in Ecumenical Relations* (New York, 1973); *The Greek Orthodox Archdiocese of North and South America* (New York, 1990); *Patriarch Dimitrios in the United States* (New York, 1991).

STYLIANOPOULOS, THEODORE GEORGE   (1938, Mouzakion, Greece–   ). *Education:* B.A., Holy Cross School of Theology, 1962; S. T. M., Boston University School of Theology, 1964; Th.D., Harvard Divinity School,

1974. *Career:* ordained a priest, 1965; pastorates in Boston; Concord, NH; Lexington, MA; Keene, NH, 1965–present; faculty member, now professor of New Testament and orthodox spirituality, Hellenic College–Holy Cross Greek Orthodox School of Theology, 1967–present.

Theodore Stylianopoulos has devoted special attention in his teaching and writing to New Testament studies and to the characteristic features of Orthodox spirituality. A priest of the Greek Orthodox archdiocese, he has also been active in religious education and ecumenical dialogues, having served as a member of the Orthodox-Roman Catholic Consultation and the Central Committee of the World Council of Churches.

Bibliography

A. *Gospel of Christ* (Brookline, MA, 1981); *The Good News of Christ* (Brookline, MA, 1991).

T

TARASAR, CONSTANCE J.   (3 February 1938, Minneapolis–). *Education:* B.S., University of Minnesota, 1960; certificate, Ecumenical Institute, Geneva, 1966; M.Div., St. Vladimir's Seminary, 1968; Ed.D., State University of New York, Albany, 1989. *Career:* teacher, Fridley, MN, 1960–62; consultant in religious education, 1966–present; executive secretary, Department of Religious Education, 1967–78; executive secretary, Orthodox Christian Education Commission, 1969–78; lecturer in religious education, St. Vladimir's Seminary, 1970–present; managing editor, *The Orthodox Church,* 1985–90; associate general secretary, National Council of Churches, 1991–93; associate in Faith and Order, 1993–present.

Constance Tarasar has done pioneering work in formulating programs and in writing texts in the area of Orthodox religious education. She has also been active in ecumenical witness and service within both the National Council of Churches and the World Council of Churches. She is presently a member of its Faith and Order Commission.

Bibliography

A. Editor, *Orthodox America: 1794–1976* (Syosset, NY, 1975); editor, *Orthodox Women: Their Role and Participation in the Orthodox Church* (Geneva, 1977); editor, *Perspectives on Orthodox Education* (Syosset, NY, 1983); *Eyes to See, Ears to Hear* (New York, 1987).

TARAZI, PAUL NADIM   (2 October 1943, Jaffa, Palestine–). *Education:* diploma, French School of Medicine, Beirut, 1965; Lic. Theol., Theological Institute, Bucharest, Romania, 1969; Th.D., 1975. *Career:* lecturer, St. John School of

Theology, Balamand, Lebanon, 1970–76; ordained a priest, 1977; lecturer, St. Vladimir's Orthodox Theological Seminary, Crestwood, NY, 1977–79; pastorates, Danbury, CT, 1977–81; Uniondale, NY, 1981–present; assistant professor, 1980–83; visiting professor of biblical studies, St. John Institute of Theology, Balamand, Lebanon, 1981–present; associate professor, 1983–present.

Paul Tarazi is one of the outstanding beneficiaries of the Orthodox youth movement in the Middle East and the spirit of renewal in the patriarch of Antioch. Since coming to this country in 1976, he has been active in producing a commentary on the Old and New Testaments and has been a leader in renewing the interest in Scripture study among the Orthodox. A priest of the Antiochian Orthodox Christian Archdiocese, he has also been associated with the movement to reemphasize importance of biblical preaching in the Orthodox Church.

Bibliography

A. *I Thessalonians: A Commentary* (Crestwood, NY, 1982); *Old Testament: An Introduction* (Crestwood, NY, 1991); *Galatians: A Commentary* (Crestwood, NY, 1993).
B. *WWR* (1994), 511.

TOPPING, EVA CATAFYGIOTU   (23 August 1920, Fredericksburg, VA–   ). *Education:* B.A., Mary Washington College, 1941; M.A., Radcliffe College, 1943; graduate studies, University of Athens, 1950–51. *Career:* research and writing, 1977–present.

Eva Topping has been active in associations dealing with ecumenical relations and church renewal. In her recent historical studies, she has investigated the role of women in the church of the Byzantine period.

Bibliography

A. *Sacred Stories from Byzantium* (Brookline, MA, 1977); *Holy Mothers of Orthodoxy* (Minneapolis, 1987); *Saints and Sisterhood* (Minneapolis, 1990).
B. *WWR* (1992), 522.

TOTH, ALEXIS GEORGIEVICH   (14 March 1853, Presov, Slovakia–7 May 1909, Mayfield, PA). *Education:* diploma, University of Presov, 1878. *Career:* ordained a priest, 1878; professor of canon law and director of the Greek Catholic Seminary of Presov, 1881–89; sent as missionary priest to America, 1889; received into the Russian Orthodox diocese of Alaska and Aleutians together with his Minneapolis parish, 1891; proclaimed a saint, 1994.

Alexis Toth came to the United States to serve the Eastern-Rite Catholic immigrants from the Austro-Hungarian Empire who were known as Carpatho-Russians or Ruthenians. Their Orthodox ancestors had entered into a union with the Roman Catholic Church at the Union of Brest in 1596 and the Union of Uzhorod in 1646.

Toth immediately encountered opposition to his missionary work from Archbishop John Ireland of Minneapolis. Desirous of a rapid process of Americanization for the immigrants, Ireland also had little appreciation for the particular characteristics of the Eastern Catholic Churches, which were usually known then as Greek Catholic. Objecting particularly to the practice of a married priesthood, Ireland refused to give Toth, who was a widower, permission to organize his parish.

Almost immediately, Toth initiated contacts with Bishop Nicholas of San Francisco, the head of the Russian Orthodox diocese of Alaska and the Aleutians. On 25 March 1891, Bishop Nicholas traveled to Minneapolis to receive Toth and his entire parish into the diocese. For the next twenty-eight years, Toth was a powerful force in encouraging about fifty other Eastern Catholic priests and their parishes to enter the Orthodox Church.

Bibliography

A. *Letters, Articles, Papers and Sermons,* ed. George Soldatow (Chillwack, B.C., 1978).
B. Keith Russin, "Father Alexis G. Toth and the Wilkes-Barre Litigation," *SVSQ* 16:3 (1972), 128–49.

TRAKATELLIS, DEMETRIOS (1 February 1928, Thessaloniki, Greece–). *Education:* diploma, University of Athens, School of Theology, Athens, Greece, 1950; Ph.D., Harvard Divinity School, 1977; University of Athens, School of Theology, Th.D., 1977. *Career:* consecrated a bishop in Athens, 1967; distinguished professor of biblical studies and Christian origins, Hellenic College–Holy Cross Greek Orthodox School of Theology, 1984–93; visiting professor of New Testament, Harvard Divinity School, 1984–85, 1988–89; metropolitan of Vresthena, Athens, 1991–present.

Metropolitan Demetrios Trakatellis is a preeminent Orthodox biblical scholar who is highly regarded for his studies in Scripture and early Christianity. Since his student days at Harvard Divinity School, he has been a much sought-after speaker at scholarly symposia, retreats, and conferences both in this country and abroad. In recent years, Metropolitan Demetrios has been active both in ministerial service and in scholarly circles in Greece and in the United States.

Bibliography

A. *Presence of the Holy Spirit* (Thessaloniki, 1984); *Authority and Passion* (Brookline, MA, 1987); *The Transcendent God of Eugnostos* (Brookline, MA, 1991); *Christ, the Pre-Existing God* (Athens, 1992).

TRIFA, VALERIAN VIOREL (28 June 1914, Campeni, Romania–27 January 1987, Estoril, Portugal). *Education:* graduate studies, University of Bucharest, Romania, 1931–41; diploma, Chisinau Theological School, Besarabia, Romania, 1935. *Career:* political and student organizer, 1935–41; exile in Germany, Austria, and Italy, 1941–50; admitted to the United States, 1950; elected bishop of the Romanian Orthodox Episcopate of America, 1951; ordained deacon, priest, and bishop, 1952; reordained, 1960.

Valerian Trifa and others fled Romania in 1941 after being involved in student political activities. He entered the United States in 1950 as a displaced person. From that time, charges were frequently made that he had a role in the persecutions of Romanian Jews and that he been a Nazi sympathizer. Inconclusive investigations were carried out by a number of government agencies between 1950 and 1957, when, on 13 May, 1957, Trifa became a naturalized citizen.

Trifa became active in affairs of the Romanian Orthodox Church in this country. A division within this diocesan jurisdiction occurred in 1950, chiefly regarding its relationship with the Church in Romania. Claiming Communist interference in Romanian church affairs, some clergy and laity refused to recognize the election of a new bishop for America, Andrei Modavan, in 1951. They established an independent diocese separate from the Romanian Orthodox Patriarchate in Bucharest. Although a layman at the time, Trifa was the choice for bishop due, in part, to his staunch Romanian nationalism and anti-Communism. Most other Orthodox bishops refused to establish any association with Trifa, chiefly because of concerns about the canonicity of his new diocese. After much searching, some Ukrainian Orthodox bishops eventually agreed to perform his ordinations in Philadelphia in 1952. These ordinations, however, were viewed as uncanonical and were not recognized by most other Orthodox bishops. The Patriarchate of Bucharest refused to recognize Trifa and viewed the new diocese as schismatic.

Seeking greater recognition, Trifa was eventually reordained by bishops of the Russian Orthodox Metropolia in 1960. From that time, Archbishop Valerian and his approximately thirty-three parishes became associated with the Metropolia, which in 1970 became known as the Orthodox Church in America. As head of his diocese, Trifa paid special attention to the development of religious education programs and the translation of liturgical texts into English to meet the needs of the growing numbers of American-born members. Known for his staunch anti-Communism, he was also active in the National Council of Churches and World Council of Churches.

The American government opened a new inquiry into Archbishop Valerian Trifa's background in 1974. It was demonstrated that he had lied about his background at the time of his immigration. While Trifa recognized that he misrepresented himself at the time of his immigration, he rejected all other charges against him. Facing the possibility of deportation, he surrendered his certificate of naturalization on 26 August 1980 on the advice of counsel. In poor health, he left the country and settled in Portugal in 1984, where he died three years later.

Bibliography

B. Gerald J. Bobango, *Religion and Politics: Bishop Valerian Trifa and His Times* (New York, 1981); Gerald J. Bobango, *The Romanian Orthodox Episcopate of America: The First Half Century, 1929–1979* (Jackson, MI, 1979).

TSOUMAS, GEORGE (1912, Lowell, MA–22 October 1979, Boston). *Education:* B.A., University of Connecticut, 1936; Lic. Theol., Patriarchal Theological School of Halki, 1938; S.T.M., Hartford Theological Seminary, 1943; Ph.D., Boston University, 1953. *Career:* ordained a priest, 1948; pastorates in Manchester, NH, 1948–50; Nashua, NH, 1950–58; Boston, 1957–62; and Somerville, MA, 1970–78; professor of church history, Holy Cross Greek Orthodox School of Theology, 1938–71; emeritus professor, 1971–79.

George Tsoumas was one of the founding faculty members of Holy Cross Greek Orthodox School of Theology. Known for his devotion to the teaching of church history and patristics, he both taught and inspired generations of students during his distinguished career. In his weekly column in the *Hellenic Chronicle,* Tsoumas had a special ability to communicate the history and teachings of the Orthodox Church to a popular audience. As a priest of the Greek Orthodox Archdiocese, he was also called upon to undertake administrative responsibilities in the Boston district.

Bibliography

A. *Patrology: A History of the Fathers of the Church* (Pomfret, CT, 1942); *A History of the Holy Cross Greek Orthodox School of Theology* (Brookline, MA, 1973).
B. *OO* 45 (1979), 10.

U

UPSON, STEPHEN (21 April 1911, Lockport, NY–). *Education:* B.A., University of Buffalo, 1936; M.A., 1937; Ph.D., Harvard University, 1940. *Career:* ordained a priest, 1941; pastorates in Pittsburgh; Boston; Toronto, Ont.; Rochester, NY, 1954–present.

A priest of the Antiochian Orthodox Christian Archdiocese, Stephen Upson is among the pioneers responsible for new liturgical translations and the publication of literature on the Orthodox faith in the United States, especially in the period after World War II. For over fifty years, he has been among the driving forces for Pan-Orthodox religious education, a unified youth movement, and greater jurisdictional cooperation.

Bibliography

A. *A Catechism of Christian Doctrine of the Holy Eastern Orthodox Catholic and Apostolic Church* (New York, 1944); *The Divine Liturgy of Our Fathers Among the Saints, John Chrysostom* (New York, 1948); *A Brief Synopsis of the Orthodox Church Year* (New York, 1949); *Service Book* (New York, 1949); *Orthodox Church History* (New York, 1953); *A Pocket Prayer Book for Orthodox Christians* (New York, 1956).

V

VAPORIS, NOMIKOS MICHAEL (20 July 1926, Kalymnos, Greece–). *Education:* diploma, Holy Cross School of Theology, 1949; S.T.M., Berkeley Divinity School, 1951; Lic. Theol., University of Athens, 1954; M.A., Columbia University, 1963; Ph.D., 1970. *Career:* ordained a priest, 1953; pastorates in Pittsburgh; Brooklyn, NY; Easton, PA; Somersworth, NH, 1953–present; faculty member, Hellenic College–Holy Cross School of Theology, now professor of Byzantine history, 1965–present; editor, *The Greek Orthodox Theological Review,* 1971–present.

A priest of the Greek Orthodox Archdiocese, Nomikos Vaporis has concentrated his writing and research on the role of the Orthodox Church and the place of Greek culture, especially during the Ottoman period. He is regarded as an expert on this period.

Bibliography

A. *Some Aspects of the History of the Ecumenical Patriarchate of Constantinople in the Seventeenth and Eighteenth Centuries* (New York, 1969); *The Controversies That Arose as a Consequence of the Translations of the Scriptures into Modern Greek* (Ann Arbor, MI, 1970); *Father Kosmos: Apostle to the Poor* (Brookline, MA, 1977).

B. *DAS* (1974), 648.

VENIAMINOV, INNOCENT JOHN (26 August 1797, Anginskoe, Russia–31 March 1879, Moscow). *Education:* diploma, Irkutsk Seminary, 1818. *Career:* ordained a priest, 1821; arrived in Unalaska in Russian America, 1824; transferred to Sitka parish, 1834; consecrated bishop of Kamchatka, the Kuriles, and Aleutian

Islands, 1840; named archbishop with see at Yakutsk, 1852; Metropolitan of Moscow, 1858–79; proclaimed a saint, 1977.

John Veniaminov arrived in Unalaska with his wife, son, mother, and brother on 29 July 1824. At the age of twenty-seven, the young missionary immediately began to serve the natives, who has been without a priest for about two years. In order to do his missionary work, Veniaminov created an Aleut alphabet based upon the Cyrillic characters. A dictionary and grammar soon followed. These provided a basis for his translation of the gospel of Matthew and portions of the liturgy into Aleut. He also wrote a basic catechism entitled *Indication of the Pathway into the Kingdom of Heaven.*

Veniaminov also taught the Aleuts agricultural techniques, carpentry, and metalworking. He established a meteorological station and wrote three volumes on the natives entitled *Notes on the Islands of the Unalaska District.* He constructed a new church building on Unalaska in 1826. During the ten years of service on the island, he also supervised the construction of a school and an orphanage, as well as a number of chapels on nearby islands.

Veniaminov was persuaded by the Russian governor to move to New Archangel (Sitka) in 1934 to continue his missionary activity among the natives. There, Veniaminov immediately began to learn the language and culture of the Tlingits, who were generally hostile to the Russians. Veniaminov managed to gain the confidence of many of the natives when he struggled to combat an epidemic of smallpox. While stationed at New Archangel, Veniaminov traveled extensively to many missionary outposts. In 1836, he visited Fort Rus in Northern California, which had been established in 1812. During this trip, he also visited a number of Roman Catholic missions staffed by Franciscan missionaries.

During a return visit to St. Petersburg to seek assistance for the mission, Veniaminov's wife died. Within less than two years of this tragedy, Veniaminov was elected bishop of a new diocese that included Alaska and Eastern Siberia. Taking the name Innocent, he was consecrated in the cathedral in St. Petersburg on 15 December 1940. With his return to New Archangel, the region began to experience a new period of missionary activity. A mission house was constructed in 1842, and a seminary was established in 1845. In 1848, the Cathedral of St. Michael was consecrated. Innocent became an archbishop in 1852 and began to devote more attention to missionary work in Eastern Siberia. By 1860, there were about 12,000 native Alaskan Christians. Innocent was elected Metropolitan of Moscow in 1868 and subsequently founded in 1870 the Russian Orthodox Missionary Society. He was formally proclaimed a saint by the Church of Russia in 1977 and given the title Apostle to America.

Bibliography

A. *Indication of the Pathway into the Kingdom of Heaven,* trans. Paul Garrett in *Alaskan Missionary Spirituality,* ed. Michael Oleska (New York, 1987), 80–119.
B. Paul Garrett, *St. Innocent, Apostle to America* (Crestwood, NY, 1979).

VERHOVSKOY, SERGE S.   (1907 Sarzha, Russia–4 August 1986, Crestwood, NY). *Education:* St. Sergius Theological Institute, Paris, 1932–36. *Career:* professor, St. Sergius, 1944–52; professor of dogmatic theology, St. Vladimir's Theological Seminary, New York, 1952–81.

Serge Verhovskoy emigrated with his parents to Prague following the Russian revolution of 1917. After receiving his early education there, the family went to Paris, then the center of Russian émigré life in the decades following World War I. He undertook theological studies at St. Sergius Theological Institute in Paris and became an early leader in the Russian Student Christian movement. Not long after graduation, he began teaching at St. Sergius in the area of ancient and medieval philosophy and later in dogmatic theology. During this period, he was also involved in discussions with Roman Catholic theologians, a rare occurrence in those days.

Following Father Georges Florovsky, Verhovskoy arrived in New York in 1952 with his wife and three daughters in order to teach at St. Vladimir's. As the dean, Florovsky was eager to establish the reputation of St. Vladimir's by attracting former colleagues from Paris. Teaching in the areas of moral and dogmatic theology, Verhovskoy was known for his strong emphasis upon the importance of the scriptural basis of Orthodox doctrine.

Bibliography

A. *God and Man* (in Russian) (Paris, 1955); *Orthodoxy in Life* (in Russian) (Paris, 1955); *The Light of the World* (Crestwood, NY, 1982).
B. *SVQR* 30:4 (1986), 283–84.

VERONIS, ALEXANDER   (7 September 1932, Paterson, NJ–   ). *Education:* B.A., Lafayette College, 1954; B.D., Holy Cross School of Theology, 1958; S.T.M., Boston University, 1960; Lic. Theol., University of Athens, 1961. *Career:* ordained a priest, 1961; pastor, Annunciation Orthodox Church, Lancaster, PA, 1961–present.

A priest of the Greek Orthodox Archdiocese, Alexander Veronis has combined pastoral and ecumenical activities in south central Pennsylvania with a deep commitment to the development of Orthodox missions. He has been among the leading advocates for a renewed emphasis upon Orthodox missions both here and abroad. In recent years, he has joined with his wife, Pearl, in leading spiritual life and renewal retreats as well as lecturing on topics related to missions and social concerns. In recognition of their service, the Alexander and Pearl Veronis Endowment Fund for Orthodox Missions was established in 1981 to promote missions.

Bibliography

A. "Eastern Europe: An Historic Challenge for Orthodoxy," *Mission* 8:1 (1992), 12.

Appendix I
CHRONOLOGY

1741   The Eucharist is celebrated on a boat off Alaskan coast.

1768   Colony of Greek Orthodox in St. Augustine, Florida.

1794   Russian Orthodox missionaries arrive on Kodiak Island.

1798   Father Joseph Bolotov consecrated first bishop.

1812   Chapel at Fort Rus, California.

1824   Father John (Innocent) Veniaminov arrives in Unalaska.

1825   Father Iakov Netsvetov, first native priest.

1834   The liturgy and catechism translated into Aleut.

1840   Consecration of Bishop Innocent.

1841   Pastoral school established in Sitka.

1848   St. Michael Cathedral consecrated in Sitka.

1864   Holy Trinity Church in New Orleans established. Subsequently becomes first Greek Orthodox parish.

1867   Alaska sold to the United States.

1868   Founding of parish in San Francisco.

1870   Father Bjerring establishes parish in New York City.

1878   *Oriental Church* magazine published.

1891   St. Mary parish in Minneapolis enters Orthodox church.

1892   Holy Trinity Greek Orthodox parish in New York founded.

        First Serbian Orthodox parish in Jackson, California.

        Father Sabastian Dabovich first American-born person ordained.

1895   First Syrian Orthodox parish in Brooklyn, New York.

First conference of Orthodox clergy, Wilkes-Barre, Pennsylvania.

1897   Missionary school opens in Minneapolis.

Russian-American Messenger begins publication.

1898   Bishop Tikhon arrives in America.

1902   St. Nicholas Cathedral in New York built.

1904   Father Raphael Hawaweeny, first bishop consecrated in United States.

First Romanian Orthodox parish in Cleveland, Ohio.

1905   Russian Orthodox Archdiocese see transferred to New York.

1906   St. Tikhon Monastery dedicated.

Service Book translated by Isabel Hapgood.

1907   First Sunday of Orthodoxy Service in New York.

Theofan Noli ordained.

First Bulgarian Orthodox parish in Madison, Illinois.

1908   Albanian Orthodox parish in Boston.

1909   Death of Father Alexis Toth.

1912   First Orthodox Sunday school, in Holy Trinity Church, New York.

1913   Serbian Orthodox clergy come under Church of Serbia.

1914   Patriarchate of Antioch sends bishop to organize parishes.

1915   First monastery for women, Springfield, Vermont.

1922   Greek Orthodox Archdiocese established.

Father Antony Bashir arrives.

Metropolitan Platon heads Russian Orthodox Archdiocese.

1923   Father Theophan Noli consecrated a bishop in Albania.

1924   Russian Orthodox Archdiocese declares autonomy.

1926   Russian Orthodox Synod Abroad establishes a diocese.

1928   A Ukrainian Orthodox diocese is established.

1929   Romanian Orthodox Episcopate is established.

1931   Archbishop Athenagoras heads the Greek Orthodox Archdiocese.

1933   Father Benjamin Basalga, first American-born bishop.

Patriarchate of Moscow establishes exarchate.

1934   Metropolitan Theophilus heads Metropolia.

1935   Bishop Policarp Morusca heads the Romanian Orthodox diocese.

1936   Metropolitan Antony Bashir heads the Syrian Orthodox Archdiocese.

Metropolitan Samuel David heads Toledo diocese.

1937   Holy Cross Seminary established in Pomfret, Connecticut.

Ukrainian Orthodox diocese established by Constantinople.

Father Bohdan Shpilka consecrated bishop in Constantinople.

1938	St. Vladimir's Seminary established in New York.
	St. Tikhon's Pastoral School is established.
	The Metropolia unites with the Synod Abroad.
	Bulgarian Orthodox diocese established.
	Carpatho-Russian diocese established by Constantinople.
	Father Orestes Chornok consecrated bishop in Constantinople.
1939	Father James (Iakovos) Coucousis arrives.
1944	The Federated Orthodox Greek Catholic Primary Jurisdictions (The Federation) established.
1945	Bulgarian Orthodox diocese established.
1946	The Metropolia severs relationship with the Synod Abroad.
1950	Synod Abroad moves headquarters to New York.
	Metropolitan Leonty heads Metropolia.
1951	Archbishop Michael heads Greek Orthodox Archdiocese.
	Independent Romanian Orthodox diocese created.
1953	Orthodox designation recognized by Defense Department.
1954	Toledo diocese recognized by Patriarchate of Antioch.
1956	Orthodox Christian Education Commission created.
1959	Archbishop Iakovos heads Greek Orthodox Archdiocese.
1960	Standing Conference of Canonical Orthodox Bishops in America (SCOBA) created.
1963	Autonomous Serbian Orthodox diocese established.
1964	Autonomous Bulgarian Orthodox diocese established.
	Metropolitan Philaret heads Synod Abroad.
1966	Metropolitan Philip Saliba heads the Syrian Orthodox Archdiocese.
1970	Church of Russia grants autocephaly to the Metropolia.
	Metropolia takes name Orthodox Church in America.
	Herman of Alaska is canonized.
1972	St. Herman Pastoral School opens in Sitka, Alaska.
1975	Unification of Syrian Orthodox dioceses.
	Antiochian Orthodox Christian Archdiocese established.
1977	Innocent of Alaska is canonized.
	Metropolitan Theodosius heads Orthodox Church in America.
1985	Metropolitan Vitali heads Synod Abroad.
1989	Patriarch Tikhon is canonized.
1990	Ecumenical Patriarch Dimitrios visits the United States.
1994	Bicentenary of Alaskan mission.

Appendix II
THE AUTOCEPHALOUS AND AUTONOMOUS ORTHODOX CHURCHES

The Ecumenical Patriarchate of Constantinople

The Patriarchate of Alexandria

The Patriarchate of Antioch

The Patriarchate of Jerusalem

The Patriarchate of Russia

The Patriarchate of Serbia

The Patriarchate of Romania

The Patriarchate of Bulgaria

The Patriarchate of Georgia

The Church of Cyprus

The Church of Greece

The Church of Poland

The Church of Albania

The Church of the Czech Lands and Slovakia (Autonomous)

The Church of Finland (Autonomous)

The above order is that followed in Inter-Orthodox gatherings. The Orthodox Church in America, formerly the Russian Orthodox Metropolia, was granted autocephalous status by the Patriarchate of Moscow in 1970. This status, however, is not recognized by all churches. Likewise, the autonomous status of the Church of Japan is not recognized by all churches.

Appendix III
THE STANDING CONFERENCE OF CANONICAL ORTHODOX BISHOPS IN AMERICA

Albanian Orthodox Diocese of America
  (Patriarchate of Constantinople)

American Carpatho-Russian Orthodox Greek Catholic Diocese in the U.S.A.
  (Patriarchate of Constantinople)

Antiochian Orthodox Christian Archdiocese of North America
  (Patriarchate of Antioch)

Bulgarian Eastern Orthodox Church
  (Patriarchate of Bulgaria)

Greek Orthodox Archdiocese of North and South America
  (Patriarchate of Constantinople)

Orthodox Church in America
  (formerly, Patriarchate of Russia)

Romanian Orthodox Missionary Archdiocese in America and Canada
  (Patriarchate of Romania)

Serbian Orthodox Church in the United States and Canada
  (Patriarchate of Serbia)

Ukrainian Orthodox Church in America
  (Patriarchate of Constantinople)

BIBLIOGRAPHIC ESSAY

This essay is intended to be a guide for further investigation into aspects of Orthodox Christianity in general and the Orthodox in America in particular. It is not meant to be an exhaustive bibliography. Special attention is given to the writings of American Orthodox theologians and church historians.

GENERAL HISTORIES AND INTRODUCTIONS
TO ORTHODOX THOUGHT

General introductions to the history of the Orthodox Church can be found in John Meyendorff's *The Orthodox Church* (Crestwood, NY: St. Vladimir's Seminary Press, 1981) and Alexander Schmemann's *The Historical Road of Eastern Orthodoxy* (Crestwood, NY: St. Vladimir's Seminary Press, 1977). The most popular general history, and often more accessible than the two books previously mentioned, is from the British Orthodox bishop Timothy (Kallistos) Ware, *The Orthodox Church* (New York: Penguin Books, rev. ed., 1993).

For studies dealing with particular historical periods of the Orthodox Church, see John Meyendorff, *Imperial Unity* (Crestwood, NY: St. Vladimir's Seminary Press, 1989) and *Byzantium and the Rise of Russia* (Crestwood, NY: St. Vladimir's Seminary Press, 1989); Richard Haugh, *Photius and the Carolingians* (Belmont, MA: Nordland, 1975); Anthony-Emil Tachiaos, *Cyril and Methodios of Thessalonica: The Acculturation of the Slavs* (Thessaloniki: Rekos, 1989); Demetrios Constantellos, *Byzantine Philanthropy and Social Welfare* (New Brunswick, NJ: Rutgers University Press, 1968); J. M. Hussey, *The Orthodox Church in the Byzantine Empire* (Oxford: Clarendon Press, 1986).

Among the best general histories of the Byzantine period are George Ostrogorsky, *History of the Byzantine State* (Oxford: Oxford University Press, 1968) and Dimitri Obolinsky, *The Byzantine Commonwealth: Eastern Europe, 500–1453* (London: Cardinal, 1971).

Issues related to the schism between Eastern and Western Christianity are discussed in John Meyendorff's *Byzantine Theology* (New York: Fordham University Press, 1974). Some aspects of the church under Ottoman rule are covered in Steven Runciman's *The Great Church in Captivity* (Cambridge: Cambridge University Press, 1968).

For developments of the Orthodox Church in Russia in more recent times, see James Cunningham, *A Vanquished Hope: Movements for Church Renewal in Russia* (Crestwood, NY: St. Vladimir's Seminary Press, 1981); Nicholas Zernov, *The Russian Religious Renaissance of the Twentieth Century* (London: Darton, Longman and Todd, 1963); Dimitri Pospielovsky, *The Russian Church Under the Soviet Regime 1917–1982* (Crestwood, NY: St. Vladimir's Seminary Press, 1984). Essays on recent developments of a number of regional Orthodox churches and jurisdictions are found in Petro Ramet, ed., *Eastern Christianity and Politics in the Twentieth Century* (Durham, NC: Duke University Press, 1988).

A valuable introduction to the Oriental Orthodox churches is Azziz S. Atiya, *A History of Eastern Christianity* (Notre Dame, IN: University of Notre Dame Press, 1965). For some aspects of the recent developments between the Orthodox and the Oriental Orthodox, see William Lazareth and Nikos Nissiotis, *Does Chalcedon Unite or Divide?* (Geneva: World Council of Churches, 1981) and Thomas FitzGerald, "Towards the Reestablishment of Full Communion: The Orthodox-Oriental Orthodox Dialogue," *The Greek Orthodox Theological Review* 36:2 (1991), 169–82.

The fundamental themes of Orthodox doctrine and spirituality can be found in Kallistos (Timothy) Ware, *The Orthodox Way* (Crestwood, NY: St. Vladimir's Seminary Press, 1979). Somewhat less accessible is the classic work by Vladimir Lossky, *The Mystical Theology of the Eastern Church* (Cambridge: James Clarke, 1951). See also his essays in *In the Image and Likeness of God,* ed. John Erickson and Thomas Bird (Crestwood, NY: St. Vladimir's Seminary Press, 1974). Also of importance for the development of Orthodox spirituality is John Meyendorff's *St. Gregory Palamas and Orthodox Spirituality* (Crestwood, NY: St. Vladimir's Seminary Press, 1974). A popular presentation of Orthodox faith and practice is Anthony Coniaris, *Introducing the Orthodox Church* (Minneapolis: Light and Life, 1982). A valuable introduction to the Orthodox Church is Jordan Bajis, *Common Ground: An Introduction to Eastern Christianity for the American Christian* (Minneapolis: Light and Life, 1991).

A very comprehensive study of Orthodox doctrine as it was explicated in its historical context is Jaroslav Pelikan's *The Christian Tradition: A History of the Development of Doctrine, Volume 2, The Spirit of Eastern Christendom (600–1700)* (Chicago: University of Chicago Press, 1974). Pelikan also makes reference to the Orthodox, especially in volume 5, *Christian Doctrine and Modern Culture* (Chicago: University of Chicago Press, 1989). The author's bibliographical information is exceptional.

The extensive writings of Georges Florovsky have had a powerful influence on Orthodox theologians both in this country and elsewhere. Few themes in Orthodox history and theology escaped his attention. Many of his most important essays have been published in *The Collected Works of Georges Florovsky, Volumes I–XIV* (Belmont, MA: Nordland-Buchervertriebsanstalt, 1972–89). On Florovsky's career, see Andrew Blane, ed., *Georges Florovsky: Russian Intellectual and Orthodox Churchman* (Crestwood, NY: St. Vladimir's Seminary Press, 1993).

Alexander Schmemann's many works on Orthodox worship are most valuable in discussing the relationship between worship and belief. See especially *The Eucharist* (Crestwood, NY: St. Vladimir's Seminary Press, 1988); *Of Water and the Spirit* (Crestwood, NY: St. Vladimir's Seminary Press, 1974); *For the Life of the World: Sacraments and Orthodoxy*

(Crestwood, NY: St. Vladimir's Seminary Press, 1973); *Great Lent* (Crestwood, NY: St. Vladimir's Seminary Press, 1969).

With a rich bibliography of theological sources in Greek, Alkiviadis Calivas addresses a number of issues related to the development of the liturgy in his *The Divine Liturgy: The Time of Its Celebration* (Thessaloniki: Patriarchal Institute, 1988). The relationship between Scripture and worship is explored by John Breck in his *The Power of the Word in the Worshiping Church*. Kyriaki FitzGerald relates Orthodox worship to faith development in her *Religious Formation and Liturgical Life: An Orthodox Perspective* (Ann Arbor, MI: University Microfilm, 1982).

A very popular series containing statements on the spiritual life from the early patristic tradition is *The Philokalia*, Vols. 1–3, trans. and ed. G.E.H. Palmer, Philip Sherrard, and Kallistos Ware (London: Faber and Faber, 1979–84). A popular expression of Orthodox spirituality is *Way of the Pilgrim*, trans. R. M. French (London: S.P.C.K., 1963).

The intimate relationship between Orthodox teaching and the organization of the church and the characteristics of its ministries are found in the classic study by John Zizioulas, *Being as Communion* (Crestwood, NY: St. Vladimir's Seminary Press, 1985). John Erickson takes up a number of questions regarding church organization in his *The Challenge of Our Past* (Crestwood, NY: St. Vladimir's Seminary Press, 1991).

A number of recent reference works have been especially sensitive to the need to include essays dealing with the Orthodox. *Dictionary of Christianity in America*, ed. Daniel Reid, Robert D. Linder, Bruce L. Shelley, and Harry S. Stout (Downers Grove, IL: InterVarsity Press, 1990) has a number of essays devoted to the Orthodox themes, as does *Dictionary of the Ecumenical Movement*, ed. Nicholas Lossky *et al.* (Geneva: World Council of Churches, 1991). *The Encyclopedia of the American Religious Experience*, ed. Charles H. Lippy and Peter W. Williams (New York: Charles Scribner's Sons, 1988) has a valuable essay on "Eastern Christianity" by Paul Garrett. The three volumes of *Christian Spirituality*, ed. Bernard McGinn and John Meyendorff (New York: Crossroad, 1989) have very valuable essays by Orthodox contributors. Edwin S. Gaustad's *A Documentary History of Religion in America Since 1865* (Grand Rapids: Eerdsmand, 1983) includes a few documents related to the Orthodox. A Roman Catholic theologian, Michael A. Fahey, has produced two valuable bibliographical essays dealing especially with the writings of Orthodox theologians. See his "Orthodox Ecumenism and Theology: 1970–1978," *Theological Studies* 39:3 (1978), 446–85; and "Orthodox Ecumenism and Theology: 1978–1983," *Theological Studies* 44 (1983), 625–92. Another Roman Catholic theologian, Thomas Bird, has provided a valuable chronicle to events in the Orthodox Church in the journal *Diakonia* from 1970 to 1975.

THE ORTHODOX CHURCH IN THE UNITED STATES

Extensive studies dealing with aspects of the development of the Orthodox Church in the United States are few. Early movements toward greater unity up until 1970 are discussed in Serafim Surrency's *The Quest for Orthodox Church Unity in America* (Saints Boris and Gleb Press: New York, 1973). A general history of the Metropolia/Orthodox Church in America with some references to other jurisdictions is *Orthodox America: 1784–1976*, ed. Constance Tarasar and John Erickson (Syosset, NY: Orthodox Church in America, 1975). Some aspects of the Greek Orthodox Archdiocese are discussed in *History of the Greek Orthodox Church in America*, ed. Miltiades Efthimiou and George Christopoulos (New York: Greek Orthodox Archdiocese, 1984) and in George Papaioannou's *From Mars Hill to Manhattan* (Minneapolis: Light and Life, 1976). A brief account of the development of the

Greek Orthodox Archdiocese is found in Demetrios Constantelos, *Understanding the Greek Orthodox Church: Its Faith, History and Practice* (New York: Seabury Press, 1982). The same author has collected a number of documents related to the Greek Orthodox Archdiocese in his *Encyclicals and Documents of the Greek Orthodox Archdiocese, 1922–1972* (Thessaloniki: Patriarchal Center for Patristic Studies, 1976). Of historical value is the work done by the Historical Records Survey in its *Eastern Orthodox Churches and the Armenian Church in America* (New York: Works Project Administration, 1940). This text contains a number of general essays on various jurisdictions, together with a review of their activities in New York City prior to 1940. Although his text is somewhat outdated, Arthur Piepkorn provides a valuable introduction to various Orthodox jurisdictions in his *Profiles in Belief: The Religious Bodies in the United States Volume I: Roman Catholic, Old Catholic and Eastern Orthodox* (New York: Harper and Row, 1977).

LATE EIGHTEENTH- AND NINETEENTH-CENTURY DEVELOPMENTS AND CONCERNS

Valuable documents related to the Alaskan mission have been collected by Michael Oleska in his *Alaskan Missionary Spirituality* (New York: Paulist Press, 1987). For a historical introduction to the mission, see his *Orthodox Alaska: A Theology of Mission* (Crestwood, NY: St. Vladimir's Seminary Press, 1992). Also of importance are the works by Barbara Smith, *Russian Orthodoxy in Alaska* (Anchorage: Alaska Historical Resources, 1980); *Orthodoxy and Native Americans: The Alaskan Mission* (Crestwood, NY: St. Vladimir's Seminary Press, 1980); and *Russian America: The Forgotten Frontier* (Tacoma: Washington Historical Society, 1990). Paul Garrett's *St. Innocent: Apostle to America* (Crestwood, NY: St. Vladimir's Seminary Press, 1978) is a comprehensive study that emphasizes the missionary activity of this major personality.

References to the relationship between the immigrants and the early parish and diocesan developments are found in Charles Moschos, *Greek Americans: Struggle and Success* (Englewood Cliffs, NJ: Prentice-Hall, 1980); Theodore Saloutos, *The Greeks in the United States* (Cambridge: Harvard University Press, 1964); Henry Fairchild, *Greek Immigration to the United States* (New Haven, CT: Yale University Press, 1911); Lawrence Barringer, *Good Victory* (Brookline, MA: Holy Cross Orthodox Press, 1985); Paul Robert Magocsi, *Our People: Carpatho–Rusyns and Their Descendents in North America* (Toronto: Multicultural History Society of Ontario, 1984); Jerome Davis, *The Russians and Ruthenians in America: Bolsheviks or Brothers* (New York: George H. Doran, 1922). A handy introduction to various immigrant groups can be found in Stephen Thernstrom, ed., *Harvard Encyclopedia of American Ethnic Groups* (Cambridge: Harvard University Press, 1980).

More direct references to the church in this period can be found in Alexander Doumouras, "Greek Orthodox Communities in America Before World War I," *SVTQ* 11:4 (1967), 177–78; Peter Haskell, "American Civil Religion and Greek Immigration: Religious Confrontation Before the First World War," *SVTQ* 18:4 (1974), 166–92; Dimitry Gregorieff, "The Historical Background of Orthodoxy in America," *SVTQ* 5:1 (1961), 2–53; Vasile Hategan, *Fifty Years of the Romanian Orthodox Church in America* (Jackson, MI: Romanian Orthodox Episcopate, 1954).

The movements of Eastern-Rite Catholics into the Orthodox Church are discussed in Keith Russin, "Father Alexis Toth and the Wilkes-Barre Legislation," *SVTQ* 16:3 (1972), 128–48 and James Jorgenson, "Fr. Alexis Toth and the Transition of the Greek Catholic Community of Minneapolis to the Russian Orthodox Church," *SVTQ* 32:2 (1988), 119–38.

EARLY TWENTIETH-CENTURY DEVELOPMENTS
AND CONCERNS

Two prominent leaders of this period are discussed in Leonid Kishkovsky, "Archbishop Tikhon in America," *SVTQ* 19:1 (1975), 9–31 and George Bebis, "Metaxakis in Profile," in *History of the Greek Orthodox Church in America,* ed. Miltiadis Efthimiou and George Christopoulos (New York: Greek Orthodox Archdiocese, 1984).

The difficulties related to the establishment of the Greek Orthodox Archdiocese are discussed in George Papaioannou, *From Mars Hill to Manhattan* (Minneapolis: Light and Life, 1976) and his *The Odyssey of Hellenism in America* (Thessaloniki: Patriarchal Institute, 1985). The work of Patriarch Athenagoras in America is discussed in Dimitrios Tsakonas, *A Man Sent by God* (Brookline, MA: Holy Cross Orthodox Press, 1977) and Peter Kourides, *The Evolution of the Greek Orthodox Church in America and Its Present Problems* (New York: Greek Orthodox Archdiocese, 1959). The interplay of church and culture is discussed in Ekaterini Brown, *Religion and Ethnicity in Greek Americans* (Ann Arbor, MI: University Microfilm, 1977).

The various divisions that afflicted the Russian Orthodox beginning in the 1920s and 1930s are discussed in Joseph Hayden, *Slavic Orthodox Christianity in the United States* (Ann Arbor, MI: University Microfilm, 1973); Marvin Schrank, "Problems of Orthodoxy in America: The Russian Church," *SVTQ* 6:4 (1962), 185–205; Michael Lopuchin, "The Russian Orthodox Church in America: A Psycho-Social View," *SVTQ* 8:3 (1964), 131–38; Boris Burden, "The Holy Eastern Orthodox Catholic and Apostolic Church," *Orthodox Catholic Review* 1:1 (1927), 1–35.

The perspectives of the Metropolia are found in Basil Benson, *A History of the Russian Orthodox Greek Catholic Church of North America* (New York: Colonial, 1941) and Metropolitan Leonty, "Problems of the Eastern Orthodox Church in America," *SVTQ* 1:1 (1952), 6–12. The positions of the Exarchate of the Moscow Patriarchate are found in Makarios Illinsky, "The Church of Russia and Her American Branch," *One Church* 2:11 (1948), 1–12. Finally, the views of the Russian Orthodox Synod Abroad are expressed in John Maximovitch, "The Russian Orthodox Church Outside of Russia," *Orthodox Word* 8:2 (1972), 54–65 and Michael Rodzianko, *The Truth About the Russian Church Abroad* (Jordanville, NY: Holy Trinity Monastery, 1975). Nicholas Zernov provides some valuable background to the origins of the Synod Abroad in his "The First Council of the Russian Orthodox Church Abroad: Notes of One of the Participants," *Eastern Churches Review* 7:2 (1975), 165–77. Anton Ugolnik discusses some of the aspects of the development of these jurisdictions in *The Illuminating Icon* (Grand Rapids, MI: Eerdsmans, 1989).

A thorough presentation of the European background for the Russian Orthodox divisions in America can be found in Dimitri Pospielovsky, *The Russian Church Under the Soviet Regime 1917–1982* (Crestwood, NY: St. Vladimir's Seminary Press, 1984) and Marc Raeff, *Russia Abroad: A Cultural History of Russian Immigration, 1919–1939* (New York: Oxford University Press, 1990).

LATE TWENTIETH-CENTURY ISSUES AND CONCERNS

Alexander Schmemann produced three significant essays that deal with the problems of the Orthodox as they moved out of their isolation and began to be more concerned with unity and mission. See "Problems of Orthodoxy in America: I The Canonical Problem,"

SVTQ 8:2 (1964), 67–85; "II The Liturgical Problem," *SVTQ* 8:4 (1964), 164–85; and "III The Spiritual Problem," *SVTQ* 9:4 (1965), 171–93.

The story of an early ecumenical witness by American Orthodox theologians, especially prior to 1960, has not as yet been fully explored. For some perspectives, see Nicholas Arseniev, "Roots of Russian Ecumenism," *SVTQ* 6:1 (1962), 3-15, and "Some Thoughts Concerning the Possibility of Union Between the Orthodox Church and the Catholic Church," *SVTQ* 3:2 (1959), 6–10. The observations of Greek Orthodox Archbishop Michael are also of interest; see "The Tensions of the World and Our Unity in Christ, *SVTQ* 3:1 (1954), 37–40. Early contacts between Orthodox and Anglicans in this country are reviewed in Peter Haskell, "Archbishop Tikhon and Bishop Grafton: An Early Chapter in Anglican-Orthodox Relations in the New World," *SVTQ* 11:4 (1967), 193–206 and 12:1 (1969), 2–16.

American Orthodox theologians since 1960 have produced many essays on various aspects of the ecumenical movement. The following collections contain a number of significant essays with further biographical information. John Meyendorff et al., *The Primacy of Peter in the Orthodox Church* (London: Faith Press, 1963); John Meyendorff, *Living Tradition* (Crestwood, NY: St. Vladimir's Seminary Press, 1978); Alexander Schmemann, *Church, World, Mission* (Crestwood, NY: St. Vladimir's Seminary Press, 1979); Demetrios Constantelos, ed., *Orthodox Theology and Diakonia* (Brookline, MA: Hellenic College Press, 1981); Thomas Hopko, *All the Fulness of God* (Crestwood, NY: St. Vladimir's Seminary Press, 1982); Theodore Stylianopoulos, *Good News of Christ* (Brookline, MA: Holy Cross Orthodox Press, 1991). A valuable analysis of Orthodox participation in ecumenical dialogues, together with a rich bibliography, is found in Robert Stephanopoulos's, *A Study of Recent Greek Orthodox Ecumenical Relations* (Ann Arbor, MI: University Microfilm, 1970). Gregory Wiggenbach has produced a valuable introduction to Orthodox ecumenism in his *Broken, Yet Never Sundered* (Brookline, MA: Holy Cross Orthodox Press, 1987). A valuable collection of documents dealing with Orthodox participation in the ecumenical movement is Constantin Patelos, ed., *The Orthodox Church in the Ecumenical Movement, 1902–1977* (Geneva: World Council of Churches, 1978). A brief review of Orthodox involvement in the contemporary ecumenical movement is Thomas FitzGerald, *The Ecumenical Patriarchate and the Quest for Christian Unity* (Brookline, MA: Holy Cross Orthodox Press, 1990).

Bishop Maximos Aghiourgoussis of Pittsburgh is regarded as one of the foremost Orthodox theologians involved in Orthodox relations with Roman Catholics. See his most recent essay on this topic, "East Meets West: Gifts of the Eastern Tradition to the Whole Church," *SVTQ* 37:1 (1993), 3–22.

The grant of autocephaly to the Russian Orthodox Metropola by the Church of Russia led to the publication of a number of articles and books that dealt with this theme. Alexander Schmemann discusses the position of the Metropolia/Orthodox Church in America in his "A Meaningful Storm: Some Reflections on Autocephaly, Tradition and Ecclesiology," *SVTQ* 15:1/2 (1971), 3–27. Alexander Bogelepov provides direction for the actions of the Metropolia in his *Towards an American Orthodox Church* (New York: Moorehouse Barlow, 1963). A number of valuable documents related to autocephaly are contained in *The Autocephaly of the Orthodox Church in America* (Crestwood, NY: St. Vladimir's Seminary Press, 1971) and in Nicon Patrinacos, ed., *Russian Autocephaly and Orthodoxy in America* (New York: Greek Orthodox Archdiocese, 1972). A critique of the act is offered by the Greek theologian Panagiotis Trembelas in his *The Autocephaly of the Metropolia in America* (Brookline, MA: Holy Cross Theological School Press, 1973).

The position of the Ecumenical Patriarchate of Constantinople and its role in the church today are discussed by Metropolitan Maximos of Sardis, *The Oecumenical Patriarchate in the Orthodox Church* (Thessaloniki: Patriarchal Institute, 1976); Lewis Patsavos, "The Primacy of the See of Constantinople in Theory and Practice," *GOTR* 27:3/4 (1992), 233–58; John Meyendorff, "The Ecumenical Patriarchate, Seen in the Light of Orthodox Ecclesiology and History," *GOTR* 24:2/3 (1979), 226–43.

Three recently published volumes contain valuable essays by American Orthodox theologians dealing with a number of contemporary themes. See John Breck, *et al.*, eds., *The Legacy of St. Vladimir* (Crestwood, NY: St. Vladimir's Seminary Press, 1990); Theodore Stylianopoulos, ed., *Orthodox Perspectives on Pastoral Praxis* (Brookline, MA: Holy Cross Orthodox Press, 1988); and Joseph Allen, ed., *Orthodox Synthesis: The Unity of Orthodox Theological Thought* (Crestwood, NY: St. Vladimir's Seminary Press, 1981); Thomas Hopko, ed., *Women and the Priesthood* (Crestwood, NY: St. Vladimir's Seminary Press, 1983). A group of Orthodox clergy and laity has produced a number of provocative essays dealing with unity and renewal in Stephen Sfekas and George Matsoukas, eds., *Project for Orthodox Renewal* (Chicago: Orthodox Christian Laity, 1993).

A number of editorials by John Meyendorff that appeared in the newspaper *The Orthodox Church* between 1965 and 1984 have recently been published in two volumes. These succinct statements express the views of Meyendorff on a number of critical issues. See John Meyendorff, *Vision of Unity* (Crestwood, NY: St. Vladimir's Seminary Press, 1987) and *Witness to the World* (Crestwood, NY: St. Vladimir's Seminary Press, 1987).

The recent major work by Stanley Harakas, *Living the Faith: The Praxis of Eastern Orthodox Ethics* (Minneapolis: Light and Life, 1992) is destined to become a classic introduction to social ethics from an Orthodox perspective. Harakas is the foremost Orthodox theologian dealing with issues of ethics and the relationship of church and society. His recent work is a valuable complement to his earlier study *Toward Transfigured Life* (Minneapolis: Light and Life, 1983). The biographical notes in both provide rich guidance for further investigations. See also his *Health and Medicine in the Eastern Orthodox Tradition* (New York: Crossroad, 1990).

A valuable guide to Orthodox parishes is *Directory of Orthodox Parishes and Institutions in North America,* ed. Philip Tamouch (Torrance, CA: Orthodox People Together, 1992).

INDEX

Page numbers in **bold** refer to the biographical entries in Part Two.

About the Author

THOMAS E. FITZGERALD is Executive Director of the Program Unit on Unity and Renewal at the World Council of Churches in Geneva, Switzerland. He is also Professor of Religious Studies and History at Hellenic College and Holy Cross Greek Orthodox School of Theology. He has been a Visiting Professor at St. Vladimir's Orthodox Theological Seminary and the Ecumenical Institute of the World Council of Churches in Geneva. He has published in the areas of Orthodox studies, church history, and ecumenical relations.

ISBN 0-313-26281-0

HARDCOVER BAR CODE

DATE DUE

MAR 04 '97			
			Printed in USA

HIGHSMITH #45230